D0933065

Education for Peace

Testimonies from World Religions

Haim Gordon and Leonard Grob,
Editors

ORBIS BOOKS

Maryknoll, New York 10545

The Catholic Foreign Mission Society of America (Maryknoll) recruits and trains people for overseas missionary service. Through Orbis Books Maryknoll aims to foster the international dialogue that is essential to mission. The books published, however, reflect the opinions of their authors and are not meant to represent the official position of the society.

Copyright © 1987 by Orbis Books, Maryknoll, NY 10545
All rights reserved
Manufactured in the United States of America

Manuscript editor: William E. Jerman

Library of Congress Cataloging in Publication Data

Education for peace.

Includes index.
1. Peace—Religious aspects.   I. Grob, Leonard.
II. Gordon, Haim.
BL65.P4E38   1987   291.1'7873'07   86-31083
ISBN 0-88344-359-7 (pbk.)

To the memory of Bilhah Garinkol
and
to Susan

Contents

BUDDHISM

HINDUISM

PART THREE
PEACEMAKING IN ACTION

PART ONE

INTRODUCTION

Leah Goldberg

Odysseus's Lament

Enough wandering. Odysseus, gray-haired and sated, descended
   to Hades
to seek his friends killed in the war.
At the gate their shadows blessed him,
the cry of their death and their weeping came back to his
   ear—
how heroes have fallen!

A man and his horse sank on the battlefield.
Blood of cattle and men—rivers of darkness spilled.
The wailing of widows and the clanging of metal.
Orphans sobbing, broken walls crumbling.
A horror to eyes meeting death.
A horror to lips going dumb—give me water!
how heroes have fallen!

The vulture swoops on stench and decay.
Among the dead a survivor walks lonely.
I have come to Hades to ask your forgiveness
for then, for when the trap burst and we escaped.
On my forehead lies the mark of shame for a brother's death.
On my forehead lies the mark of shame for my life;
the sound of your dying cry rings in my ear—
how heroes have fallen.

translated by Myra Shapiro

1

Leonard Grob

Spiritual Politics: Introductory Remarks

In the current climate of heightened tension between nations possessing the capability to destroy the planet many times over, the need to deepen current efforts and to develop new initiatives in educating for peace is apparent. Indeed, it is no longer adequate to educate toward the goal of avoidance of conflict or warfare; peace educators must involve themselves with the contents and skills that will promote the positive art of peacemaking. Parents, teachers, community leaders—religious and lay—must come to acknowledge that education for peace is not merely one theme among others to be considered in the field of education, but rather its central or core concern: both the spiritual and material survival of the race demand that all education become, in essence, education for peace.

It is this last claim that serves as the impetus for the present collection of writings. "Educating for peace" is understood by the editors in its broadest sense as a grassroots pedagogy to be employed in a wide variety of settings by parents, teachers, and community leaders. This pedagogy has as its goal the creation of a climate of thought within which political leaders will be spurred to work for the resolution of conflict between nations through nonmilitary means. Yet more needs to be said: education for peace sets its sights on nothing short of the goal of fostering reconciliation at the deepest levels of the humanity of all parties to conflict. Indeed, any peace that extends beyond the mere cessation of hostilities is a peace that must be sought through a fundamental rethinking of those schemas of thought that grant primacy in the realm of politics to the play of power amid an allegedly inevitable clash of interests among the parties involved. In particular, the largely unexamined assumptions of realpolitik, which have dominated political thinking since Machiavelli, and, in subtler terms, beforehand, must be scrutinized anew. Such a scrutiny reveals

5

that realpolitik may indeed fail to bear adequate witness to the "reality" to which it allegedly adheres. That is to say, it may be argued that realpolitik is an essentially reductive schema operating under fixed assumptions concerning patterns of behavior of individuals and peoples, patterns seen to have led to human history as a history of war, spelled by relatively brief interludes called "peace."

The majority of contributors to this anthology take issue with this often implicit set of preconceptions about the rule of power on that battlefield of competing individual and group interests most often equated with politics. This is not to say that the authors of the articles in this volume deny the existence of the harsh realities of conflict in the name of some facile or superficial notion of reconciliation. Like the philosopher Martin Buber—a major source of inspiration for contemporary peace studies—the authors acknowledge the potential for, indeed, the brute actuality of conflict among humans; at the same time, however, the potential on the part of these same fallible humans for overcoming the "play for power" in the process of achieving truly dialogical encounters is here celebrated. What emerges, in other words, is a call for an alternative politics, a politics that would enlarge the "realism" of realpolitik to encompass the reality of authentic reconciliation between peoples and nations. In Buber's words:

> What I mean is not a vague idealism, but a more comprehending, more penetrating realism. . . . Man is not to be seen through, but to be perceived ever more completely. . . . Only if this happens and in so far as it happens, can a genuine dialogue begin between the two camps into which mankind is today split. They who begin it must have overcome in themselves the basic mistrust and be capable of recognizing in their partner in dialogue the reality of his being.[1]

This volume is informed by a vision of what may be called a "politics of peace" in which individuals and nations alike are seen as able to transcend "self-interest," narrowly conceived, in order to recognize in dialogue *not* that other who is objectified, subjected to my schemas of concern, but rather that other whom I approach in "the reality of his being" as a co-subject. Again, in Buber's words, "In a genuine dialogue each of the partners, even when he stands in opposition to the other, heeds, affirms, and confirms his opponent as an existing other."[2]

The notion of transcendence, alluded to above, is in this text not to be equated with any mere shifts in the cognitive or affective capabilities of conflicting parties. Dialogical peacemaking proceeds neither on the level of the mere exchange of ideas, nor on the level of an exchange of good feeling. Rather, what is called for here as the work of the peace educator is nothing short of fundamental or ontological change, a change in the way of being of the parties involved in conflict, a change, therefore, that underlies both cognition and affectivity—and their sum.

Having rooted the peacemaking process in an ontological event, the editors do not mean to imply that such fundamental reeducation of self can occur outside the concrete framework of cultural context. On the contrary, it is the central claim of this volume that guidance in authentic peacemaking must be provided by the great spiritual traditions at the center of cultures. Indeed, without heeding the peace-teachings of these religious traditions, peace education runs the risk of adopting a notion of peace that demands less than the transformative processes of ontological change. It is, then, to five major currents of religious thought—Judaism, Christianity, Islam, Hinduism, and Buddhism—that this volume turns for instruction as to the nature of the peacemaking process it wishes to advance.

At this juncture, however, several issues arise that must be addressed before these religious "witnesses for peace"—these "testimonies of spirit"—can be heard. Is it not the case, first of all, that these very traditions to be presented are ones that have often been perceived, at least popularly, as failing to serve, concretely, the course of peace to which they allegedly speak? Have not the religions themselves served as rallying points for warring parties—as the locus of, if not the motive force behind, much of the conflict the world has suffered? And can it not be asserted that even the sacred texts of these religions, apart from how they are realized in the world, are far from unambiguous with regard to their claims concerning the primacy of the goal of peace?

The contributors to the present volume assume the responsibility for addressing these questions—and others like them—in part 2, "Witnessing for Peace." The reader will find a response to these queries in the introductory chapter of each set of two chapters devoted to the five spiritual traditions under consideration. In the course of these individual expositions the reader will be informed, more specifically, of the attitudes toward peace and war of the founders and leaders of each religion; its scriptural and other written statements concerning peace; and, finally, its concrete initiatives for peacemaking.

For the purposes of this general introduction, the thesis underlying this section can be stated briefly and in more general terms: at the core of these five major spiritual traditions lies a basic teaching on peace that—though often disputed, covered over by arid institutional forms, or even betrayed from within—remains to instruct peace educators with regard to their vocation of fostering peace through dialogue.

To the question, then, of "who" addresses the other-as-subject in peacemaking dialogue, this anthology responds by acknowledging the unique contributions of these five spiritual traditions. More pointedly, each tradition advances a response to the question of "who" makes peace by recalling the aspect of divinity that attends to human beings qua human. This is not to say that the authors argue for the existence of some abstract notion of personhood posited as lying at the foundation of an empirical or ordinary self. No, the aspect of divinity alluded to here is no substantive, no-thing, but rather a flowering of the spirit, *an activity (of peacemaking) to be witnessed to, rather than predicated or argued for by the powers of discursive reasoning.* Hence the emphasis on "witness" and "testimony" in both the title of this section and the title of the anthology itself. What is embodied in this section is thus nothing short of the religious wellsprings of peacemaking attested to by the person who gives witness to it.

The above, however, is not to be understood as an endeavor to "homogenize" the teachings of the traditions here presented. The task of uncovering a kernel of peace-teaching at the core of five religions does not imply a unity in the spiritual voices to be heard. Just as dialogue between individuals is a dialogue between persons whose uniqueness is preserved in—indeed, is indispensable to—creation of "lines of tension," which constitute authentic communication, so the interreligious dialogue central to this volume must be grounded in a listening to the distinct and unique longing for peace of each tradition addressing every other. The road to understanding the role of spiritual traditions in advancing teachings about peace is thus not *around* the distinct cultures in which such teachings are born, but rather *through* them to a ground that demands of all of them the supreme effort to turn to one another in dialogue. As the meeting of peace-teachings both within a given tradition and among the traditions themselves, this anthology, we hope, will be illustrative of its own claim concerning the primacy of dialogue in the educational process in general and in peace education in particular. Again, Buber's insight in this regard is instructive:

> When a man is singing and cannot lift his voice, and another comes and sings with him, another who can lift his voice, the first will be able to lift his voice too. That is the secret of the bond between spirits.[3]

The second chapter in this introductory section, Eugene Fisher's "The Interreligious Dimension of War and Peace," constitutes an initial endeavor to allow the voices of these five religious traditions to be heard in dialogical tension with regard to one another—to be heard in the process of each enabling the other to sing!

I have argued above that this volume questions the often hidden assumptions on which realpolitik is based. An alternative to realpolitik—a "politics of peace"—must nonetheless remain a *politics:* the vision of peacemaking that emerges in this anthology must be one firmly directed toward *praxis,* toward the concrete interactions among inhabitants of the polis. The teachings of the spiritual traditions must be acknowledged as living teachings to be realized in the context of the complex and demanding world of interpersonal and international relationships. Such a spiritual legacy must guide us, in Buber's words, not in "renouncing the world but [in] placing it upon its proper ground,"[4] the ground of the divine. The spiritual teachings concerning peace must inform—and thereby hallow—the realm of the political.

The authors of the second of each set of two chapters in part 2, "Witnessing for Peace," wrestle with precisely this task. A witness from each of the five religions devotes a chapter to some aspect of that religion's peace-teaching as it confronts issues challenging it in the context of twentieth-century political life. What emerges in one instance is a discussion of the tensions between freedom and "fatalism" in aspects of contemporary education for peace in Israel; what is presented in another instance is an analysis of the Bible as peace teacher in an age tottering on the brink of nuclear conflict. A third chapter is an interview (conducted by co-editor Haim Gordon) with Egyptian author Naguib Mahfouz, in which an Islamic perspective on peace is aired in the context of the current crisis in the Middle East. A fourth selection deals with the unique nature of a Buddhist contribution to peace education in postwar Japan—Japan after the bomb. And, finally, the last in this series of chapters is devoted to Mahatma Gandhi's application of Hindu teachings toward the creation of a strategy for peace-making in the twentieth century.

A volume whose creation is spurred by the desire to develop and deepen the peacemaking process must not conclude without reference to concrete problems encountered by educators for peace. Hence part 3, "Peacemaking in Action." And, indeed, this section is a celebration of the *concrete,* as we hear of the trials—and successes and failures in meeting these trials—of the (flesh-and-blood) peace educator. Betty Cannon's chapter serves to illustrate one genre of problems facing the practitioner in this field: such an educator must grapple with the "Demonic Double," the projection onto another of the evil that I find it is within me to commit. She ends her selection with a series of pedagogical principles and exercises appropriate for helping young children prepare for a life in which the specter of the "Demonic Double" remains everpresent as a threat to peace. In the second chapter in this section, Antony Flew sounds a pedagogical note from another direction: his essay abounds in criticism of those university-level peace programs and curricula that—insofar as they refuse to encourage the amalgam of critical thinking and historical awareness essential for success in the educational enterprise in general—are most certain to prove problematic in educating others to promote peace in the world. Professor Flew's "dissenting voice"—alone in this volume in its outspoken critique of beliefs held in common by peace educators from a variety of traditions—serves to alert such educators to some of the challenges they must meet and endeavor to counter if they are to be faithful to their vocation.

A third chapter in this section, by coeditor Haim Gordon, readdresses the pitfalls to be avoided by the peace educator as brought to light by the two preceding authors. Gordon goes further, however, in his contention that even when one has overcome these difficultuies, one has not yet arrived at the essence of the peace education process as that process has been illuminated thus far in this volume. Drawing on insights advanced throughout this volume—and illustrating some of them by reference to his own work as peace educator in the context of a project with Arab and Jewish participants in Israel—Gordon concludes with a reaffirmation of the need to embody the "peacemaking core of one's religious heritage" in the course of entering into a dialogue with another in which each partner relates with the fullness of their being. Only as peace educators heed, in life, the teachings of spiritual traditions can they attest to the ontological movement at the root of authentic reconciliation.

Finally, there is an epilogue "Fun, Fantasy, and Failure in Educating for Peace." Here the somewhat more discursive arguments of the previous chapter are supplemented and further fleshed out by the praxis evidenced in an exchange of letters between Gordon and co-educator Diana Dolev, an exchange that attests to successes and failures in the Arab-Jewish peace project alluded to earlier. This most "concrete" of all chapters in this volume brings to a fitting close a work celebrating the engagement of spirit in that realm of the political in which the peacemaker works.

NOTES

1. Martin Buber, *Pointing the Way* (New York, Harper & Row, 1958), p. 227.

2. Ibid., p. 238.

3. Martin Buber, *Ten Rungs: Hasidic Sayings* (New York, Schocken Books, 1947), p. 84.

4. Martin Buber, *I and Thou* (New York, Scribner's, 1970), p. 127.

2

Eugene J. Fisher

The Interreligious Dimensions
of War and Peace

In announcing the Camp David accords, each of the three national leaders—Begin, Carter, and Sadat—all appealed to central aspects of their own (and the others') religious traditions concerning peace to justify the national commitments each was making. Ironically, appeals to religious tradition have been and are being made by national leaders to justify intergroup conflict throughout the world. This article will seek to examine the interreligious component of the peace/war equation and some of the ways ecumenical and interreligious movements can be seen as contributing to a solution.

Religious components are not difficult to discern in the major conflicts of this century. The slaughter of Armenians at the beginning of the century, for example, involved the near destruction of a largely Christian group by Muslim Turks. The division of the British Raj in India was necessitated by the fact that Muslims felt that their safety would not be ensured by the Hindu majority population in the subcontinent. World War II saw professed Christians committing genocide against Jews who had lived peacefully in their midst for centuries, as well as related crimes, such as the massacre of close to half a million Orthodox Serbs by Catholic Croatians set in power by the Nazis.

INTERRELIGIOUS CONFLICT IN THE PRESENT AGE

This century has also seen antireligious wars perpetrated by great ideologies of our times. Just as Stalin sought to bring the Orthodox Church to heel in the Soviet Union, so one of the first acts of the Nazi regime in Poland during World War II was to undertake the destruction of the Polish Catholic clergy. Totalitarian ideologies, which aim to control all aspects of individual and communal life, rightly see religion as a major potential source of unrest, because the world religions are transnational in character and hold the potential for bringing a people of any given culture into contact with the ideas and potentialities of peoples of other cultures. Afghanistan today witnesses Muslims taking up arms against an ideological as well as imperial invader.

Buddhism and Confucianism, the hereditary religions of China, are likewise beseiged and dwindling due to the aggressive ideology of communism since the Maoist revolution, though an easing of pressure seems to be occurring at present.

Interreligious conflict can thus occur not only between religious groups (Hindus/Muslims, Jews/Christians, etc.), but also between the religious vision and other world visions that seek to replace religion as such on the world stage. It can also be internal to a particular religion because no world religion is truly monolithic in character. Thus, Protestants and Catholics, continuing today an internecine strife that at one point in history threatened to engulf all of European civilization, are pitted against one another in Northern Ireland. And distinctions between Shiite, Sunni, and other Muslim groups, once only of academic interest in the West, are part and parcel of any understanding of the nature of the conflicts in the Middle East, such as Lebanon and the Iran/Iraq war. In some situations, for example Muammar Qaddafi's Libya, one finds elements of religious fundamentalism combining with a modern secular ideology to produce a volatile mixture threatening many other nations.

Although it is relatively easy to see interreligious conflict as widespread in the world, it is far more difficult to pinpoint with precision the extent to which religion as such dominates or merely contributes to a given conflict. Religious apologists often argue that the "real" reasons for this or that conflict are, in fact, social or economic or historical, and that religious belief is only being used (i.e., abused) by various groups or national leaders to "rally the troops." Religion as such (at least *their* religion), they maintain, properly motivates its adherents toward peace and justice, and it is "the state" that abuses it for its own mischievous ends.

This argument, to judge from the sacred texts and scriptures of the various religions with which I am conversant, has a certain validity. Every great religion, in its own way, orients its adherents towards the pursuit of peace and justice, not only for themselves but for humanity as a whole. But the argument can be carried too far. Most of the leaders of the groups involved in intergroup and international conflict today, I would hazard, feel that they are sincere adherents of the particular religious or ideological tradition that they espouse. Few are successfully disabused of this exalted self-image by the official religious authorities of their own communities. (When national authority *is* religious authority, as in the case of the Ayatollah Khomeni or the ruling family of Saudi Arabia, the chances of a successful religious challenge to state authority move from slim to nonexistent.)

In this vein, I remain sadly bemused by those authors who would "defend" the churches from the charge of complicity by silence in the Holocaust with the assertion that those Christians who were Nazis or Nazi sympathizers were in fact apostates (and thus not "ours"). In one sense this is correct. Nazism represented an ideology in essence inimical to Christian tradition, and in its own eyes was, like communism, a replacement of Christian hopes and beliefs. But although technically correct, this notion is morally inadequate. Apostasy and murder are heinous sins in the Christian view. And the fact that so many persons raised as Christians in nations "christianized" for centuries fell so easily and so quickly into the practice of the worst sort of crimes known to humanity can only signify a tremendous *Christian* failing. As we Christians justly take pride in the great spiritual accomplishments of our saints and martyrs, so we must assume an equivalent measure of responsibility for evils perpetrated in our name. This, I believe, is the stringency of a truly religious (as opposed to philosophical) moral view. We are responsible for what our coreligionists do, not on the level of personal or collective guilt, but on the level of ensuring that such abuses of our faith will never happen again.

Thus the churches since World War II have rightly sought to root out the negative teaching of contempt against Jews and Judaism that over the centuries had become encrusted on authentic Christian teaching. The story of this effort, virtually unprecedented in human history, is the subject for other essays. But it remains a positive paradigm for interreligious amity to which I shall return in the proper section of this discussion.

Interreligious conflict, is, then, characteristic of the present age. It is a factor in numerous conflicts around the world, threatening the lives of millions. This is a fact that cannot and should not be masked by religionists. Religion, further, is not a factor that acts in isolation from other factors. We have seen the capacity for intergroup conflict in world ideologies that also marks our age. Questions remain. What is it about the religious (or ideological) view that generates the capacity for intolerance of others and hence for intergroup violence? Why is this type of violence so particularly bitter? What is it about religion that makes it so often so susceptible to causes other than its own professed aims (as is true of all the world religions) of justice and peace for all?

RELIGION AND INTERGROUP TENSION

Briefly put, religion carries with it the capacity for increasing intergroup tension by reason of its nature as a means of self-identity, individual and group. We know ourselves *through* our religious self-identification, which is to say that religion is a basic way we orient ourselves in terms of other members of "our" group as distinguished from others.

In much of the world, religion and ethnicity (and often religion and nationalism) are intermingled inextricably. For eight centuries the Irish held to their ethnic, national identity by identifying with Catholicism over against the Anglican religion of their English conquerors. And Polish Catholics do this today vis-à-vis the Soviets.

I would argue that a similar dynamic fuels the rise of Islamic fundamentalism today. The perception among many Muslims is that the West is a threat not only militarily, as at the time of the Crusades, but even more so spiritually and culturally, and that modern European ideas of statecraft and social polity are fundamentally anti-Islamic, or at least intolerably non-Islamic. Hence the appeal to return to "pure" Islam has largely replaced the pan-Arabism of the 1950s and 60s as a rallying cry for contemporary Islamic movements. The "secular" or "enlightened" regimes of the Middle East, North Africa, and Asia are feeling more and more the pressure to base their internal legal structures (and to some extent external foreign policies) on the rubrics of Islamic law, *sharī'ah,* even though nationalism, itself a European import somewhat at odds with the ideals of the universal Islamic *al ummah* ("peoplehood"), remains a potent countervailing force. Whereas earlier Muslims gave their primary loyalties to the family, on the one hand, and to the *uamah,* the people, on the other, with little room left for loyalty to the various states in which they lived (seeing these as a result of Western influence), Muslims more and more show increased loyalty to their states, altering significantly the Middle East equation.

The pressure to islamicize carries with it inevitable areas of interreligious conflict. The Bahai's are no longer even tolerated in Iran, the birthplace of the movement. Christians in the Sudan are being physically punished under new, *sharī'ah*-based criminal codes for violating laws that bind Muslims but not Christians (e.g., the possession of alcohol, when wine is religiously *required* of Christians in sacred worship). Saudia Arabia has laws prohibiting public worship by non-Muslims and restricting Christian places of religious assembly to "foreign" compounds.

Whether such interpretations of *sharī'ah* are consonant with the quranic traditional tolerance of other religions, especially the "peoples of the book," is not the point of the present essay. But these are some of the many samples from various parts of the world that are potential trouble spots in interreligious, and therefore in international, relationships.

The ethnic component of religious self-identification has the potential of reducing a universal ethic to a dangerous we/they frame of intergroup relating. Interreligious polemic, which is part of all religious traditions, can thus be called upon by national leaders to justify hostilities on various levels, whether internal or external. Hitler, for example, dismissed attempts by church leaders to criticize his antisemitic policies by referring to medieval Christian polemics and canonical legislation against Jews. That the ambiguities of medieval legislation on the Jews were neither racially motivated nor logically conducive to genocide (forced conversion and the Inquisition, not death camps, were their tragic outcome when the medieval system began to break down) bothered the Nazis not a whit. They were looking for a veneer for ends already decided upon and, all too conveniently, found them.

The mingling of religion and politics represents a constant theme of religious history. The Hasmonean dynasty used religious appeals to rationalize the forced conversion of neighboring peoples. And the early Christian thinker Eusebius virtually equated the Roman empire with the eschatological kingdom of God in his efforts to celebrate the adoption of Christianity as the state religion of the empire in the post-Constantinian era. Augustine's careful delineation of the proper spheres of the heavenly kingdom (city of God) and of the earthly kingdom (human city) was an attempt, whether successful or not, to restore a balance and a certain distance between the two. Equating the visible church with God's kingdom is considered in classic Christian thought as an abuse (technically, "triumphalism"). Many Catholics, if only in retrospect, thus rejoiced when the days of churchly "temporal power" represented by the papal states finally came to an end.

Along with the interweaving of ethnocentrism and nationalism with religion, a third factor stemming from the religious thought structure itself is often mentioned in the literature as a "contribution" of religion to intergroup intolerance and conflict. This is the very universality of religious claims, which first relativize and then see as a threat the religious claims of other groups.

Monotheism, history has shown, has the capacity to engender intolerance. If there is only one God, and if this God has been revealed to my group, the reasoning goes, then other groups not only cannot but should not be tolerated. Indeed, love for other groups, concern for their very salvation, must logically manifest itself in attempts to convert them. To leave them to their own devices is to leave them in grave spiritual danger. Jews, Christians, and Muslims all show remarkably parallel levels of intolerance of paganism and idolatry, and toward each other.

It is not only the Abrahamic, or monotheistic traditions, however, which show in their histories interlocking origins, geographicopolitical rivalries, and subsequent levels of mutual tension and intolerance.

The word "Hinduism," for example, derives from the word "Hindustan," a geographical designation given by the Muslims to the peoples of the Indus River valley and beyond. The term suggests the Western penchant for systematizing internally diverse religious spheres into "simple" (perhaps, better, "simplistic") categories, but it does reflect the reality of what has been common among the varied peoples of the Indian subcontinent for millennia.

Although not "monotheist" in the Western sense of the term, Hinduism, for example in the Vedas, speaks of "God as one, but the wise call him by many names." Rich religious concepts and practices, such as rebirth, karma, and moksha (liberation/transcendence) pervade an Indian life in which religious belief and the caste structure intermingled and supported each other.

The Buddha, Gautama Siddhartha, was born of the princely *(kshatriya)* caste in what is now Nepal. His teaching took hold, however, not so much among the Hindus among whom it was born, as on the Indochinese peninsula and in Tibet, China, Korea, and Japan. Later ideas, as we shall see again with regard to Jewish/Christian/Muslim relationships, are not always considered "better" ideas by those who hold the earlier tradition. By 1000 C.E., Buddhism had virtually disappeared from the subcontinent.

Buddhism in turn mingled with Confucianism in China and Shintoism in Japan. The "Neo-Confucianism" of Chu Hsi (1130–1200 c.e.,) arose in part in reaction to Buddhist metaphysics, affirming change as the source of transformation where Buddhism saw it as the source of suffering, and emphasizing the balances of life in opposition to what was felt to be Buddhist "withdrawal" from the world into meditation. Shintoism, meanwhile, often functioned as an ally of Japanese nationalism.

The dynamics of interreligious rivalry discussed in this chapter, then, are by no means the exclusive prerogative of the "Western" (more properly, "Middle Eastern," given their origins) traditions of Judaism, Christianity, and Islam, though the special focus of this chapter is on those traditions.

WAR AMONG THE CHILDREN OF ABRAHAM

Judaism, Christianity, and Islam, all holding a common monotheism, a deep historical linkage, and a claim of descent from a common ancestor, Abraham, have a unique set of historical and interreligious relationships worth a closer look as a particularly critical "test case" of interreligious conflict (and potential for reconciliation).

Catholic scholar F. E. Peters outlines that relationship, both conceptually and historically, in a remarkably useful book, *Children of Abraham* (Princeton University Press, 1982). He traces the development of each, not only in isolation but also in terms of its interrelatedness with the other two, illustrating that the way in which each worked out its beliefs and practices in response to parallel historical challenges had important political and sociological consequences. His study shows that the development of such essential structures of the three traditions as community, hierarchy, law, scripture, tradition, liturgy, asceticism, mysticism, and theology was dependent not only on internal factors but also on the view each had of the other two.

Asymmetrical realities, of course, abound in Peters's analysis. Rabbinic Judaism and early Christianity, on the one hand, underwent their formative periods (roughly the first six centuries of the common era) in concert with one another, often facing the same external threats (e.g., the destruction of the temple, Hellenism, Gnosticism, etc.), whereas the third partner, Islam, came into being only after the formative periods of the earlier two were virtually concluded. On the other hand, and my own experience in trilateral dialogue with the Jewish/Christian/Muslim Trialogue sponsored by the Kennedy Institute of Ethics at Georgetown University over a period of six years verifies this, there is remarkable similarity in the reactions of each to the others.

Christianity had to take into account the existence and role of Judaism within its own understanding of the divine plan of salvation because the God it worships, the God of Jesus, is the God of Israel, and because its central beliefs, institutions, and spiritual understandings are essentially Jewish in origin. It did so in the New Testament itself and subsequently, at first apologetically (Justin Martyr's *Dialogue with Trypho*) and soon polemically (Chrysostom), because it had to define its own identity over against that of its "elder brother" in the faith. Rabbinic Judaism, on the other hand, though doubtless influenced over the centuries by Christianity more than either group would care to admit today, did not feel such a burning need to account for the existence of Christianity in its central self-articulation, the Talmud.

Likewise, Islam, in the Qur'ān and subsequently, felt the need to devote central attention to the earlier revelations of the two historically prior "peoples of the book," and to develop a polemic against their continuing religious validity. The Jewish prophets and Jesus, Islam proclaims early on in its history, were valid prophets. But Judaism has simply gotten wrong the teachings of Moses and Christianity the teaching of Jesus in their respective scriptures. The Hebrew Bible and the New Testament stand before the final judgment of the Qur'ān, the revelation to Muhammad, which supersedes the earlier, and in present form seriously flawed, scriptures. Jesus, for example, was not crucified; hence claims concerning his resurrection are spurious. So too did Christianity claim to supersede Judaism in God's scheme of sacred history.

Just as Judaism is not quite sure what to do with Christianity, which proclaimed answers to needs never felt by the older tradition, so neither Judaism nor Christianity knows quite what to do with Islam, which has admittedly brought millions to the knowledge of the one God but persists in the notion that its later religious idea is a better one, effectively replacing the other two, which now become mere remnants of an ancient past.

Christianity and Judaism alone among the world religions share a major block of writings that both adhere to as sacred scripture. Islam and Judaism, on the other hand, seem closer in articulating a "pure" monotheism and in eschewing claims to the divinity of Jesus.

The stage is thus set for inevitable conflict at the outset on the conceptual level. Historical events would greatly exacerbate that conflict. And history is differently remembered. The Qur'ān recalls as "teaching" the refusal of the Jewish tribes of the Arabian peninsula to convert to Islam, and recalls the Arab-Jewish wars of that time as necessary self-defense. Jewish memory, on the other hand, views that particular conflict as but one more example of religious and cultural persecution at the hands of gentiles.

Similarly, Western Christians view the Crusades and the Muslim-Christian battles of ensuing centuries as essentially self-defense moves to halt the Muslim conquest of Christian countries and to free the Holy Land from Arab invaders who inhibited Christian pilgrimage to the Holy Places. Here, Jews and Eastern Orthodox Christians would join vociferously with Muslims in condemning the brutality and barbarism of the way in which the Crusaders conducted their war, a point that Western Christians would today freely acknowledge. They would, however, persist in reminding Muslims that the Crusaders were not without Islamic provocation and that the spread of Islam constituted a very real threat to Christendom.

Muslims, however, see nineteenth-century Western imperialism as simply an extension of the Crusades, a religious as well as material threat to their way of life. The existence of the state of Israel, viewed through this historico-theological prism, is seen by Muslims as an extension into the twentieth century of the Crusades and Western imperialism. Israel, they believe, was set up by the West as a means of solving its own "Jewish problem"—by imposing it on Islam.

The fact that the majority of Israeli Jews are refugees, not from Europe but from Muslim countries, where they were often suppressed and mistreated (reduced to *dhimmī* status, etc.), is not likely to shake this Muslim perception in the near future. In a part of the world where the mayors of Rome and Tunis could solemnly sit down, as they did in January 1985, to sign a treaty officially ending the Third Punic War, historical grievances are always fresh. They are present realities, not part of the "past," which Americans, with their own history of immigration and new beginnings, are almost casually capable of putting behind them in order to seek out a better future.

POSSIBILITIES FOR PEACE THROUGH INTERRELIGIOUS DIALOGUE

Intergroup dialogue, which begins with the process of building trust, thus faces nearly insuperable historical barriers. Rivers of blood, and not merely incompatible doctrinal conceptions, stand between the communities involved. It is crucial to keep this factor in mind at the outset. Religion in general, and certainly the three monotheistic traditions that concern us here, can by no means be understood simply as an equation formed of varying amounts of theological doctrine plus certain pious practices. The Abrahamic faiths are in the first instance "peoples," not just creedal or liturgical systems. (Islam may acknowledge this best in its deceptively simple phrase, "peoples of the book.")

One can see this immediately in the scriptures of all three. Torah, the first five books of the Bible, which in Jewish eyes form its heart, is framed above all as history, as the story of a people seen against the story of all humanity. Thus the sections that to Christian eyes are among its dullest (genealogies, lists of laws, etc.) are not peripheral but biblically central. Judaism is not a structure of beliefs demanding adherence, but a peoplehood, a way of life demanding commitment. It begins with an interpretation of historical events. How did the people come to be? How did it come to be where it was, in a particular land? The interpretation is that these events did not take place by chance but reflect specific actions (saving actions as in the exodus) of the divine within human history. To respond to this awesome fact is to assume responsibility, not only for oneself but for the people brought into being by this action. "Jewishness" is thus not racial or even cultural, but a deeper response to community-in-history.

Christianity likewise begins with an interpretation of events: the death and resurrection of Jesus, and the interpretation of these events (incarnation, for Christians the definitive though not necessarily exclusive incursion of the divine into the human condition). Christians are grateful for positive views of Jesus by Islam, which see him as a prophet, and Judaism, which can see in

Jesus a great Jewish teacher of the period, but they hold a deeper significance of his life, which for them is determinative of how humanity and human history are to be understood.

Islam in a real sense begins with a reinterpretation of the founding events of the earlier two traditions, seeing the revelations given to Moses and Jesus as valid, if improperly recorded in the Bible. Just as Christianity has felt a theological embarrassment at the continuing existence of a people who felt no need for its later revelation, so too does Islam have a theologically ambivalent attitude toward Jews and Christians. As peoples of the book, they are to be protected. But as peoples who have failed to accept the revelation of the last of the prophets, they must be kept in a distinctly subservient position. The loss of Muslim Spain to Christians was thus a theological as well as political blow to Islam. And the loss of even as small a section of the Middle East to the Jews is interpreted in this way as virtually a theological impossibility. Hence there is a mingling of religious and historico-political factors in the current conflict.

Because of this mingling of factors, interreligious dialogue alone is not capable of providing a solution. Political factors, such as the Israeli invasion of Lebanon, can chill dialogues between Jews, Christians, and Muslims taking place in the United States, far from the actual scene of the conflict. Again, the strong sense of family and peoplehood shared by Jews and Muslims makes the political equation an inevitable part of religious dialogue.

Any attempt at dialogue, then, must include an honest confrontation of historical grievances. Until fully aired and honestly acknowledged by all sides, there is little hope for progress. Although such a discussion is best framed in a recitation of the spiritual resources for peace and reconciliation in the name of the one God, which form a basic thrust of the religious message of all three traditions, such articulations of biblical and quranic passages will remain superficial until the deeper historical grievances are fully confronted.

Here I can speak out of my experience with the Kennedy Institute Trialogue (see the *Journal of Ecumenical Studies,* 19 [1982] 197–200). As a pioneering group in the field, it has seen both remarkable progress and continuing difficulties. In that group, it early became clear that the bilateral relationships involved (Jewish-Christian, Christian-Muslim, Muslim-Jewish) were all at different levels. Most advanced, at the outset, was the Christian-Jewish relationship.

In one sense, this might be seen as startling: of the three combinations, the history of Christian-Jewish relationships has seen by far the worst treatment of one side (the Jewish) by another (the Christian). The crusaders fought a brutal war with Islamic armies over some centuries, but Muslims were not exactly helpless in the encounter and, in the final event, won militarily by repulsing the invaders. The Crusaders, however, massacred hundreds of thousands of totally helpless Jews throughout Europe, and the Crusades were only the first act of a tragic drama of expulsions, forced conversions, massacres, and pogroms that took place over a millennium of history and culminated in the Holocaust. The historical picture is not one of unrelieved persecution (as evidenced by the fact that so large a percentage of the Jewish peoples lives in Christian lands), but it is a tragic one.

Statements by the churches after World War II reassessing the relationship, condemning antisemitism, and calling for thorough revisions of Christian teaching concerning Jews and Judaism on all levels, led to an embryonic dialogue. There was, in short, an official acknowledgment of the problem on the Christian side, most dramatically, perhaps, by the Second Vatican Council, and real steps taken in a concrete way within the churches to eradicate any potential source of anti-Jewish attitudes among Christians. Such realities and acknowledgments of past wrongs are a necessary first step to dialogue.

It must be said at the same time, of course, that dialogue between various Jewish and Christian leaders occurred *before* the issuance of those official statements and as a necessary prerequisite. These dialogues, once they had gone beyond the initial "tea and sympathy" stage, quickly found themselves turning to the historical record as the first agenda item to be tackled seriously. Rev. Edward Flannery's *The Anguish of the Jews* (Macmillan, 1967), for example, had immense impact not only within the Catholic community, but in a different way within segments of the Jewish community because Jews began to realize that the church was at last willing to begin the process of honestly confronting the sinister side of its own history vis-à-vis the Jewish community. Only on such a basis of acknowledgment that "I" have unjustly hurt "you" and will take what actions are possible to redress that fact, can Martin Buber's version of I and Thou begin to take place in interreligious encounter. The process that ensues is the slow development of trust. Only when they trust each other can they begin to search in common for the deeper spiritual bonds that do link Christians and Jews together religiously.

Jewish/Muslim relationships, which might on one level logically have been expected to advance more quickly than Christian/Jewish relationships—there being no doctrine of the Trinity to separate them—have not in fact advanced very far. The reasons, I suggest, are partly political (the Middle East), perceived as a theater of war between the two, and partly religious. In the case of Jewish/Christian relationships there exists a shared body of scripture acknowledged as such by both, and a shared means, modern biblico-critical methodology, to approach the common text. Judaism and Islam, although sharing much in practice and style, and having cognate sacred languages (Hebrew and Arabic), do not share a common text. And, given the unique nature of the Qur'ān, the notion of applying the methodology of modern biblical scholarship as practiced by Jews and Christians to the quranic text is viewed as repugnant.

Muslims and Christians, meanwhile, have not yet moved to the point, in my opinion, of coming to grips commonly with their histories vis-à-vis one another. There have been numerous excellent meetings on several levels, and several very good statements on the part of the churches, but not yet the building of trust to allow dialogues and statements to have the impact that *Nostra Aetate* §4 (§3 is devoted to Islam) has had upon Christian-Jewish relationships. The political mix, given some twenty-two Arab nations and the lingering consequences of Western imperialism, is also extremely complex.

There remain, however, rich sources of spiritual vitality in all three traditions that can be tapped. The vision of universal harmony and justice under one God is shared by all three equally as a constituent element. It is a vision that calls on its adherents to transcend history in response to the call of the transcendent God who is the ruler of history.

This is a powerful motivation and, although seldom achieved, is never to be underestimated. Anwar Sadat's evocation of the Qur'ān and of the Hebrew scriptures during his visit to Jerusalem broke down barriers of mistrust most objective political observers of the time would have judged unbreakable. The one God who calls, we all believe, gives the strength to answer the call. Interreligious dialogue, properly so called, has limitless potential for changing hearts, and therefore the overall reality of even the most intractable situations of intergroup conflict.

Pope John Paul II captured this vision of the potential of dialogue among the Abrahamic traditions in an address given to the Jewish community of Mainz in November 1980:

[the three religions are called], as children of Abraham, to be a blessing for the world (Gen. 12:2). They engage themselves jointly to work for peace and justice among all persons and peoples and in the fullness and profundity that God has disposed for us and with readiness for the sacrifice that this high goal may impose on us. The more this holy duty inspires our encounter, so much the more will it become for us a blessing. . . . In all this it is not only a question of correcting a false religious view of the Jewish people, which caused in part the misunderstandings and persecution in the course of history, but above all a question of the dialogue between the two religions which—with Islam—can give to the world the belief in one ineffable God who speaks to us and which, representing the entire world, wish to serve him [*Origins,* Dec. 4, 1980].

JOINT ACTIONS FOR PEACE IN A NUCLEAR AGE

There is in the pope's vision a sense in which the urgency of the search for a just peace, whether in the Middle East or globally, is so pressing that it cannot wait for interreligious reconciliation to run its full, difficult course before launching joint actions to address the many conflicts now besetting the world. On this level the world religions, drawing directly upon the sources for peace in their traditions, can begin to challenge world leaders to make the practical adjustments and, indeed, political concessions necessary to diminish the horrifying potential for nuclear war that hangs over all of us like the sword of Damocles by a precariously frayed thread.

In the United States, the Catholic bishops' pastoral letter, *The Challenge of Peace,* appears to have ignited some of this potential, which "brackets" the ecumenical and interreligious equations (though not ignoring them) in order to build a solid interfaith coalition capable of having some impact on nuclear arms questions. The process of developing the bishops' pastoral, for example, was unique in including the viewpoints not only of a wide political spectrum within the Catholic community, but also of society at large, and specifically the voices of non-Catholic religious communities (see James Castelli, *The Bishops and the Bomb,* 1984). The acclaim with which the peace pastoral was met by other Christian and Jewish groups (though each would have its own particular caveats) revealed a remarkable and perhaps unprecedented consensus among American religious bodies on the critical nature of the nuclear issue.

Most of these bodies had already issued, though few in such detail, their own statements on nuclear warfare and its potential for being the mechanism of the suicide of the human race. All seemed to find in the bishops' pastoral an enabling force to come together on the issue. Though condemned by a few "experts" as naive, and even dangerously naive, the pastoral did succeed in taking the issue out of the hands of the experts and the think tanks and making it a matter of public debate. The genie, in short, was let out of the jar, perhaps never to be returned.

Evidence of this is not difficult to find. Catholic parishes and Protestant congregations are gathering to discuss and jointly probe the issues. Protestant denominations circulated the pastoral widely within their own communities. The official Catholic/Presbyterian-Reformed bilateral consultation has made analysis of the bishops' pastoral and parallel Presbyterian and Reformed pastorals a major agenda item of its current round of dialogue.

In 1985, the Interreligious Affairs Department of the Union of American Hebrew Congregations and the Secretariat for Catholic-Jewish Relations of the National Conference of Catholic Bishops announced the joint publication of a discussion guide on the bishops' pastoral for Catholic/Jewish study groups entitled *The Challenge of Shalom.* Only a short time ago "living room dialogues" between Catholics and Jews were considered the foolish dreams of isolated visionaries. And the prospects that a major Jewish agency would exert its institutional energies to assist Jews in understanding and implementing an official church document would have been less than nothing. But new energies release new possibilities and ancient enmities can be overcome in search for the good of all. Future generations (if there are any) will have to judge the ultimate efficacy of such movements on the world scene. In the meantime the struggle, frustrating and fruitless as it often can seem to those involved, impels action where least anticipated.

Interreligious dialogue between "West" (Judaism, Christianity, Islam) and "East" (Hinduism, Buddhism, Shinto, Confucianism) is facilitated (and sometimes frustrated) today by the presence of so many of the adherents of each tradition within the geographical areas normally associated with the others. The Eastern traditions have as essential elements beliefs and practices embodying the urge toward peace with justice that can provide a sound basis for such dialogue and cooperation.

The most vivid symbol of West-to-East outreach on this level remains the figure of Thomas Merton, whose works and life are rightly being given renewed attention today. Merton died pioneering intermonastic dialogue with Buddhists and Hindus, a practice that has increased in frequency and depth since his untimely death. (Interestingly, the Benedictine monk who was with Merton, and said the last rites for him, Rembert Weakland, is now, as archbishop of Milwaukee, in charge of the committee of U.S. Catholic bishops preparing the economics pastoral, so a circle of sorts has been closed.)

Hinduism, with its ancient concept of "no-killing" *(ahimsa)* and Buddhism, with its great emphasis on "no-harming," can offer invaluable and deeply profound aspects to any interreligious search for a workable peace. The figure that stands out here, just as Jewish thinker Martin Buber does in the concept and practice of dialogue, is, of course, Mahatma Gandhi, who was deeply influenced by the "Western" ideals of Christian thinkers such as Leo Tolstoy, and who in turn has so deeply influenced the European and American peace movements. Again, a circle can be drawn around a shrinking globe.

Most recently the worldwide "Live Aid" rock concert, celebrated simultaneously all over the world and linked together by satellite in order to raise money for relief of famine victims in Africa, reveals something of the new possibilities opening up. One could not help but observe the surprisingly religious character of the lyrics of so many of the songs, from Joan Baez's opening "Amazing Grace" to the concluding "We Are the World." Here again the human ability, when faced with the urgency of need, to tap the riches of diverse spiritual traditions for the sake of others is at least glimpsed, tantalizing our deepest hopes.

PART TWO

WITNESSING FOR PEACE

Myra Shapiro

Passover, 1983

for Rebecca

A broken Hebrew fills our mouths
around a table
set with wine, soup, to each
a chopped piece of fish,
the ritual of this family for years.
This year a sister is dying.
She stands to bless us;
all other years her husband
has been the one to rise.
She prays—*Oh shit*—
to regain speech from tears.

We sing *Dayenoo;* my husband's palm
taps mine to make his father's rhythm
stay alive. Plagues have fallen
diminishing our cups, ten drops
of wine. We sing sorrow
and we sing satisfied, grateful
for protection, for the soul
set free. Linked
to this house of my will
how will I separate to speak a rage
rising. On my milk-white plate
a coral cobra's running wild.

•

Die Ay Nooooo . . . all night
I hear in broken sleep the kitchen
clock start stop start
stop, the spigot
driveling in the basin.

27

At 3 the stammer of this quiet house
I want to throw against the wall.

By 5 the faint rose of morning
dabs the top of the windowpane.
Birds echo the sun. I turn
to lie west toward the still clear
full moon, a tablet
held in the fingers of a budding tree.
Oh moo. Open.
Let me in. Fill me.

Judaism

3

Leonard Grob

Pursuing Peace:
Shalom in the Jewish Tradition

The scholar engaged in the search for a *core* teaching in the record of Jewish attitudes toward peace and war is confronted at the outset by a seemingly Herculean task. How are we to choose between one biblical characterization of God as a "warrior" (Exod. 15:3) and another proclaiming (as Gideon's name for God's altar) that "the Lord is peace" (Judg. 6:24)? How are we to choose between the depiction of a people carrying the holy ark into battle as the representation of God's presence on the side of the victor, and the depiction, in a well-known legend, of this same people rebuked by their God for rejoicing at the defeat of the Egyptian enemy—God's creatures also—at the Red Sea?

In the face of such conflicting evidence are we merely to throw up our hands and adopt the historicist claim that any such endeavor to seek a root or "grounding" tradition is spurious—that every such quotation makes sense only in its own historical context, a context behind or beneath which one cannot legitimately delve? Are we to dismiss such a quest—a quest that lies at the core of this anthology—in the endeavor to reconcile solely by reference to their contexts such opposing injunctions as Isaiah's "They shall beat their swords into plowshares, and their spears into pruning hooks" (2:4) and the prophet Joel's "Beat your plowshares into swords, and your pruning hooks into spears" (3:10)?

In this chapter I shall contend that although the historicist claim is one that, yielding a partial truth, is not to be dismissed easily, the goal to discern amid more than three millennia of a people's history a dominant current of thought and practice with regard to war and peace is by no means specious. Moreover, just as "success" in the conduct of such a quest cannot be reduced to the

30

product of any merely *quantitative* measure—as if counting up the number of references supporting either position would suffice to answer our question— just so must we resist the temptation to adopt any reductive practice of viewing the presence or absence of a teaching on peace as the function of sharp vicissitudes in the *quality* of Jewish experience in the disparate historical settings in which Jews have found themselves throughout the ages.

Just as we should wish to resist any inclination to understand the presence of the many biblical passages depicting—and sometimes glorifying—Jewish militarism as the function of the status of ancient Israel as a people residing, for long periods, in its own territory, just so must we refuse the temptation to attribute the two thousand years of a strong tradition of peace within diasporatic Judaism to the absence of statehood. Underlying the vicissitudes of history that affect but never *determine* the Jewish people's attitudes toward peace and war resides what I will contend is nothing short of a foundational teaching. It is my endeavor in this chapter to argue for the presence of such a core teaching as a teaching of shalom.

Let us begin, then, with the first strands of evidence of this people's attitudes toward war and peace: attitudes manifesting themselves in the Old Testament. Scholars have repeatedly cited the numerous references to the Lord's might in battle—as well as the allegedly vengeful nature of the Lord—as evidence for a fundamentally militaristic spirit pervading the annals of ancient Israel. And, indeed, the people Israel is born in its deliverance by force from servitude in Egypt. Moreover its entry into the promised land of Canaan, sealing the bond between a nation and its territory, is an entry gained by force of arms as well:

And I brought you into the land of the Amorites, which dwelt on the other side of the Jordan; they fought with you; and I gave them into your hand, that you might possess their land; and I destroyed them from before you [Josh. 24:8].

The multitude of references to reliance on arms, with the sometimes total destruction of the enemy as its result, finds a yet more developed and vivid expression in the "historical" books of Judges, Samuel, and Kings. The essentially tribal God of the early sections of the Pentateuch, it has been argued, is gradually transformed into the national God of the historical books of the canon, with a concomitant increase in the degree and extent of this deity's use of force to defend an expanded and well-defined territorial stake.[1] How are these references to a people and its God embroiled in a seemingly never-ending series of wars—in this regard, a people no different from its ancient contemporaries—how are these chronicles to be reconciled with the tradition of peace to which I have alluded above?

The response to this query is by no means a simple one. But just as our point of departure in ancient texts has served as the locus for a posing of the problematic in the terms sketched above, so must we look to this same text for evidence that may give our initial inclination to pass judgment some pause. For even in its earliest chronicles the Old Testament yields evidence of *troubled* attitudes toward the violence so frequently depicted. As related in chapter 34 of Genesis, two of Jacob's sons, Simeon and Levi, resort to treachery to avenge their sister's honor and succeed in promoting the wanton slaughter of the community to which the wrongdoer belongs. In a later speech delivered just prior to his death, Jacob is unrestrained in his condemnation of the violence thus perpetrated:

> Simeon and Levi are brethren; the instruments of cruelty are in their habitations. . . . Unto their assembly mine honor be not thou united; for in their anger they slew a man. . . . Cursed be their anger, for it was fierce; and their wrath, for it was cruel [Gen. 49:5-7].

Numerous other citations from these same books of the Pentateuch and from the historical books can be brought to bear as counterreferences to those celebrating violence cited in the paragraph above: Abraham's role as mediator on behalf of the wicked inhabitants of Sodom (Gen. 18:23); the purity of trust exhibited by the peaceful Jacob in a God who would save him from the grasp of the warlike Esau (Gen. 32:10-13); God's injunction to Moses to desist from building an altar of hewn stones, seemingly so that tools of iron—the metal used in forging arms—would not make their mark upon a sacred site of worship (Exod. 20:22); Elisha's compassion for the Arameans who had been led into Samaria (2 Kings 6:8-23); and, finally, God's refusal to allow David, a man of war, to build the holy temple (1 Chron. 28:2-3).

VIOLENCE AND MORAL TENSION

The point of listing these citations is not primarily to enumerate instance and counterinstance of attitudes toward war in some early books of the Old Testament. Rather, it is to show that although violence most certainly exists in these chronicles of ancient Israel, such violence is seldom recounted outside the context of *moral tension.* As John Ferguson, in his *War and Peace in the World's Religions,* puts it, "while the way of violence exists [in the Old Testament], it stands under judgment."[2] The military heroics of the God of the Old Testament are not in themselves the essential subject matter of the many passages in which they are often so graphically depicted. Rather, the tension between the deed of violence and the condition of peace—between war and a vision of an ideal state of peace that it disrupts—takes its initial shape in these books of the Pentateuch and in the historical books that follow, only to be more fully celebrated in the writings of the later prophets and the psalmists.

The prophetic judgments of violence, moreover, are extended and elaborately argued by the authors of the Talmud and other exegetical texts in the early centuries of the common era, as well as by Jewish thinkers in more recent epochs. Indeed, the twentieth century bears witness to this moral tension as Judaism struggles with issues of war and peace in the context of its need to relate to a reunion of people and territory in the form of a contemporary Jewish nation-state defining its (disputed) place in a troubled region of the world. In what follows I shall endeavor to make this, what I have termed *moral tension,* more palpable as it evidences itself throughout the annals of Jewish history.

As we have begun to see, the God of ancient Israel is no mere proprietary deity defending the Israelites', and thus God's own, honor and territory in the accepted mode of an exercise of military might. God was the protector of the people *on condition that* certain ethical injunctions to which it had freely committed itself in a covenant relationship were fulfilled. This set of injunctions, moreover, was interpreted, especially by the prophetic tradition, as providing the basis for a moral code that would finally be realized only in its free acceptance by all nations in the universal arena. On this interpretation, the fulfillment of the divine hegemony whose seeds are sown in the early books of the Old Testament can be nothing other than the affirmation—in both word and deed, and by all of humankind—of peace as a normative state of being.

It is only in this context, then, that the words of Isaiah 2 alluded to above can be comprehended. Not as some apocalyptic vision thrust upon a favored people are Isaiah's words to be understood, but rather only as an injunction to be heeded, as a summons to what (in this anthology) is called education for peace, can they be fully understood:

> And it shall come to pass in the last days that the mountain of the Lord's house shall be established in the top of the mountains, and shall be exalted above the hills; and all nations shall flow unto it. And many people shall go and say, Come ye, and let us go up to the mountain of the Lord. . . . And they shall beat their swords into plowshares, and their spears into pruning hooks; nation shall not lift up sword against nation, neither shall they learn war any more [Isa. 2:2–4].

Amid the all-too-human acts of violence recounted in the Old Testament, then, the voice of Isaiah and that of several of his fellow prophets ring out in stirring counterpoint. Such a voice, I have argued, sets forth a vision of peace not as some eschatological doctrine to be realized in a dimension of being fundamentally alien to the everyday practitioners of war and peace to which it is directed. Rather, the norm of peace is announced as that to which humankind—born of the dust of the earth—must aspire if it is to realize a dimension of spiritual existence that is, and has eternally been, the ultimate criterion for its achievement of a life lived in God's image. Indeed, it is the very essence of the prophet's mission to awaken this aspiration to the life of the spirit in ancient Israel.

The ideal of peace to which the people is called in its endeavor to transcend the "is" in the name of the ultimate "ought" of universal peace is an ideal that, as I have pointed out, receives ever fuller treatment in the biblical writings of the later prophets and in the songs of the psalmists. Hence, for example,

Micah's version of the culmination of the vision he shares with Isaiah: "But they shall sit every man under his vine and under his fig tree, and none shall make them afraid" (4:4); Zechariah's familiar refrain, uttered in God's name: "Not by might, nor by power, but by my spirit" (4:6); Hosea's rendering of the Lord's vision of universal peace: "I will abolish the bow, and the sword, and war from the land" (2:18); Habakkuk's admonition to the practitioner of violence: "Woe to him that buildeth a town with blood" (2:12); and, finally, the vision of the psalmist: "He maketh wars to cease unto the end of the earth" (46:9), and again, "seek peace and pursue it" (34:14).

This last injunction of the psalmist, to "seek peace and pursue it," can well serve as a point of departure for a discussion of those postbiblical accounts of attitudes toward peace and war in which the normative vision of shalom finds its fullest expression in Jewish thought. Indeed in the context of a tradition given over to intense debate concerning the relative weight of certain commandments vis-à-vis others, one finds among the authors of the Talmud and other postbiblical texts an astounding confluence of thinking on the primacy of peace. The psalmist's directive to "pursue peace," for example, is echoed both in the writings of Hillel around the turn of the common era ("Be of the disciples of Aaron, loving peace and pursuing peace")[3] and in a later exegetical text devoted to the Book of Numbers. This latter text evidences most strikingly the primacy given by the rabbis to the commandment to pursue peace over other commandments:

> The Torah did not insist that we should actually go in pursuit of the commandments but said: "If a bird's nest chance to be before thee" (Deuteronomy 22:6); "If thou meet thine enemy's ox" (Exodus 23:4). . . . In all these cases, if they come your way you are commanded to perform the duties connected with them, but you need not go in "pursuit" of them. In the case of peace, however, "seek peace" wherever you happen to be, and "pursue it" if it is elsewhere [Midrash, Bemidbar Rabbah, Seder Chukkat, part 19, §27].

The rabbinic tradition spared little in its designation of peace as the cornerstone of God's creation:

> Therefore one man was created . . . to teach you that he who kills one soul, of him it is said that it is as if he had killed an entire world for he destroys all future generations that would have come from that one person, and he who saves the life of one person, of him it is as if he had saved an entire world [Sanhedrin, 37a].

Peace is likened by the rabbis to a leavening agent of creation: "Great is peace, because it is to the earth what yeast is to the dough" (Baraita de Perek ha-Shalom); at times the primacy of peace in the rabbinic storehouse of values is simply proclaimed outright: "Great is peace, for it is equal to everything"

(Bemidbar Rabbah, 11:7). And if doubts remain as to the value to be ascribed to pursuing peace in comparison with the value—so fundamental to any monotheistic system—of renouncing the worship of idols, all one must do is attend to the words of Genesis Rabbah:

> Great is peace, because if the Jews were to practice idolatry, and peace prevailed among them at the same time, God would say, "I cannot punish them, because peace prevails among them" [38:6].

In a sustained and concerted effort to readdress and reinterpret the many references to militancy in the Pentateuch, the rabbis went so far in their exegesis as to embrace the refusal to obey a command of God in the name of the pursuit of peace:

> God commanded Moses to make war on Sihon, as it is said, "And contend with him in battle" (Deuteronomy 2:24), but he did not do so. God said to him: "I have commanded you to make war with him, but instead you began with peace; by your life, I will confirm your decision; every war upon which Israel enters, they shall begin with a declaration of peace" [Deuteronomy Rabbah 5:12].

What was termed at the beginning of this chapter the existence of violence "under judgment," what was termed a "moral tension" regarding accounts of violence in the early books of the Old Testament, now, in the hands of the authors of the Talmud, becomes nothing less than an explicit celebration of a creature's right to contest aspects of the morality of a sometimes warring deity. Such contestation, in the eyes of the rabbis, can meet with success: the Lord is, so to speak, a good learner:

> When the Holy One, Blessed be He, said to him "visiting the iniquities of the fathers upon the children" (Exodus 20:5), Moses responded: "Lord of the Universe! Many are the wicked who have begotten righteous men. Shall the latter really partake of the iniquities of their fathers? Terach worshipped idols, yet his son Abraham was a righteous man. Hezekiah, too, was righteous, though his father, Ahaz, was wicked. . . . Is it proper that the righteous should suffer for the iniquity of their fathers?" The Holy One, Blessed be He, said to Moses: "You have taught me something! By your life, I shall nullify My words and affirm yours" [Bemidbar Rabbah Seder Chukkat, part 19, §33].

What are we, given over to the task of inquiring into the possibility of a dominant current of thought regarding peace and war in the Jewish tradition, to make of this evidence gleaned from the rabbinic tradition? First of all we must take care not to see the rabbinic celebration of the primacy of peace as any totally innovative current in Jewish thought. As I have endeavored to argue, a moral tension vis-à-vis acts of violence is already in evidence in the earliest biblical writings, a tension that, although reaching a height in the Talmudic corpus, is never relaxed on the continuum of Jewish thought.

Nor must we fail to recollect that in Judaism it is not a matter of relegating to some inferior status a line of thinking developed by Talmudic authorities in comparison with that expressed in holy scripture. Indeed, holiness pervades the tradition as a developing whole. Not only was it the case that for many interpreters of Judaism the Talmud was itself understood to be in harmony with the revelation at Sinai, but it could also be argued that divine revelation covered, "in the words of the third-century Rabbi Joshua ben Levi, 'even the comments some bright student will one day make to his teacher.' "[4] The shalom tradition in the Talmud can thus never be assigned a secondary weight vis-à-vis any alleged "true" depiction of Jewish attitudes recorded in the canonical writings as such.

SELF-CRITICISM

More than this needs to be said, however. That self-criticism whose seeds are to be found in the Old Testament and whose flowering manifests itself in postbiblical literature *at one and the same time thematizes the shalom teaching in Judaism and serves as a living example of the essence of peacemaking itself.* That is to say, in its ability to challenge its own word, this tradition exemplifies the very openness to critique that lies at the core of the activity of making peace. Without a receptivity to the activity of dialogue in its very midst— without an awareness of the need for some self-scrutiny—the voices of scripture and its exegetical offshoots run the eternal risk of serving merely ideological ends, of mirroring the dominant thought of a given time and place, rather than of fulfilling the "sacred" task of exhorting their readers to ever transcend the alleged givens of existence in pursuit of the realization of the spirit. The dialogical give-and-take in Jewish tradition is thus not merely accidental to any message about war and peace that might be conveyed therein; the enactment of moral tension concerning violence in the tradition is itself a crucial aspect of its teaching concerning shalom.

The postbiblical authorities, moreover, do more than extend in degree and scope the beginnings of self-criticism found in scripture. Individual actions and even whole characters of biblical personages are here reinterpreted and ultimately reinvested with the Talmudic emphasis on shalom. The same "trained men" who followed Abraham into battle, as recounted in Genesis 14:14, are referred to as "scholars" in the Talmud.[5]

In a much-quoted passage concerning the character of Jacob, the Talmudic authorities explain the seeming redundancy of "fear" and "distress" in a passage from Genesis, "Then Jacob was greatly afraid and was distressed" (32:7), in this manner: Jacob felt "fear" that he would be slain by his brother Esau, but "distress" at the thought that he, Jacob, might himself be a slayer.[6]

David, whose aggressive traits and feats of prowess in battle begin to be called into question even within the text of the Old Testament, is largely transformed in the Talmud from military hero to a sweet and pacific psalmist; at midnight, we are told, David would be awakened by the strings of his harp—vibrating on their own—so that he might pursue his essential vocation as a student of the Torah.[7]

Not only were personages of the Bible thus recast in their fundamental attributes of character; key terms and concepts referring to power and military might also undergo a process of reinterpretation by the authors of the later tradition. Jacob's "sword" becomes "prayer"; his "bow" is now a "supplication."[8] In the yet later mystical treatise, the Zohar, the Hebrew letter "zayin," a word that also means "weapon," is for this reason refused the privilege—sought by each of the letters of the alphabet as they present their credentials before God—of serving as the first letter of the Torah.[9] The very notion of "might" is spiritualized: "Who is mighty?" ask the sages. The response: "He who subdues his desires" (Avot 4:1). And again, Isaiah 28:6, "For strength to them that turn the battle to the gate" is understood to be alluding to those who are victorious in scholarly disputations.[10]

The festival of Chanukah is reinterpreted so as to put aside the heroic deeds recounted in the Books of the Maccabees in favor of the recitation of the tale of the miracle of God's intervention resulting in the burning of oil in the rededicated temple for eight days, instead of the anticipated one day. Indeed, the name of the military hero of Chanukah, Judas Maccabeus, is notably absent from the Talmudic corpus.

None of these citations from postbiblical writings, however, is here adduced in order to make a case for any principled pacifist position as a dominant mode of thinking in the Jewish tradition. As we shall see below, the Talmudic authorities were quite vocal concerning those instances in which killing was permitted. Support for pacifism as a moral position in postbiblical Judaism is not lacking, however. In the celebrated dispute between Rabbi Yochanan ben Zakkai and the zealots who wished to preserve Jewish independence from Roman rule at all costs, it is the open advocacy of nonresistance on the part of the former that is remembered as providing for the very continuity of Jewish learning—and thus of Jewish life: by secretly negotiating a military surrender with the Romans, Rabbi Yochanan received in return the guarantee that he could establish the academy at Yavneh, which, according to tradition, made possible the cultural survival of his people.

Moreover, a tradition proclaiming (in the ethics of Rabbi Nathan) that the greatest hero is one who is successful in transforming a foe into a friend is a tradition that is no stranger to *active* pacifist strategies for peacemaking. (Striking examples of such activist strategies are recounted in Reuven Kimelman's notable paper on "Nonviolence in the Talmud."[11] Commenting on a verse concerning Aaron, Rabbi Meir, for example, is quoted as follows:

> When two men had quarreled with each other, Aaron would go and sit down with one of them and say to him: "My son, mark what thy fellow is

saying! He beats his breast and tears his clothing, saying 'Woe unto me! How shall I lift my eyes and look upon my fellow! I am ashamed before him, for it is I who treated him foully.' " He would sit with him until he had removed all rancor from his heart, and then Aaron would go and sit with the other one and say to him: "My son, mark what thy fellow is saying! He beats his breast and tears his clothing, saying, 'Woe unto me! How shall I lift my eyes and look upon my fellow; I am ashamed before him, for it is I who treated him foully.' " He would sit with him until he had removed all rancor from his heart. And when the two men met each other, they would embrace and kiss each other [Abot de Rabbi Nathan, XII].

Or we can cite the case of the third-century Rabbi Alexandri who attributes to God, through the agency of the Torah, the responsibility for the resolution of conflict through nonviolent means:

Two donkey-drivers who were walking by the way hated each other. One of their donkeys sat down. His companion saw it, and passed on. When he had passed, he thought: It is written in the Torah, "If you see the ass of one who hates you . . . you shall surely help him to lift it up." Immediately he returned and loaded with him. He [the former] began to say to himself: So-and-so is thus my friend and I did not know. Both entered an inn and ate and drank. Who is responsible for their making peace? The fact that the latter had looked into the Torah. Accordingly, it is written: "Thou hast established righteousness" (Psalms, 99:4) [Tanhuma Yashon, Mispatim I].

One should not wonder that a people who adhere to a tradition in which it is claimed that "Whenever destruction of the wicked takes place, there is grief for them above" (Zohar I:576), should endeavor to make the means of conflict-resolution commensurate with its end.

Even if it is the case, as Kimelman has argued and as we have seen evidenced in the above examples, that "alongside the normative legal tradition there existed in this period of third- and fourth-century Palestinian Talmudic authorities a concomitant undercurrent,"[12] an undercurrent of pacifism as a moral absolute, it has been my contention throughout this chapter that the so-called normative legal tradition is itself one in which all sanctioning of violence is subject to moral scrutiny. Yes, mainstream Jewish thought throughout the ages upholds the duty to preserve one's own life. Yet the Talmudic sages render the fulfillment of this duty in terms that are ethically complex:

In every other law of the Torah, if a man is commanded, "Transgress and suffer not death," he may transgress and not suffer death, excepting idolatry, incest, and shedding blood. . . . Murder may not be practiced to save one's life. . . . Even as one who came before Raba and said to him,

"The governor of my town has ordered me, 'Go, and kill so-and-so; if not, I will slay thee.' " Raba answered him: "Let him rather slay you than that you should commit murder; who knows that your blood is redder? Perhaps his blood is redder" [Sanhedrin, 74a].

These same authorities went so far as to qualify, ethically speaking, even the apparently clear right of individuals to defend themselves from an attacker with murderous intent: the same authors of Sanhedrin 74a caution the pursued against using any more force than is necessary to deter pursuers from their purposes. Any excess of force applied to one's own pursuer, or to that of a bystander, is outlawed:

If one is able to save a victim at the cost of only a limb of the pursuer and does not take the trouble to do so, but saves the victim at the cost of the pursuer's life by killing him, he is deemed a shedder of blood and he deserves to be put to death. He may not, however, be put to death by the court, because his true intention was to save life; he must be punished rather than put to death [Mishneh Torah, Hilchot Rozeach I:13].

Nor does a profound set of moral ambiguities surrounding violence against the enemy in war escape the attention of the rabbis. First of all, it should be noted that although war against other nations was by no means proscribed in the tradition—indeed, wars undertaken against "Amalek" (the brutal aggressor and the symbol of all nations that commit unprovoked aggression against the Jewish people) were considered "obligatory" (a term under which the rabbis also included the ancient conquest of Canaan)—limitations of the extent and kind of permissible destruction are clearly in evidence. According to the Code of the great Maimonides, "When seige is laid to a city for the purpose of capture, it may not be surrounded on all four sides, but only on three in order to give an opportunity to escape to those who would flee to save their lives . . ." (Mishne Torah, Hilchot Melachim, VII:7). And Maimonides forbids, in the same treatise, both the cutting down of fruit-bearing trees outside a city under seige and the wanton destruction of household furniture, clothing, and food.

Indeed, the rabbis dare to take exception with the word of the Torah that demands the *total* destruction of "Amalek" and the inhabitants of the seven original nations of Canaan. The sages of the Talmudic era and later refuse to take it upon themselves to subscribe to the concept of an enemy's annihilation. Thus Maimonides—recalling the spirit familiar to us from earlier rabbinic sources—proclaims:

No war is declared against any nation before peace offers are made to it. . . . If the inhabitants make peace and accept the seven commandments enjoined upon the descendants of Noah, none of them is slain [Mishneh Torah, Hilchot Melachim VI:1-3].

It should be noted that the acceptance by individuals of the seven Noachian commandments—most of which are incorporated into the decalogue—was equivalent, for the rabbis, to their affirmation of their moral agency—and thus of their humanity.[13]

SCRUTINY

What are we to glean from the spirit of these judgments of the rabbis, which, although not prohibiting violence, constitute attempts to question it? The strength of the Jewish contribution to peace advocacy, I contend, lies not in any moral absolutism regarding acts of violence, but rather in a firm tradition of moral scrutiny vis-à-vis such violence, a scrutiny that can be fully understood only against the horizon of the prophetic and rabbinic vision of the ideal of universal peace. To realize this vision—to fulfill Isaiah's glorious imperative—one must take as point of departure an observation concerning the nature of our humanity, which seems hardly glorious! Judaism has never cast doubt on the paradoxical nature of God's human creatures as the locus of a meeting of earth and heaven, of the mundane and the holy. As the twentieth-century philosopher Martin Buber suggests, we would do well to begin articulating an attitude toward peacemaking with the Hasidic Rabbi Bunam's command that each of us have "two pockets, so that he can reach into the one or the other, according to his needs. In his right pocket are to be the words: 'For my sake was the world created,' and in his left: 'I am earth and ashes.' "[14] A Jewish teaching on peace and war, in other words, must originate in the firm acknowledgment of the admixture of good and evil "urges" that we most fundamentally are.

The above, however, is *only* a point of departure. The Hasidic movement, born in eighteenth-century Eastern Europe and reaffirmed by Buber as occupying an important, though often unacknowledged, role in the larger tradition, asks us to deal with the urge toward violence, as with all evil, by not averting our eyes from its presence, but rather by facing it and transforming it in acts that can be called nothing short of redemptive. That is to say, one must follow the advice of Rabbi Abraham who proclaimed that "what is needed is not to strike straight at evil, but to withdraw to the sources of divine power, and from there to circle around evil, bend it, and transform it into its opposite."[15]

Heeding the rabbinic injunction to serve God with both one's good and one's evil "inclination"—the word in Hebrew connotes "creative impulse"—one must take the "raw matter" of human existence and strive to sanctify or hallow each and every element therein. No human inclination is in and of itself—or of some eternal necessity—evil.

How might this teaching shed light on a peculiarly Jewish view of peace? The activity of judgment or moral scrutiny of violent conflict that has served, in this chapter, to characterize the tradition's mode of relating to violence in its midst is a judgment and scrutiny that, although acknowledging the existence of such inclinations toward violence—and the ever-present possibility of their realization in overt deeds of force—can exist only against the backdrop of a vision of peace. Such a peace of the future is no static end to be achieved "once and for all," but a living goal eternally to be achieved—and renewed—in the everyday conduct of individuals and nations alike.

This vision of peace, most fully articulated by Buber in the contemporary period but consonant, I contend, with the shalom tradition as a developing whole, foresees no idealized sense of "reconciliation" that would be based on an avoidance of conflict among human, all-too-human, creatures. Rather, the ideal of peace that serves as the norm against which all acts of conflict are to be judged is a "peace of dialogue," a peace consisting of the refusal to see either oneself or one's partner in conflict as, in principle, primary; primacy is reserved for the dialogical encounter itself! In Buber's words:

I believe, despite all, that the peoples in this hour can enter into dialogue, into a genuine dialogue with one another. In a genuine dialogue each of the partners, even when he stands in opposition to the other, heeds, affirms, and confirms his opponent as an existing other. Only so can conflict certainly not be eliminated from the world, but be humanly arbitrated and led towards its overcoming.[16]

In learning to thus confront one another as individuals, and as groups of individuals formed as nation-states, we will be achieving a dialogical peace-making that is nothing short of the essence of a spiritual transcendence to which I alluded above. Within this frame of reference for understanding an ideal of peace, moreover, we are in a better position to grasp what I have argued earlier to be the self-illustrating character of that moral scrutiny of acts of violence that pervades Judaism: in thus challenging the early teachings of their tradition, the prophets and sages of Israel engage in dialogical activity that is a living enactment of the peacemaking of which the tradition speaks.

This notion of dialogical encounter, which emerges from the peace tradition in Judaism, is no equivalent of any abstract moral postulate. The resistance, by and large, to what I have termed a "principled" condemnation of the use of force in Judaism is well illustrated in the writings of Buber. He refuses to reject, in absolute terms, the use of violence in a context in which the life of the human creature is in danger of being sacrificed on the altar of a seemingly "dried up," dogmatic rendering of a strategy of nonviolent resistance. In his 1939 letter to Mahatma Gandhi, Buber tenders his reply to the latter's suggestion that Jews in Germany use satyagraha, "truth-force," as the most effective response to Nazi persecutions of the Jews. Gandhi had argued three months previously:

If the Jewish mind could be prepared for voluntary suffering, even a massacre would be turned into a day of thanksgiving and joy that Jehovah had wrought deliverance of the race even at the hands of the tyrant. For to the God-fearing, death has no terror.[17]

Buber's response to Gandhi must be understood in the context of the former's well-documented praise of the living spirit of Gandhi's approach, a spirit that he believes has been betrayed by a mechanical application of abstract principle:

> And do you think perhaps a Jew in Germany could pronounce in public one single sentence of a speech such as yours without being knocked down? . . . An effective stand may be taken against unfeeling human beings in the hope of gradually bringing them thereby to their senses, but a diabolical steamroller cannot be so withstood.[18]

Although the right to self-defense, acknowledged consistently throughout the Jewish tradition, is to be exercised with great care by the dialogical peacemaker—often alternative modes of confrontation in the spirit of dialogue are called for, even at the risk of one's very life—this right is not to be sacrificed to any ideology abstracted from situations as such.

VISION OF PEACE

I have argued, finally, that the vision of universal peace that constitutes the horizon against which judgments concerning human conduct are to be made is a vision perpetually to be renewed in the everyday situations in which human creatures find themselves cast. Resources for peacemaking derive from both the so-called good and evil inclinations within us. The Hebrew word for "inclination"—*yetzer*—I have noted, connotes "creative impulse." And here the notion of a "creative" role for the peacemaker is to be understood in earnest: Judaism proclaims the essentially incomplete nature of creation, the notion that the world is in need of repair. The concept of *tikkun olam,* literally, "fixing the world," assigns to God's creatures the task of co-creation, the task of assuming partnership with God in the building of a world at peace. Again Buber's words are instructive, as he urges us to become no less than God's fellow workers in the task of redeeming history![19] In the work of the repair of the universe, the peacemaker, according to Judaism, is God's essential companion.

The very meaning of the Hebrew word *shalom* confirms the interpretation, argued above, of the centrality of a vision of (dialogical) peace in the Jewish tradition. The origins of *shalom* are strikingly different from those of the English word "peace." The Latin *pax,* from which "peace" is derived, not only refers to what is in large measure a negative state of being—the absence of conflict—but was also used to denote that "absence of conflict" imposed by one nation upon another by force. *Pax Romana,* for example, was precisely what the term implies: a suspension of war in the name of a decidedly Roman peace! *Shalom* on the other hand, derives from a Hebrew root meaning "wholeness" or "completeness," the state of positive well-being that, I have argued, it is our task as God's co-workers to help realize.

This state of shalom is no different from Isaiah's envisioned kingdom in which "the wolf also shall dwell with the lamb, and the leopard shall lie down with the kid; . . . They shall not hurt or destroy in all my holy mountain; for the earth shall be full of the knowledge of the Lord, as the waters cover the sea" (11:6–9). Furthermore, we must resist the temptation to view Isaiah's prophecy as an eschatological truth to materialize only in some epoch beyond human time. In Buber's words:

> The prophecy of peace addressed to Israel is not valid only for the days of the coming of the Messiah. . . . It holds for today. "And if not now, when?" (*Sayings of the Fathers,* I:14). Fulfillment in a Then is inextricably bound up with fulfillment in the Now.[20]

We may well conclude, then, with a word directed to the "now" of Jewish existence in the 1980s. With a vision of peace-as-wholeness as its norm, contemporary Jewry is faced with challenges to realize its ideal, challenges that are unique in its recent history: statehood has provided a testing ground, a crucible, in which is to be forged a contemporary response to the summons of Isaiah. These words, I have argued, are no proclamation of an apocalyptic certainty. Rather they are a call, a demand to realize in action—ever to be renewed—the vision of making-whole. Isaiah's call must be heard as criticism and demand, as the incessant reminder that Jews committed to the building of a true Zion must avoid the employment of means that would be incommensurate, ethically speaking, with the ends of the shalom tradition sketched in this chapter. In a critical phase of a people's struggle to remain faithful to itself, it can only be hoped that Israel—together with its neighbors—will heed the eternal injunction to hasten in the pursuit of peace.

NOTES

1. D. Martin Dankin, *Peace and Brotherhood in the Old Testament* (London, Bannisdale Press, 1956), pp. 13–15.

2. John Ferguson, *War and Peace in the World's Religions* (New York, Oxford University Press, 1978), p. 80.

3. *Sayings of the Fathers,* I:12.

4. Cited in Israel Shenker, *Coat of Many Colors: Pages from Jewish Life* (Garden City, N.Y., Doubleday, 1985), p. 46.

5. Nedarim 32a.

6. Tanhoma, Vayishlah 4.

7. Sukot 26b and Berachot 36.

8. Mechilta Jethro 25.

9. Zohar I:3a.

10. Megillah 15b.

11. Reuven Kimelman, "Nonviolence in the Talmud," in *Roots of Jewish Nonviolence,* Allan Solomonow, ed. (Nyack, N.Y., Jewish Peace Fellowship, 1981).

12. Ibid., p. 43.

13. A fuller discussion of this point and a complete list of the commandments can be found in Richard G. Hirsch, *Thy Most Precious Gift* (New York, Union of American Hebrew Congregations, 1974), p. 28.

14. Martin Buber, *Tales of the Hasidim: Later Masters* (New York, Schocken Books, 1948), pp. 249–50.

15. Quoted in Maurice Friedman, "Hasidism and the Love of Enemies: A New Approach to Reconciliation," *Fellowship* (November 1964) 10.

16. Martin Buber, "Genuine Dialogue and the Possibilities of Peace," in *Pointing the Way* (New York, Harper and Row, 1962), p. 238.

17. "Gandhi's Statement from the *Harijan*, November 26, 1938," in *Pamphlets of the "Bond"* (Jerusalem, Reuben Mass, 1939), p. 42.

18. Ibid., pp. 4–5.

19. Martin Buber, "And If Not Now, When?" in *Israel and the World: Essays in a Time of Crisis* (New York, Schocken Books, 1948), p. 239.

20. Ibid.

4

Haim Gordon

Beyond Fatalism:
Education for Peace within Judaism

The thrust of this essay is that the fatalist is the enemy of the educator for peace; hence the educator must learn how to respond to this enemy. Although, as a Jew, I will be showing how one may confront this enemy on the basis of Judaism, it is clear to me that the core of each world religion is antifatalistic, simply because fatalism undermines the spirit of any religion that emphasizes human freedom. For instance, the Jew's freedom to choose—between slavery and freedom, between faith in God and denial of God, between adhering to God's commandments and ignoring them—is central to the Jewish faith and is crucial for the emergence of the spirit of Judaism. In Christianity, Islam, Buddhism, and other faiths one can find a similar emphasis on freedom at the core of religious belief.

Fatalism, as the belief that all is either in the hands of God or is a result of necessity or of chance, effaces personal freedom. It allows persons to abdicate all responsibility for what occurs in the world and in their specific lives.

One should add that fatalism and fanaticism are Siamese twins, born of the same wish: to allow one *not* to assume personal responsibility for one's life, especially for one's passions. Fatalists deny the importance of one's passions in developing a relationship with God and with one's fellow humans, a denial leading to a repression of those passions; fanatics allow their passions to erupt, primarily because they cannot cope with them in establishing relationships with God and with other persons. Both fatalists and fanatics speak about faith in God but refuse to acknowledge that such faith demands that one learn to live with one's passions while assuming responsibility for one's life and for what occurs in the world. In short, such a life is the embodiment of a lie.

45

In Judaism, Christianity, and Islam, all persons, with their passions, deeds, failings, and misgivings, are called upon to relate to the personal God. When they respond to this calling, their act of faith is also an act of courage. Fatalists and fanatics are unwilling to take the risk of establishing such a personal relationship, which daily demands accountability for one's decisions and one's deeds. Hence they project themselves as inert objects within God's domain: they are rocks in God's edifice of reality or pebbles in God's slingshot. And these rocks, these pebbles—these inert beings who do not have the courage to be persons—proclaim that they epitomize true faith.

Here is a major source of their living as a lie. A rock in God's masonry, a pebble in God's pouch, cannot establish the communion with God necessary for true faith. Yet the distortion of these Siamese twins goes deeper. The fatalist and the fanatic cannot efface their subjectivity, and they know it, even if they attempt to eradicate their freedom by projecting themselves as God's inert tools. One must be human in order to be able to imagine or project oneself as, or to demand of oneself to be, a tool of God. One must have freedom in order to be able to suppress one's personal responsibility and one's freedom. One must have passions in order to be able to be frigid, or to resign oneself to inertness. By using one's subjectivity to suppress oneself as a subject, by using one's freedom to deny that freedom, by directing one's passions to the suppression of passions, fatalists create a powerful dialectic, a dialectic that endows them with power. But it is not the dialectic of communion, neither with one's fellow humans nor with God. Hence living as a fatalist or as a fanatic is a way of distorting one's freedom and of lying to God by denying the depth, the uniqueness, and the godly image of one's own human face.

All this is not new. Condemning the fatalist and the fanatic in certain sections of Western society is like burning a straw effigy. And yet fatalism has made inroads into Western existence and thought, and has created a situation in which education for peace is very difficult, at times nearly impossible. (Fatalism also manifests itself in many corners of the contemporary Islamic world, giving rise to phenomena such as the fanaticism in Iran; it also prevails in many areas in the Far East. But addressing the problems of these fatalistic societies and regimes is beyond the scope of this essay.)

The problem with Western neofatalism is that the wolf parades in many a sheepskin: that of liberalism, apologetics, orthodoxy, racism. It is not the strict fatalism that one encounters among poverty-stricken Egyptians in the back alleys of Cairo. Ours is rather a seeping fatalism, waving banners reading "Be Realistic!" or hiding itself under a nostalgic apologetics that advocates: "We have to be nice and let those in power make the appropriate decisions; after all they know what really is happening." In short, this seeping fatalism is not only a flight from personal responsibility, it is a rejection of joy in life, a refusal to embrace a just and human vision based on one's religious heritage, and, in a world on the brink of nuclear disaster, it is also a denial of the need to educate for peace.

Enough. Now let me prove all this, using Judaism and the situation in Israel as a case study.

FATALISM AND FANATICISM IN CONTEMPORARY ISRAEL

Jewish history in the twentieth century is very much the history of the involvement of Jews in devastating wars. In previous centuries Jews suffered because of wars; in this century the question of Jewish existence was central to what the wars were all about. Hitler declared clearly his intention to make the world *judenrein* (free of Jews); and the rhetoric of many Arab leaders before Sadat's peace initiative, and even after the signing of the Egyptian-Israeli peace treaty, has not fallen far behind. The very existence of the Jewish people has been repeatedly called into question. Hence, almost every Jew has learned a disturbing truth: one must take the rhetoric of the avowed enemies of Israel very seriously; it is a rhetoric that may lead to horrendous deeds.

Jews have been affected personally. I do not recall ever having met Jews above the age of thirty-five who could not describe a personal involvement in these wars. Either they had personally participated in one of the Israeli-Arab wars or in the Holocaust, or some close relative or friend had gone through these experiences. Many had friends or family members who had been killed. The shedding of Jewish blood is not an external abstract phenomenon for the adult Jew; it is a phenomenon that has to do with pages in the family album, with personal memories, with disturbing nightmares. And because history is central to the experience of living as a Jew—the God of Abraham is revealed to Abraham and his progeny as the God of history—this sad and terrifying history has left a deep imprint upon the Jewish people. Unfortunately, the response of many Jewish persons to this history has often not accorded with the spirit of Judaism. It has often been fatalistic.

Indeed fatalism and fanaticism have been growing in Israel during the past decade. One immediate reason for this development was the government of the right-wing Likud Party, which was in power from 1977 to 1984, and explicitly supported political bodies that professed fatalism and fanaticism. Another reason is that fanaticism has been on the upsurge among Arabs and Muslims in the Middle East in recent years. But the growth of fatalism in Israel was also an outcome of the fact that the religious establishment and religious leaders in Israel have ignored the messages of peace and dialogue within Judaism for years. Judaism and Jewish chauvinism have lately merged in greater or lesser degrees in the minds of most Jews. An antichauvinistic Judaism seems impossible. But that is the kind of Judaism I shall be advocating, while indicating how it can help counter fatalism, and educate for dialogue and peace.

Consider the following from the *Sayings of the Jewish Fathers:* "Hillel said, Be of the disciples of Aharon; loving peace and pursuing peace; loving mankind and bringing them nigh to the Torah" (I, 13). Working for peace is an active undertaking according to Hillel. One must pursue peace; the Hebrew word he uses, *rodef,* is closer to "chasing after." Thus one should chase after peace, not only strive to attain it by some passive design. Hillel also indicates that loving peace and pursuing peace are parallel to loving humankind and bringing it closer to God's word, the Torah. (The translation is somewhat faulty. Hillel says to love each man, *haadam,* not the abstract concept of humanity.) Hence the precept to work passionately for peace resides within Judaism: Jews should passionately, actively, wholeheartedly pursue and love peace, much as they strive to love their fellow humans and bring them close to the Torah. Peace is not a result of fate, but of your own personal doing, says Hillel. Hence he entreats every Jew: Be of the disciples of Aharon.

In the light of Hillel's saying let us examine some of the self-justifications presented by Jewish fatalists to peacemakers. One such justification comes from the "impotent serialist." (I am here borrowing a term from Jean Paul Sartre, who described at length the dialectic of the serial nature of human existence and its resultant social impotency.) Although agreeing that what Hillel said was "edifying," this type of fatalist will counter by describing the futility of one's personal actions in a world governed by economic and social developments that render the strivings of any individual insignificant. They hold that movement toward peace or war in the Middle East or in the world will be an outcome of economic and social developments that are beyond the reach of the educator, or even of most politicians. Of course, these fatalists may add, the educator should educate for the possibility of peace, but to be realistic one should understand how impotent one is in relation to, say, the power of the world military-industrial complex. Power struggles, economic developments, social upheavals, such as occured in Iran, are the stuff from which history is made. Hence, educating for peace, or for Jewish-Arab dialogue, or for mutual trust, can contribute little—if anything at all—to the dialectical developments of history.

Thus, serial fatalists strive to put their listeners (or readers) in a no-win situation. Often the fatalists have much to gain, but that will be discussed a little later. First it is important to point out the logical fallacy in their presentation. Even if we grant the most dismal view of history that these fatalists wish to present, and they usually do not wish to be too dismal, we cannot escape the fact that a necessary component of the economic or social developments that they describe is human praxis. (Economic or social developments do not occur outside human society, outside the realms where human beings engage in praxis.) Whether fatalists like it or not, these developments are partially a result of persons engaging their freedom to attain certain results, to surpass certain situations, to create certain goods. Human freedom is the fuel of economic and social developments; human beings make the decisions and engage in the work that help bring about these developments.

In other words, these fatalists are only half dialecticians. They have chosen the deterministic half of dialectics, purposely ignoring the importance of human freedom. This half truth often serves their purposes. If they are politicians, it allows them to convince their listeners of their social impotence: that they should not engage in efforts to influence or alter political decisions. Politicians also know that leaving the search for peace in the hands of Big

Brother, "because there is nothing realistic one can do," accords with the lack of courage, indolence, and self-indulgence of much of their constituency.

If the half dialecticians are theoreticians, they are lazy, finding it much easier to describe a situation as developing according to fixed criteria, than to engage in the hard historical research that might help one to understand a specific development, or to seek new ideas on how a specific situation could be changed.

In both cases, they are dishonest. And there are rewards for their dishonesty. Such fatalism allows for a general milieu of nonaccountability, in which the wielders of power are united with their adherents in negating the significance of personal responsibility. And by negating the possibility of new possibilities, fatalists are attuned to the laziness and unwillingness of many to seek new ideas.

These fatalists will often endeavor to prove that God is on their side. Only enemies will not encounter God or the millennium on their itinerary. Hence the serial fatalists never present too dismal a picture of historical developments: it might cast doubt on the inevitability of their presentation, or on the general consensus that they need not be accountable. Thus, even though it is very dismal to consider the amount of nuclear weapons stockpiled in the U.S.A. and their potential power of annihilation, few politicians dare present this situation as a Pandora's box that does not include hope.

More recently, to strengthen their case, these fatalists have been establishing a covenant with social scientists and philosophers of the analytic or behavioral school. The basis of this covenant is the wish to accept as final the structure of deep alienation in contemporary life, coloring it with scientific determinism. All participants in this covenant deny the existence and the significance of human freedom, responsibility, dignity. They have nothing to suggest to the educator for peace, who must begin by affirming what they deny.

Most politicians are serial fatalists. They adopt this approach intuitively as a way of consolidating their power. Ideas do not move them, only the wish to attain and to hold on to power. To that end they manipulate ideas. In Israel since the mid-1960s (at least) we have been ruled by serial fatalists, whatever their party affiliation. These political serialists find it easy to communicate with each other, despite seeming party differences, because they all share a fatalistic *Weltanschauung*. The two general elections in Israel in 1981 and 1984 were especially characterized by a poverty of ideas in relation to Israel's problems, including the problem of peace. Each party merely colored its serial fatalism with some political taint, be it liberalism, or labor, or racism.

Serial fatalists as politicians should arouse concern when they are in power in any nation. In Israel the rule of political fatalists is toxic to our spiritual life. Remember, Israel is a nation born of a specific covenant with God, a nation with a spiritual message to bear and to daily realize. In biblical times prophets arose again and again to remind the children of Israel and their political leaders of the covenant with God, and of the need to counter political leaders who degraded and betrayed the spirit of that covenant. Today we have no prophets, and those who hold themselves to be speakers for the people—novelists, artists, journalists, some scholars—sadly fail the people. I will return to these false guardians of the spirit of Judaism shortly, but first it is important to add a few comments. The main point is that most political fatalists know how to conceal their fatalism by calling themselves "realists." But the realm of the ethical, the realm of spirit, emerges only when one transcends such "realism." The fatalist is really concealing a cowardice to confront and to relate to such realms as the ethical and the spiritual.

I am saying categorically that one of the reasons why the peace process stalled in the Middle East, and why educating for peace receives no support from the political establishment, is that most of the leaders of our country during past decades have been cowards. As politicians they did not dare to take an ethical risk; they feared the realm of the spirit and did their best to ignore it. The only risks they took were political risks. But as President Jimmy Carter seemed to have sensed when he initiated the Middle East peace talks, working for peace begins with an ethical risk that has political implications.

The challenge facing the Jewish educator for peace is to break through a vicious circle of fatalism and cowardice. In other words, educating for peace begins and can only be sustained through acts of courage. Here is the reason I entitle this essay "Beyond Fatalism." Without the courage to take the risk of peace we Jews are falling prey to the antispiritualism of the political fatalist and endangering the spirit that sustains us as Jews. What I find most lacking in Israel today is the courage to educate for peace.

FAITH AND DOGMA

Hold it, someone may say. You are overlooking history. The establishment of the state of Israel in 1948, following half a century of Zionist activities and the terrible experience of the Holocaust, was done by the United Nations against the explicit wish of Israel's neighbors. Since then very few Arabs have whole-heartedly accepted a Jewish presence in the midst of a part of the world dominated by Arabs and Muslims. Hence many Jews would say that even thinking about observing Hillel's precepts is today an act of foolishness.

Furthermore, this same someone may say, you seem to have forgotten that five wars initiated by the Arabs and one by the Israelis have created an atmosphere of existential mistrust between Jewish and Arab citizens of Israel. (There are three million Jewish citizens in Israel and six hundred thousand Arab citizens. But there are in addition a million and a quarter Palestinians on the West Bank and in the Gaza Strip who have no government of their own and are citizens of no land, although they are currently under Israeli rule.) Existential mistrust is a relationship that arises between two persons (or two nations) when one believes that the other denies its right to exist and to realize its potential in that portion of the world to which one is attached. The relationship is expressed by the attitude: if I want to exist, I must *not* trust you. If you add to this mistrust the mistrust and explicit wish to destroy Israel professed by Arab nations such as Syria and Libya, you will understand why the person you call a serial fatalist relies on history. Furthermore, this situation is hardly conducive to the acts of courage you have been demanding from politicians.

One can present arguments back and forth concerning history; yet it would be very hard to find, within Israel or between Israelis and Egyptians, attempts to address the concrete problems of mistrust and hatred that exist between Jews and Arabs. It is precisely by ignoring this concrete situation of hatred and mistrust, and instead discussing history in general, that the serial fatalist attempts to induce the educator to be passive. But peacemaking is a doing, not a discussing or arguing about historical developments. Hillel called it "a chasing after"; one cannot chase after anything while sitting in an armchair and analyzing history. Education for peace in Israel means addressing Jewish-Arab hatred and mistrust here and now in one's daily life. And as stated above, such a doing has been ignored by mainstream and establishment Israel, because such a working for peace demands courage.

Here is where religious fatalists would intervene. "We agree with your emphasis on everyday doing and with your holding that Hillel is right," they would say, "but one must view Hillel's saying not as an isolated statement, but rather as a statement within the entire halakic literature. This literature tells us what to do in our daily life. Only by following the precepts of the Halakah, including the *Sayings of the Jewish Fathers,* can we, as Jews, continue to uphold the covenant with God. Hence, studying the Halakah and performing all the precepts of orthodox Judaism are the only way for the Jew to fulfill God's will on earth. Any attempt to deviate from this path is wrong."

Much has been written about how the embracers of a religious dogma are worshiping an idol and not the true God. As can be seen from their arguments, religious fatalists are primarily concerned with dogma and not at all concerned with faith. They seem to have forgotten that faith without dogma is difficult for the religious believer, but dogma without faith is sacrilegious. True faith must precede dogma; and without freedom there is no such faith. For instance, I find it very wrong to read the Bible (or any truly religious text, such as the New Testament or the Qur'ān) as these religious fatalists often suggest, primarily as a book of precepts serving as the basis of dogma. The Bible is the written account of the encounter between Abraham and God, and between Abraham's progeny and God. A living encounter. An encounter in which the children of Israel, as free persons, struggle within history to develop a personal relationship with God.

Religious fatalists are trying to eliminate two aspects of that encounter—that it occurred between free persons and God, and that it occurred within history. They wish to freeze Jewish history at the halakic stage or at the Diaspora stage of its development. But Jewish history is the history of the Jewish people, of that unique community that is the progeny of Abraham, of its life and struggles to fulfill the covenant Abraham made with God. It is not only the history of Jewish learning, or of the development of arguments in the Talmud, as religious fatalists seem to suggest. They forget that God is portrayed in the

Bible as concerned with the actions of the children of Israel within history, with political actions, with cultivating the land of Israel, with the pursuit of justice and peace. The development of Halakah and its recapitulation came much later, as a response of Jews to their living outside the land of Israel, and to some extent outside history. The halakic fatalists wish us Jews to forget history and to ignore the Jew's biblical commitment to act within history. These fatalists refuse to be pebbles in God's slingshot; they prefer to be inert rocks in God's social pyramid.

In other words, I am not attacking the halakic fatalists only because their worshiping of dogma makes them idol worshipers—which many of them are. I am not attacking them only because they superciliously pronounce that *only they* know the true way to God—a superciliousness that one does not find in Moses or Abraham, who spoke with God personally. I am not attacking them only for their bad faith, by which they are seemingly outside history, but know how to use political and economic situations for their personal benefit. (Israeli governments have channeled hundreds of millions of dollars to religious groups in order to gain their support in the Knesset—the Israeli parliament. Some of these groups deny the legitimacy of the Jewish state, because it did not originate with the coming of the Messiah. Some have diverted into private coffers funds earmarked for religious education. Greed is not necessarily a characteristic of the religious fatalist but, as Max Weber and others have shown, it often goes hand in hand with the repressing of human freedom by religious dogmatists.) And finally, I am not attacking these fatalists only for their stifling of Jewish joy in life, through such practices as their degrading the Jewish woman to the status of a "pariah." (No woman is allowed to read from the Torah. Many orthodox Jews refuse to touch a woman, because she may be in her period and "unholy"!)

I am attacking them mainly because they have in their deeds and fatalistic approach to Jewish existence attempted to efface the significance and the mystery of the encounter of Abraham and his progeny with God. By denying, effacing, and ignoring this encounter they have attempted to efface, deny, and ignore the importance of human freedom for Jewish faith, for the emergence of the mystery ensconced in the ability of each person to reach communion with God. I am attacking them because without human freedom there is no communion with the God of Abraham, there is merely an eclipse of God by fatalistic dogmatism.

Actions speak louder than words. I know that orthodox Jews will find many ways of responding with words and statements to my attacks. But the actions of orthodox Jewry are there, within Jewish history, to accuse them of all that I have stated. These religious fatalists cannot help us to pursue peace, because they refuse to immerse themselves in our history, except in order to reap benefits for themselves. They cannot help us in our attempts to live up to Hillel's saying, because they have no vision of the Jew acting in history. And finally, they cannot help us in the pursuit of peace, because their understanding of Judaism is built on a denial of many of the sources of love and passion that sustain the educator for peace.

CONTEMPORARY ISRAELI WRITERS

Armchair liberals have been under attack for decades. Yet they continue to flourish, lately among an entire generation of contemporary Jewish writers. Inasmuch as these writers are representatives of much Jewish thinking of today, I must address, if only briefly, their vacuity.

Prudence is the creed of liberals. They will notify all and sundry that they abhor racism, that they believe in peace and justice. They will write newspaper articles on humanism; they will gladly sign petitions for human rights or attend protest demonstrations against the reemergence of fascism. They will repeatedly emphasize the importance of freedom for the development of civilization and culture. Intellectually, they will support the issue of peace—at the opportune moment. But *passion*—that is another matter; that has nothing to do with their personal commitments. Put otherwise, they have no commitments, only ideas. Their support of peace is intellectual, not an act of their entire being. Hence they are *not* of the disciples of Aharon. They want nothing to do with chasing after peace, with passionately committing themselves and risking themselves for justice.

Through this lack of personal commitment, liberals tacitly support serial fatalists, their assumptions, their methods, and their adherence to the system. For serial fatalists, such behavior suffices. The know that if liberals see someone breeding racism, hatred, and war—someone within the system, someone like Ariel Sharon, the Israeli defense minister, for whom the war in Lebanon was a way to gain personal political power—they will complain, but nothing more. They will never endanger their status or their popularity by pointing an accusing finger at someone who promotes war and hatred. Or if they do, it is only when they know that the support of the masses is with them, and that other fingers are pointed in the same direction. Unlike the Hebrew prophets—Samuel, Nathan, Elijah, Isaiah—the liberals never stand alone and challenge the wielders of power. They will never risk themselves for the realization of a vision, or for the fulfillment of God's word. They will never fully give of themselves—say, by acting compassionately toward the stranger, the widow, the orphan. They will always make sure that their retreat is covered.

Unfortunately, these liberal fatalists are prominent among an entire generation of contemporary Jewish writers, scholars, and journalists. There are some exceptions, some journalists who are willing to point an accusing finger at the wielders of power. But most popular writers in Israel today, including Oz, Yehoshuah, Applefeld, Kanyuk, most Israeli scholars who relate to contemporary issues, and most journalists, writers, and scholars in the Diaspora who write for Jewish readers, are "prudent" liberals to the marrow of their bones.

Like many of their liberal counterparts in Europe and the United States, Jewish liberal fatalists are playing for the crowds and to the crowds. They are speakers for freedom on the intellectual level, and stiflers of freedom on the existential level. Hence they are in bad faith, which makes their writings stale. These writings do not express a struggle for freedom, or a commitment to compassion, such as one finds in many of Saul Bellow's books; they are not an expression of a passionate search for justice, or truth, or love, or God, or peace, or other goals that have been central to Jewish existence. Rather they are a description of a life totally indifferent to these goals; they are true portraits of their authors' liberal fatalism.

Or to return to the terrible history of war and the Holocaust, which has characterized Jewish existence in the twentieth century, not one of these Jewish writers has suggested how we might relate to our tormented history in order to educate for peace. Perhaps, because we have had this terrifying experience, like the victims of Hiroshima, we can express through deeds and actions the essence of Hillel's message in a manner that will arouse the world to listen. No, such an endeavor does not interest these writers. They know that suggesting such an approach would confuse the masses; it would mean not playing to their nostalgic memories, it would mean throwing out a challenge that would also challenge the comfortable feeling that "others are guilty vis-à-vis the Jews." Yes, suggesting such an approach would mean bringing something new and perhaps unpalatable to many of one's Jewish counterparts. And that is what these authors fear most.

THE DECALOGUE AND THE TORAH

All that I have written above I learned the hard way. For six years I have been educating Jews and Arabs to relate to each other dialogically, in the spirit of the philosophy of Martin Buber. (I have described some of my work in my book, *Dance, Dialogue, and Despair: Existentialist Philosophy and Education for Peace in Israel,* University of Alabama Press, 1986.) In my search for assistance and guidance for my work among my fellow Jews, I was repeatedly confronted by the fatalistic approaches described above. Of course, most of the fatalists whom I encountered never crystalized their views. Like so many others, their views were in flux; but underlying that flux was a vigorous stream of the types of fatalism I have articulated. Furthermore, their fatalism was expressed in their decisions and in their behavior. Similar attitudes of fatalism can, of course, be found in other faiths and milieus, especially in relation to economic inequality and oppression of the weak, including women. The peacemaker must counter such fatalism in all its expressions. In another article in this book I point out how this may be done. Here I shall indicate the more positive sources that the educator for peace within Judaism may use.

But first it is important to point out that there are exceptions to the trend of fatalism in Israel. Some members of the Israeli Knesset, such as Shulamit Aloni and Yosi Sarid, are strong antifatalists. I have mentioned that a few prominent Israeli journalists continually challenge the serial fatalism of many politicians. Among the antifatalists are probably some of the leaders of the Peace Now movement, which through demonstrations and press releases has attacked and criticized pro-war decisions of the Israeli government. And of course one meets concerned antifatalistic Jews in Israel and in the Diaspora on the grassroots level.

I denote these persons as antifatalistic—that is, as negators of fatalistic trends within Judaism and within Israeli society. I cannot, yet, define them in positive terms. For such to occur one must go beyond fatalism, and beyond the rejection of fatalism. Naturally, such a positive development can begin only with the negation of fatalism, but it must be a negation that can lead to a new synthesis with Jewish sources and with the lives of Jews. In short, this synthesis must be a new expression of our attempt to live up to Hillel's teaching. I shall now present some thoughts about such a synthesis.

A Jewish legend tells us that when the children of Israel entered into covenant with God at Mount Sinai, and received the Ten Commandments, all the souls of all the Jews who would be born in the future were present. Hence, the covenant was made not only between God, Moses, and the generation that came out of Egypt, but also between God and every Jew who will ever live. You were there, at Mount Sinai, says the legend; now it is your responsibility to live up to the covenant. It is your responsibility to realize these Ten Commandments in your daily life, and more, to live up to the spirit of the godly encounter. But what does it mean to live up to the spirit of the godly encounter?

There are two ways of such a living, and the Bible describes both: one way I term closed responsibility; the other, open responsibility and trust. The Bible describes both; each of its books addresses a certain historical situation, and each situation demands a different manner of acting responsibly, of living in accordance with the spirit of the godly encounter. In general, living up to the spirit of the Sinai encounter means endeavoring through one's everyday deeds to live in a manner that accords with God's will, in the broadest sense of God's words. But because God's word is usually addressed to a particular situation, there is great danger in taking it literally. For instance, I do not agree, despite the biblical injunction, that a person who gathers firewood on the Sabbath should be stoned. Here is where the difference between open and closed responsibility emerges; here is where we may also begin to see how open responsibility is related to peace.

The giving of the Ten Commandments, at which we were all present, was an act of love; God gave this treasure because God loved the children of Israel, each one of them, even those who were not yet born. Accepting the decalogue means accepting it with joy in life and with love. Think about it! If you do not accept a godly present with a deep joy in life, with a deep love for God who gave this present as an act of love, you are not accepting the present, you are merely taking it. Remember also that love of God within Judaism must be expressed through love of one's fellow humans—not only one's fellow Jews. Thus open responsibility for the Sinai encounter can thrive only on joy in life, on love for one's fellow human beings. Such love and joy underlie Hillel's telling us to pursue peace.

During long periods of Jewish history, it was appropriate for Jews to assume a closed responsibility for Judaism. When surrounded by enemies, when antisemitism was on the rampage, Jews turned their back to the world and to historical developments, and did their best to guard and to study the Bible, their precious gift from God. Maimonides and other prominent Diaspora thinkers understood living as a Jew as accepting a closed responsibility for Judaism—that is, as refraining from any active involvement in history. They interpreted the Bible accordingly, and presented philosophical and religious justifications for their views. But these justifications, astute as they may be, should not obscure the fact that a closed responsibility for what occurred at Sinai should not, cannot, become a fetish; it can be justified only as a passing stage toward a more open responsibility whereby Jews once more take part in history. Each generation, each Jew, must attempt to express participation in the godly encounter at Sinai in a manner of open responsibility—that is, as a responsibility for what is happening here and now in the world. Only if such a responsibility is gravely hindered by persecution and murder of Jews, can the Jew assume a more closed responsibility.

Let us repeat this point. God gave the decalogue and the Torah to the children of Israel as a gift of love. God did not give it to them to covet, to study, to guard, as a treasure that one does *not* share with one's fellows. Only if these others deny this gift and organize and participate in the persecution of Jews are they allowed to turn their back on history. If the world is even only partially open to accepting and to relating to God's gift to the children of Israel, then Jewish life must try to convey this gift of love to others—through daily deeds, through trying to act in accordance with God's commandments in one's own land, with one's fellow Jews, in one's interactions with persons of other faiths, and in national interactions with other nations.

Thus the first step in going beyond fatalism is assuming open responsibility for the godly encounter at Sinai. Today, as in the biblical period, Jews are immersed in history, and in history they must act. No Jew is excluded.

NAASEH VENISHMA

Open responsibility is also prominent in the New Testament, the Qur'ān, and basic texts of other faiths. Many messages of these faiths are also presented as acts of love. In short, the coupling of love and open responsibility can be found at the core of these faiths. This coupling rejects and deprecates the fatalism and fanaticism that have arisen periodically, distorted religion, and led to war and hatred. Yet this coupling is meaningful only if love and responsibility are expressed in the peacemaker's daily deeds. Peace education may benefit from discussion, but to counter fatalism and go beyond it, doing comes first.

There are many examples within Judaism of the basic tenet that doing comes first. For instance, the well-known saying: "The burden of the Torah and the Mitzvoth was given when the children of Israel said *Naaseh venishma"*—we shall do, (then) we shall hear. Or the story read every Passover Seder from the Haggadah: when Nachshon Ben Aminadav saw that Moses had lifted his staff to part the Red Sea, because the pharaoh's chariots were drawing near, and the sea did not part—Nachshon jumped into the sea, and then it parted.

Unfortunately, *Naaseh venishma*—we shall do, (then) we shall hear—has also been used by the liberal, the serial fatalist, and the orthodox Jew promoting a closed responsibility. They all agree that the Jew must do what needs to be done at this specific moment; but they hold that what needs to be done accords with their fatalistic view of Jewish existence. The orthodox Jew will say: "Of course *Naaseh venishma;* it tells us that what we have to do is to follow all the Mitzvoth of the *Shulchan Aruch* [a book explicating Jewish dogma] even if we do not understand the importance or the significance of a specific injunction. It is, after all, the doing that counts." One can give similar responses for other types of fatalism. They all overlook, probably on purpose, two points. First, Nachshon's deed was a spontaneous act of courage and faith that had nothing to do with following a specific injunction, with adhering to a specific view. We who know that the Red Sea parted find it difficult to imagine the danger of jumping into the waves when one does *not* know that it will part, when one only hopes that the sea will part—but it might not part, and one might drown. By acting in response to the given historical situation, Nachshon was surpassing the given commandments in the direction that he believed could lead the children of Israel to freedom. He was risking his life.Through his deed he believed that he would help Moses lead the children of Israel out of their present quagmire and their life of slavery. Nothing of such an attitude is found among fatalists.

Secondly, *Naaseh venishma* without open responsibility, without love for one's fellow humans, is a farce; it allows any view within Judaism to promote its cause, including the racism of Rabbi Meir Cahane, who holds that all Arabs in Israel should be killed or deported. Hence, the way many rabbis interpret *Naaseh venishma* is almost like spitting in God's eye. They use this saying to promote their own new idolatry of the land of Israel as free from an Arab population, or their version of Judaism as racism, or their insistence that one must reduce the Jewish woman to the status of a "pariah." More often than not, such an approach plays into their own lust for power. They lack any open responsibility toward all God's creatures. They know nothing of the doing of love and faith that stems from such a responsibility, or of the courage to lead persons to freedom.

Of course one could argue that I am choosing those elements of Judaism that suit me, those legends that I like, those interpretations that accord with my views. I am. My interpretation stems from my understanding of God as a spiritual being who relates to human beings as spiritual beings, endowed with freedom. Hence, I can perceive only two dialectics in Jewish existence. The fatalistic dialectic is governed by a twisting of *Naaseh venishma* into its opposite—first we shall hear, then we shall do. First there is dogma, or a fatalistic or liberal view of history, which we must understand, examine, weigh, discuss, argue about—then there is doing in the framework of this dogma, this *Weltanschauung*. Such a dialectic is governed by closed responsibility, by a rejecting of any attempt to surpass one's situation, by an adherence to dogma, by a stifling of human freedom, by a lack of courage. This dialectic appeals to many persons because it requires few risks—it excludes the risk of love for one's fellow humans, the risk of trusting them.

The second dialectic is the dialectic of open responsibility and of *Naaseh venishma;* it is a dialectic of courage, of surpassing, of going beyond one's present situation, of expressing one's freedom by taking the risks of faith and love for one's fellows. It is the dialectic of spiritual existence.

SUFFERING AND THE STRUGGLE FOR PEACE

In all faiths the dialectic of spiritual existence is problematic. They all indicate that striving to attain a spiritual life is a struggle and a risk, and one cannot know for certain whether specific deeds will lead to a more spiritual existence, to a relating to God as a spiritual being. Faiths indicate directions for the attaining of spirit, they do not ensure results. In Judaism we know that if one endeavors to accept the decalogue and the godly encounter at Sinai in a manner of open responsibility, and to express this open responsibility through daily courageous deeds, then one is striving to live a more spiritual life.

My limited experience in such matters stems from my six years of working to educate Jews and Arabs in the Middle East to relate to each other dialogically, in accordance with the teachings of Martin Buber. I never knew which of my deeds, which of our deeds, would lead to a more spiritual existence. But I did learn that dialogue teaches us to accept a more open responsibility, to be courageous, and being courageous leads to dialogue, and the entire process leads in some indirect, and at times direct, way to a partial realization of the peace and love that Hillel emphasizes—to a more spiritual existence. When one is in this dialectic, though, one does not see oneself evolving, becoming more free, more dialogical, more courageous. We are therefore left with no assurances—only with the deed to be done and with the manner of doing it.

But that is much. Moreover, it is a gift of God. Let us briefly look a bit closer at how this gift can help the Jewish educator for peace, especially in one's attempts to cope with our history of Holocaust.

Unlike the fatalist, who nostalgically embraces one's history, who constantly remembers one's pain in order to dwell again and again on their horrors, the Bible instructs us to learn from our pains—however horrible and terrifying those pains may have been. Crime should lead to punishment, the Bible proclaims, and one must chase after justice, much as one must chase after peace. But as time passes, one must go beyond the terrible crimes inflicted upon oneself or one's people and strive for a new manner of living one's Jewish existence in one's new situation, a manner that accords with God's will. The ability to begin a new life after a period of suffering is central to the message of the Hebrew prophets; it is also a main component of the covenant between God and Abraham. In short, from the sufferings of the *Galut,* the Diaspora, the Jew can and should learn to strive for an existence that will lead to less suffering and less killing in one's own milieu, and in the entire world. In the political realities that confront us, this is not a simple matter.

I have already mentioned that one of the important lessons to learn today is to take the rhetoric of our avowed enemies seriously. Thus if Iraq is building a nuclear plant and notifies everyone that if it succeeds in developing an atomic bomb it will use it against Israel, we should believe it. (These same Iraqis used poison gas against Iranian soldiers after repeatedly announcing that they would exterminate Iranians like insects.) We dare not and must not dismiss such sayings as mere rhetoric, especially in this century, after too many of our parents and grandparents ignored Hitler's rhetoric.

But we must also remember that our sufferings and our responsibilities as partners to a covenant with God demand that we work for peace and justice. Our strength to destroy Iraq's nuclear reactor, our strength to build a constructive democracy in the Middle East—that bastion of dictatorships and reactionary regimes—must be complemented by a striving to live a more spiritual existence as Jews. In every generation we must once again educate ourselves and each other, through our deeds, to live in the spirit of the godly encounter at Sinai, the spirit of open responsibility coupled with *Naaseh venishma*. One of the main fields where this can be done is in educating for peace and dialogue with our Arab neighbors.

Of course, we must come to the encounter with our neighbors from a position of strength—dialogue never occurs when one of the parties cowers before the other partner. But because of our terrible history, becaue of our need to live a life of the spirit, we dare not allow the issues of peace and justice to be put off. For instance, due to Israel's unwillingness to allow a Palestinian state to emerge on the West Bank and the Gaza Strip, or to grant the Arabs living there any semblance of autonomy and self-government, Israel is beginning to resemble an apartheid state. Such is a grave danger for the spirit of Judaism, just as it is a degrading, tormenting experience for the Arabs living in these areas. It is an unjust situation that breeds hatred and hostility.

Our situation is complex, but clear. We must educate for strength coupled with justice, for courage coupled with a passion for peace, for love of one's Arab neighbors coupled with a wish to learn from them, for a Judaism of open responsibility coupled with the ability to reevaluate our situation in the light of Hillel's message. In our work for peace we must also go beyond our concrete situation in the Middle East and utilize what we can learn from such an experience to educate for peace worldwide. That is the challenge of a Judaism beyond fatalism.

Three points still need to be made, even if very briefly. First, I have not mentioned the fact that fatalists usually accept the unfair way the economic pie is divided in their part of the world and elsewhere. Such an attitude accords with their adhering to those in power, and with their unwillingness to strive to change history for the better. But, as is well known, economic oppression is degrading and dehumanizing and frequently leads to hatred and to war.

Secondly, there is a joy in working for peace that the fatalist will probably never understand. It is the joy of expressing one's freedom and love, the joy of giving and building, of recognizing other persons in their otherness and of relating to them as others. This joy is stifled by the spirit of gravity that emanates from fatalism.

Thirdly, working for peace is one of the ways persons may learn to develop their spiritual powers. Hence, educating to go beyond fatalism in one's quest for peace is educating others to live a more spiritual existence.

A talmudic fable relates that when God wanted to present the decalogue to the children of Israel, the angels rebelled. "Why should these sinning mortals receive such a worthy gift, and we, your unsinning immortal servants are not deemed worthy of it?" The response came from the divine presence: "The decalogue is for those who may use it, who may learn every day anew from it how to live a more just, peaceloving, meaningful existence; you, my dear angels, have no such problems." And our rabbis added: Perhaps such a learning, perhaps such a becoming educated, puts humankind on a higher rung than the angels.

Christianity

5

Timothy George

A Radically Christian Witness for Peace

On Christmas Eve in 1917, the deadly trench warfare in France was halted for a few hours. Soldiers on one side of no-man's-land could hear the faint sound of carols being sung by soldiers on the other side. "Silent Night" was rendered in English by the American and British troops; the response, *"Stille Nacht,"* echoed from the German lines. "Sleep in heavenly peace . . . *schlaf in himmlischer ruh. . . ."* For a brief moment, along that disputed and much fought-over boundary between France and Germany, soldiers from both sides, who worshiped the same God and who prayed to the same Lord Jesus Christ, were able to transcend their lethal enmity and celebrate together the birth of their Savior. Soon, of course, the singing gave way to renewed violence. Some of those who had sung together would be killed by their fellow carolers. They would be dispatched to "sleep in heavenly peace" in a manner that would seem a ghastly denial of the Christmas story.[1]

John Ferguson, in his study of war and peace in the major religions of the world, has observed that Christian peoples, despite the pacifistic origins of their faith, have a record of military activity second to none.[2] The bellicose character of Christendom cannot be understood apart from the merger of religion and civilization, the merger of the Christian church and the Roman empire in the fourth century C.E. This *corpus christianum,* as it has been called, has disintegrated only in our own century, shattered in part by the devastation, spiritual as well as physical, of World War I and by the even greater violence unleashed in the next generation. Indeed, World War II, involving Shintoist Japan and the avowedly atheistic Soviet Union along with the so-called Christian nations in both the Allied and Axis lineup, burst the boundaries of traditional Christendom to become the first truly global and pluralistic war in the history of humankind.

In the years following World War II Christians began to ponder the new situation in which they, along with everyone else, found themselves: that, after millions of years of the evolution of life on this planet, the human species stood on the verge of extinction through thermonuclear war. Or, if not complete extinction, such massive annihilation that the "survivors would envy the dead" (a phrase coined by Nikita Khrushchev). In 1959 theologian Karl Barth declared it a scandal that major Christian bodies could not pronounce a definite yes or no on the question of atomic war.[3]

In recent years most Christian churches have taken a definite stand against nuclear weapons. Popes John XXIII, Paul VI, and John Paul II have warned of the dangers of the nuclear arms race, each more urgently than his predecessor. Mainline Protestant denominations, through the World Council of Churches and separately, have placed a major emphasis on peace education and political strategies for peacemaking. Evangelical Christians, if somewhat late to get into the act, have been prolific and creative in sounding the alarm for peace. To these must be added the voices of the traditional "peace churches," the Brethren, Quakers, and Mennonites, whose consistent witness has been an important model for other groups.

If, as this anthology presupposes, the active promotion of peace requires a coming to grips with religious traditions whose banners have so often been unfurled in the interests of conflict and war, then Christians must reexamine their own history critically, paying special attention to its transforming possibilities. The aim of this chapter is to explore the rationale for peacemaking in one strand of the Christian tradition: those "radical" Christians who have consistently challenged the prevailing myths of violence and domination. They are called "radical" because the root (Latin, *radix)* of their peace witness derives from the life and teachings of Jesus. Frequently these Christians have themselves been the objects of violence and persecution by fellow Christians. After examining the biblical and historical basis of this witness, I shall then explore its implications for religious and political toleration, dialogue among competing ideologies, and nuclear disarmament.

PAX CHRISTI: JESUS AS PRIMAL METAPHOR FOR PEACE

The Christian story begins with the Christmas carol sung by angels to the shepherds in the fields: "Glory to God in the highest and upon the earth peace" (Luke 2:14). The birth of the Messiah brought the heavenly announcement of peace on earth. This meant peace for the whole inhabited world *(oikoumene)* for, in Luke's account, the birth of Jesus is set in the context of a worldwide census (Luke 2:1). Thus from its inception Christianity contained a universalistic thrust and a concern for *world* peace.

Jesus distinguished his way of peace from that which prevailed in his time. "Peace is my parting gift to you, my own peace, such as the world cannot give" (John 14:27). The *Pax Christi* stood in stark contrast to the *Pax Romana,* the system of maintaining order by means of coercion and subjugation. As Jesus said:

> You know that those who are supposed to rule over the Gentiles lord it over them, and their great men exercise authority over them. But it shall not be so among you. . . . For the Son of man . . . came not to be served but to serve, and to give his life as a ransom for many [Mark 10:42–45].

There is a certain kind of peace that can be achieved by dominative, exploitive power, power that must ultimately be prepared to destroy and to kill in order to enforce its will. The peace that Jesus embodied was of a different sort. It required a disengagement with the weapons of this world, and a transformation of hostile situations. It was the way of self-expenditure and openness to others. Ultimately for Jesus it was the way of the cross. We can identify three elements in Jesus' approach to peace.

1. Rejection of the politics of violence. Although Jesus was acclaimed the promised deliverer of Israel, he did not behave like a military messiah. It is important to remember that Jesus was born as a displaced person in a country under foreign occupation. Yet he refused to join the Zealots in their guerilla war against the Romans, just as he refused to join the Romans in their oppression of the Jews.

Jesus agreed with the Zealots in their impassioned concern for the poor and their willingness to die for the divine cause. He doubtless attracted some of their number to his following, such as Simon the Zealot and perhaps Judas ("Iscariot" may have been derived from the Latin *sicarius,* "dagger-man," assassin). But, unlike the Zealots, Jesus was willing to reach out to the enemy, to Roman soldiers and tax-gathering "scabs," the very instruments of the hated oppressors.[4]

It is in this context that we must hear Jesus' famous dictum: "Love your enemies, do good to those who hate you; bless those who curse you and pray for those who maltreat you" (Matt. 5:43–44). For Jesus the enemy has become the privileged object of love! In the context of the Sermon on the Mount this is not a maxim of privatized morality, applicable only to personal offenses. It is a call for a new kind of social behavior radically at odds with the "normal" responses made to enemies—Roman coercion and Zealot insurrection.[5]

The original disciples of Jesus found it difficult to live in accordance with their Master's command. This is evident from the scene of conflict at Jesus' arrest in the Garden of Gethsemane:

> At that moment one of those with Jesus reached for his sword and drew it, and he struck at the high priest's servant and cut off his ear. But Jesus said to him, "Put up your sword. All who take the sword die by the sword" [Matt. 26:51–52].

Luke records that Jesus touched the man's ear and healed him. Thus the last miracle Jesus performed before he died was the healing of a wound inflicted by one of his own disciples.

But what did Jesus mean, "All who take the sword die by the sword"? Perhaps he meant only the obvious: if I resort to the sword, sooner or later I will be met by someone who has a bigger sword or a sharper sword—or more nuclear weapons. Or perhaps he meant: the one who takes the sword will be destroyed by *that* sword, the one he wields. With the blade of the sword I may inflict death on another, but with the handle in my hand, I destroy my own humanity. While destroying the enemy, I destroy myself. Jesus died with the point of a sword in his side, but not with the handle in his hand.[6]

2. Reconciliation rather than retaliation. Jesus set aside the traditional *lex talionis* ("an eye for an eye") in favor of a loving response governed by compassion for the other. "Do not resist evil," he said (Matt. 5:39). Did Jesus advocate a passive submission in the face of evil? His own actions are difficult to square with this interpretation: he harshly condemned religious leaders for their hypocrisy and injustice, he protested the police brutality of the Roman troops, and he drove out with a whip the money lenders from the temple!

Clarence Jordan, a radical Christian in the Baptist tradition, has translated this verse: "But I'm telling you, *never* respond with evil."[7] Culbert Rutenber contrasts passive and active attitudes:

Whatever the damage that is done me, I must respond not in similar terms but in terms of the good of the persons involved. This is not a passive principle of supine submission, but the active effort to express the divine love by seeking my enemies' good. This active effort injects a redemptive factor of goodness into a situation which otherwise is dominated by evil.[8]

In other words, the way of nonresistance is not the path of least resistance. Rather it is resistance of a different kind, on a higher plane.

The aim of such nonretaliatory love is always the conversion of alienation into reconciliation *(katallage).* George H. Williams has defined this process as "the resolution of the impounded energy of resentment and potential violence into the power of personal exchange and social change."[9] Just as the Hebrew concept of shalom connotes more than an absence of conflict, so reconciliation in the New Testament goes far beyond the limits of passive nonviolence. In its widest meaning, including its cosmic, social, and personal dimensions, it is synonymous with salvation, liberation, redemption, the breaking into the world of a new reality aimed at ultimate and universal peace.

Justin Martyr, writing in the second century, embodied this idea as he described reconciliation as a way of life among those who followed Jesus:

We who hated and destroyed one another, and on account of their different manners would not live with men of a different tribe, now, since the coming of Christ, live familiarly with them, and pray for our enemies, and endeavor to persuade those who hate us unjustly to live conformably to the good precepts of Christ, to the end that they may become partakers with us of the same joyful hope of a reward from God the ruler of us all.[10]

3. Transforming initiatives. In the New Testament all Christians are called to a "ministry" of reconciliation (2 Cor. 5:18). This implies an active engagement in the process of peacemaking. In the Sermon on the Mount Jesus instructed his disciples to respond to violence and force by taking an unexpected, surprising initiative of their own. If someone slaps you on the right cheek, offer him the left cheek too. If anyone wants to drag you into court and take away your shirt, let him also have your undershirt. If someone makes you walk a mile for him, walk two miles. Clearly this is not merely a negative teaching about *not* doing something. It calls for positive initiatives intended to "neutralize" situations of violence and injustice so that the transforming message of God's love and reconciliation can take root.

Glen Stassen has summarized Jesus' call to active peacemaking in terms of four practical steps: (1) affirm your enemies' valid interests and pray for them; (2) talk to your adversary and seek agreement; (3) associate with the powerless, who need justice; (4) do not seek to return evil for evil. Instead, start an imaginative, transforming initiative. He interprets these steps as applying not only to interpersonal and family relationships, but also to social conflicts of war and violence and to the nuclear arms race.[11]

MILITIA CHRISTI: THE ARMY THAT SHEDS NO BLOOD

In light of Jesus' model of nonviolent love, one is struck with the prevalence of military imagery in early Christian literature. "Take up God's armor," admonished St. Paul. The word "sacrament," which came to play such an important role in the liturgy of the church, is derived from *sacramentum,* the Latin word for the military oath of allegiance that bound the Roman soldier to the "divine" emperor. Similarly, the early Christians were bound by the "sacrament" of baptism to the service of the true, heavenly Emperor. In organization and lifestyle these Christians constituted a veritable *imperium in imperio,* an empire within an empire, coexisting in polemical parallelism with the structures and values of imperial society.

As the *militia Christi,* fighting under the banner of their "captain of salvation" (Heb. 2:10), Christians did battle with the powers of evil, the demonic hosts that control so much of this present world. Yet, despite the military language borrowed from the Roman legions, Christian "warfare" was of a very different sort. Tertullian of Carthage shows the incompatibility of the two approaches:

Those whom the Christian has put to flight in the daytime by exorcisms, shall he defend them by night, leaning and resting on the lance with which Christ's side was pierced? And shall he carry a flag too that is rival to

Christ's? Shall the son of peace take part in battle when it does not become him even to sue at law? And shall he apply the chain, and the prison, and the torture, and the punishment, who is not the avenger even of his own wrongs?[12]

Writing about the same time, but from a very different theological perspective, Clement of Alexandria echoed the same sentiment:

> Now the trumpet sounds with a mighty voice, calling the
>   soldiers of the world to arms, announcing war;
> And shall not Christ, who has uttered his summons to peace
>   even to the ends of the earth,
> Summon together his own soldiers of peace?
> Indeed, O Man, he has called to arms with his blood and his
>   word an army that sheds no blood;
> To these soldiers he has handed over the Kingdom of Heaven.
> The trumpet of Christ is his gospel. He has sounded it in our
>   ears and we have heard it.
> Let us be armed for peace . . . to fight the Evil One.[13]

The ultimate alternative of this "bloodless host of peace" to the militarism of their culture was the shedding of their own blood in martyrdom. This was true not only for the military martyrs such as Maximilianus who, when called for armed service, refused, saying: "I cannot serve. I cannot commit a sin. I am a Christian"; or Martin of Tours, who, converted while a soldier, marched to the front line of battle armed only with a cross, protesting: "I am a soldier of Christ; I cannot fight."[14] Others, too, were willing to engage in mortal combat against the demonic state, including many women, such as Perpetua and Felicitas, whose courage in the arena surpassed that of their fellow martyrs. Christians revered these martyrs and preserved their bloody remains as a kind of trophy of their spiritual warfare. They remembered the occasions of their death with solemn feasts and prayed to them to intercede for the saints who remained on earth. This cult of the martyrs reflected the common belief that they, of all Christians, had succeeded in following Jesus, the great martyr, and by their identification with his passion had fulfilled what St. Paul referred to as "the full tale of Christ's afflictions still to be endured for the sake of his body, the church" (Col. 1:24).

The separatist character of early Christianity did not go unchallenged by its critics. Celsus, a Roman philosopher, charged that Christians were irresponsible for refusing to defend the empire against the savage barbarians who threatened its downfall. "What if everyone did the same as you?" he asked. Origen, a Christian apologist, responded to Celsus in two ways. First, he said, what *if* everyone did the same as we? Then "obviously the barbarians would also be converted to the word of God and would be most law-abiding and mild."[15] This was a surprising answer. Obviously Celsus had not meant "everyone" to include the barbarians! By "everyone" he had meant that persons who really counted, those on "our" side, the Roman empire and its allies. Origen takes "everyone" to mean everyone, even the enemy who, in the Christian view, is a person for whom Christ died, a person infinitely precious and redeemable. The love of Christ encompasses the other; no one is outside the pale. The Christian faith, Origen implied, was more universal in its scope than was the *oikoumene* of the Roman empire.

Realizing that this answer would not please Celsus, Origen also replied in more specific, though perhaps not more satisfactory, terms. What if everyone in the Roman empire became a Christan? There would then be no need for massive military defense, because God would protect God's own people. Origen appealed to the Old Testament precedent of Israel's deliverance from Egypt to support this view:

> For they will be praying to the Logos who *in earlier times* said to the Hebrews when they were being pursued by the Egyptians: "The Lord will fight for you, and you shall keep silence."[16]

To the charge of disloyalty Origen replied that Christians do indeed support the emperor—by their prayers. "We who by our prayers destroy all demons which stir up wars . . . are of more help to the emperors than those who seem to be doing the fighting."[17] Christians, then, were a kind of spiritual shock troops, not exempt from the tasks of the community or unconcerned with the welfare of society, but committed to fulfilling these tasks in a manner congruent with their ultimate loyalty to their Lord.

Between the conversion of Constantine in 312 and the death of Augustine in 430, Christianity underwent a political and social transformation that in retrospect can only be called a revolution. The establishment of Christianity as the official legal religion of the empire required a melding of the interests of church and society. Constantine restored the *Pax Romana,* now a *Pax Christiana,* by force of arms. Apart from the monks who were the prime transmitters of the nonmilitary tradition of the early church, Christians now generally accepted full political responsibilities including military service.

Although I cannot explore here the full meaning of what a Mennonite historian has called "the Constantinian heresy," I must point out three implications for the radical Christian peace tradition. First, the church, largely guided by Augustine, developed a theory of the just war, which set forth the conditions under which a Christian might justifiably resort to organized violence. As elaborated later, the just war theory included both the *ius ad bellum,* proper motivation and intention to enter a war, such as the desire to restore peace, and the *ius in bello,* a code of behavior to be followed during warfare, such as refusing to hurt noncombatants.

Secondly, there was a persistent tendency for a just war to become a holy war, a divinely approved crusade sanctioned by the holiness of its cause and aimed at the thorough elimination of its "evil" opposition.

Thirdly, the objects of such crusades were sometimes "barbarians" (Indians in the Americas) or "infidels" (Muslims during the Middle Ages). Frequently, however, the crusading mentality was turned inward against radical dissenters and sectarian movements such as the Donatists in the early church, the Cathari in the Middle Ages, and the Anabaptists in the Reformation.[18]

The extent to which collective violence had become the accepted norm within Christendom is reflected in the fact that Thomas Aquinas, the great master of medieval theology, treats war in one short chapter in his *Summa* while devoting twenty-four long chapters to angels! The Reformation witnessed the fracturing of Christendom into competing nation-states, and with it the rise of dynastic and religious wars and, in the case of England, a "holy" civil war.

Even in these "Dark Ages" (which certainly continue in the twentieth century under both religious and secular guises) of authoritarian conformity, a radically Christian witness for peace was present. Described as "a stream of eccentric pacifist thought," this witness subsisted in various modalities, usually in tension with the governing authorities of church and state, and always counter to the prevailing cultural consensus. Among the many types of radical peace activists in Christian history, we can distinguish three main currents that have continued into modern times in one form or another: (1) the *vocational* peace witness of the religious orders and clerics; (2) the *sectarian* peace witness of separatist groups such as the Czech Brethren, certain evangelical Anabaptists, and later groups like the Quakers; (3) the *ecumenical* peace witness of individuals like Erasmus during the sixteenth century, or the founders of the Fellowship of Reconciliation in the twentieth.

1. Vocational peacemakers. I have referred earlier to the nonmilitary status of the monastic orders. In their rigorous asceticism, in their protest against the laxity of their cultural environment, and in their explicit pacifism, the monks saw themselves as successors to the martyrs. In 376 Emperor Valens sent soldiers into the deserts of Egypt to conscript the monks into military service.[19] By and large, however, the monks were exempted from such pressures and remained, by their prayers and liturgical observance, a visible link with the *militia Christi* of the early church.

However, the idea of monks as cowled champions of Christ fighting against the powers of darkness by their prayers, fasts, and vigils became corrupted during the Middle Ages. Bernard of Clairvaux, the most famous monk of his century, preached crusade sermons urging soldiers to literally take up swords against the "heathen Turks." New military orders, such as the Knights Templar, arose fusing monastic and knightly ideals.

Against this trend Francis of Assisi embodied a recovery of the earlier meaning of *militia Christi*. Converted from a life of active soldiering to follow the poor Christ, Francis knew firsthand the devastation wrought by feudal wars, urban strife, and greed-based violence. He renounced his former career to become, as his first biographer called him, "a new soldier of Christ."

Francis's "peace movement" required a noncombatant status for all of his disciples, including those lay men and women who sought to follow his teaching while remaining in their secular occupations. "They are not to take up lethal weapons, or bear them about, against anybody," he admonished.[20] The exemption of large numbers of the laity from the obligation to draw arms and follow their lords into battle struck a blow at the heart of the entire feudal system. After much dispute Francis obtained the right of his followers to refrain from military duty. Thus these Franciscan sisters and brothers became the first adherents of the principle of "conscientious objection" long before it was known by that name.

Francis's method of peacemaking recalled Jesus' strategy of surprising initiatives to neutralize hostility and effect reconciliation. On many occasions Francis intervened to establish harmony between estranged spouses, feuding families, warring factions and towns. He was always going about "with feet unshod asking the terms of peace."[21] He took the initiative to establish common ground between seemingly implacable foes, to negotiate a pact both parties could accept as representing their best interests. Francis's famous mission to the Muslim sultan, Melek-al-Kamil, stood in stark contrast to the ruthless aggression and presumption of the Crusades. In the *Rule of 1221* he set forth regulations for his disciples who desired to undertake missionary service. They should "avoid quarrels and disputes and be subject to every human creature for God's sake, so bearing witness to the fact that they are Christians." Furthermore, he advised, they "should be prepared to expose themselves to every enemy, visible and invisible, for love of Christ."[22]

Francis remained loyal to the established church. His critique of the ways of violence was fulfilled in his vocation of reconciliation. Some of his followers, however, the "spiritual" Franciscans, seeking to imitate literally their master's example of peace and absolute poverty, fell into disfavor with the hierarchical church and moved toward the sectarian model.

2. Sectarian peacemakers. During the Reformation and early modern periods most of those Christians who were prepared to suffer violence rather than inflict it on others found themselves isolated from the mainstream of official Christendom. In part this was due to their own vision of Christian fellowship as an intentional community, consisting of committed, properly initiated disciples. In part, too, it reflected the paranoia of the established churches, Catholic, Protestant, and Orthodox, toward dissent, schism, and heresy.

The sixteenth-century Anabaptists refused to baptize their infants, swear oaths, or bear the sword. They demanded that the church be restored to the purity of apostolic times, in contrast to the more prudential reform programs of "orthodox" reformers. They tried to fuse the *militia Christi* with the *pax Christi* by applying the injunctions of love and nonresistance to every Christian. Menno Simons, one of the leading Anabaptists, described the attitude of his followers:

> Our fortress is Christ, our defense is patience, our sword is the Word of God, and our victory is the sincere, firm, unfeigned faith in Jesus Christ.

Spears and swords of iron we leave to those who, alas, consider human blood and swine's blood well-nigh of equal value.[23]

Some of the Anabaptists, such as the Polish Brethren, did concede that Christians could serve in an army so long as they did not take life, whereas others, such as the Waterlander Mennonites, permitted their members to engage in toll-collecting and other kinds of nonviolent police work. Most, however, insisted upon absolute nonconformity to the world and separation from every vestige of compliance with "the sword."

The Anabaptist movement made little headway in England, but in the seventeenth century an indigenous radical peace testimony emerged among the Quakers. George Fox, the founder of this movement, was once offered a commission as a captain in Oliver Cromwell's army. He declined the offer claiming that he "lived in the virtue of that life and power that took away the vocation of all wars."[24] The Anabaptists based their pacifism on stringent discipleship *(Nachfolge),* but the Quakers stressed the concept of the "inner light." The inner light is nothing other than Christ who is offered to everyone. All have the capacity to receive and respond to it. The inner light is the basis of reconciliation with God and of unity and love among all peoples.

Like other radical Christians, the Quakers were certainly not mere passive nonresisters. Fox urged his followers to join in the "Lamb's War" against violence and social injustice. The early Quakers carried out this mandate in a number of ways. They frequently entered church buildings (which they disparagingly called "steeples") during worship services to denounce the minister as a false prophet. They wrote government leaders demanding justice for the poor and oppressed. They protested capital punishment and abuse of prisoners. One of the most famous of the Quakers, William Penn, wrote an *Essay towards the Present and Future Peace of Europe* (1693), in which he outlined plans for a league of nations to maintain peace.

The Anabaptists and Quakers differed in their peacemaking tactics. Both groups, however, regarded Jesus' teachings on peace as normative for all Christians.

3. Ecumenical peacemakers. We have seen that one of the greatest sources of conflict in Western history has been internecine warfare among Christians, all claiming to be followers of the Prince of Peace. Certain individuals have sensed the tragic irony in this situation and have spoken against it. Desiderius Erasmus, the most notable Christian scholar of the Renaissance, found it incongruous that fellow Christians could devour one another with such studied nonchalance:

The Lord's Prayer addresses *Our Father,* but how can they call upon a common Father who drives steel into the bowels of their brothers? Christ compared himself to a hen, Christians behave like hawks. Christ was a shepherd of sheep, Christians tear each other like wolves. Christians have the same Supper of the Lord, the same heavenly Jerusalem, but they are less peaceful than the Jews who fight only with foreigners and the Turks who keep the peace among themselves.[25]

The wars of religion engulfed both Protestant and Catholic Europe from the early years of the Reformation until the end of the Thirty Years' War in 1648. The quest for religious liberty was waged most passionately by those small Christian groups that were themselves the objects of intolerance from both sides. Whereas many pleaded for toleration for *their* own belief or practice, the early Baptists in England advocated absolute, uninhibited toleration for all persons of whatever persuasion. In a treatise dedicated to King James in 1612, Thomas Helwys admonished: "Let them be heretics, Turks, Jews, or whatsoever, it appertains not to the earthly power to punish them."[26]

The modern ecumenical witness for peace owes much to these mostly forgotten, dissenting voices calling beyond the divisions and mutual recriminations of the past toward a vision of universal love and acceptance of all peoples.

CARITAS CHRISTI: THE RELEVANCE OF AN IMPOSSIBLE IDEAL?

The radically Christian witness for peace carries an evangelical mandate, an imperative that cannot be ignored. St. Paul expressed it thus:

> The love of Christ *(caritas Christi)* leaves us no choice, . . . With us therefore worldly standards have ceased to count in our estimate of any person. When anyone is united to Christ, there is a new world; the old order has gone, and a new order has already begun. . . . We come therefore as Christ's ambassadors. It is as if God were appealing to you through us: in Christ's name, we implore you, be reconciled! [2 Cor. 5:14, 17, 20].

As I have interpreted it, the radical love-imperative of Jesus embraced two actions: a saying no to war, violence, and lethal resistance, and a saying yes to the redemptive possibilities inherent in Jesus' own life and teachings.

But how on earth can it be done? What is the relevance of such an exalted ideal? By and large, traditional Christianity has rejected the radical peace witness as utterly impractical, utopian, and other-worldly. This is not to deny that these Christians have been admired for their courage and conscientious faith, or that their "perfectionist" stance has been deemed of great symbolic value for the wider church. Reinhold Niebuhr, the most trenchant critic of Christian pacifism in the twentieth century, has conceded that pacifists express "a genuine impulse in the heart of Christianity, the impulse to take the law of Christ seriously and not to allow the political strategies, which the sinful character of man makes necessary, to become final norms."[27] For all this, he judges the peace radicals to have only a marginal, at best a contrapuntal, value in the Christian tradition.

As Christian churches undertake the task of peace education in the late twentieth century, there is good reason to reexamine the role the peace dissenters have played throughout history. I want to touch on three "new" situations that call for radically different approaches from those traditionally offered.

The first is the massive stalemate of violence and enmity in which the nuclear superpowers find themselves locked. Both the United States and the Soviet Union, along with their close allies, share the common inheritance of Christendom. Yet the allegedly "Christian" theory of just war is manifestly bankrupt in the nuclear world where categories of proportionality and noncombatant immunity have become meaningless. For a world where global suicide has become a real possiblity, Martin Luther King, Jr., has expressed the new alternative: "Today the choice is no longer between violence and nonviolence. It is either nonviolence or nonexistence."[28]

The transformation in warfare brought about by the new weaponry has led many Christians who formerly accepted some variant of just-war theory to declare themselves "nuclear pacifists." A leading exponent of this view is the German theologian, Helmut Gollwitzer:

> Christians cannot participate, because the only circumstances in which it ever was permissible for them to think of taking up arms was in order to defend justice. But when the authorities urge a Christian to participate in these preparations for universal massacre, there is only one answer he can give: *Si omnes, ego non* ("Even if everyone else consents, I refuse!").[29]

Moved by similar concerns thousands of Christians have rediscovered an urgent relevance in the nonmilitarist teachings of Jesus and the early church. Many have become politically active for peace. They write their elected representatives and vote for candidates who work for disarmament. They have organized study groups and prayer groups to express their concern for peace. In the spirit of Jesus' transforming initiatives, some American peacemakers have sponsored "peace tours" of the Soviet Union. They convey a message of good will and love and return to their local congregations with names and photographs of Christians in the Soviet Union.[30] Still other Christians have become conscientious objectors to military service, have refused to work in military-related jobs, or have joined the small but growing minority who withhold the portion of their income tax used to pay for nuclear armament.

The second "new" situation is the pluralistic context in which the church today must function. Around 1900 a group of liberal Protestants founded a new journal called *The Christian Century*. Although its name has not been changed, it is doubtful whether the history of the last eight decades justifies that presumptuous title. With the breakdown of traditional Christendom, Christians find themselves again in the position of a voluntary minority. Not everyone has grasped the meaning of this new status. A famous television evangelist supports increased spending for nuclear weapons so that the Christian message may be safely proclaimed around the world: missiles to back up missionaries! However, as Christians increasingly find themselves in a position analogous to that of the pre-Constantinian church, they may need to redefine their mission in terms of its faithfulness to the model of Jesus and the early church rather than its conformity to a culture based on coercion.

Such an emphasis should lead to a vigorous commitment to religious and political toleration vis-à-vis all persons and all peoples. The violation of human rights anywhere in the world is a threat to their destruction everywhere.

A dis-established Christianity will also be in a better position to enter into genuine dialogue with the other great world religions. It is one thing to proclaim nonviolence as the ideal standard in human relationships; it is another to teach persons *how* to love their enemies. For example, the Hindu concept of ahimsa, with its structured disciplines for the learning and practice of nonharmfulness, can inform Christian traditions of nonviolence, just as Mahatma Gandhi's vision was influenced by the example of Jesus.[31]

The third "new" situation for which the radical peace witness within Christianity may have a redemptive word is the global crisis that threatens to engulf all of humanity. World peace is not an isolated issue, but one factor in a complex of problems including mass starvation, political oppression, ecological destruction, terrorism, racism, and discrimination against the most marginated members of the human community including women, children, the unborn, the aged, the illiterate, the poor, the imprisoned, the mentally and physically handicapped. The gospel of love implies a holistic ethic of life, affirming the sanctity of every living person and indeed of the cosmos itself.

The message of reconciliation is both personal and social; it encompasses both individual hatred and hostility, which are the wellsprings of violence, and also the corporate structures in which these evil intentions are objectified. A privatized interpretation of Jesus' message is not permissible in a world in crisis. What is called for now is the radical love and militant nonviolence of an intentional community whose motto might well be borrowed from the International Red Cross, an organization established during a time of war to care for the wounded and dying, *Inter Arma Caritas*—love in the midst of weaponry. Christians, followers of another cross, should prefer *Loco Armorum Caritas*—love instead of weaponry.

NOTES

1. This poignant scene is vividly retold in Erich M. Remarque's novel, *All Quiet on the Western Front.* See also Alan Geyer, ed., *The Maze of Peace* (New York, Friendship Press, 1969), p. 8.

2. *War and Peace in the World's Religions* (New York, Oxford University Press, 1975), pp. 99–122.

3. *Christianity Today.* Quoted in Jim Garrison, *The Darkness of God: Theology after Hiroshima* (Grand Rapids, Eerdmans, 1982), p. 1.

4. The Marxist philosopher Ernst Bloch, among others, has interpreted Jesus as the ultimate founder of revolutionary theology, and has found in his teachings a sanction

for revolutionary violence. See his *Thomas Münzer als Theologe der Revolution* (Munich, K. Wolff, 1921). More recently S. G. F. Brandon has argued that Jesus was allied with the Zealots in the cause of patriotic nationalism: *Jesus and the Zealots: A Study of the Political Factor in Primitive Christianity* (New York, Scribner's, 1967). For a thorough critique of this argument, see George R. Edwards, *Jesus and the Politics of Violence* (New York, Harper and Row, 1972). See also John H. Yoder, *The Politics of Jesus* (Grand Rapids, Eerdmans, 1972).

5. See the discussion in John Piper, *"Love Your Enemies": Jesus' Love Command in the Synoptic Gospels in the Early Christian Paranesis* (Cambridge University Press, 1979). See also Martin Hengel, *Victory over Violence* (London, SPCK, 1985), p. 76.

6. For this insight I am indebted to Dr. Frank Stagg, professor emeritus of New Testament theology in the Southern Baptist Theological Seminary, Louisville, Kentucky. Origen, commenting on this text at the end of the second century, interpreted it as an injunction against any warlike or retaliatory act. He warned that we should beware lest "for warfare, or for the vindication of our rights, or for any occasion, we should take out the sword, for no such occasion is allowed by this evangelical teaching" *(Works,* Berlin Corpus edition, vol. 11, pp. 221–22).

7. *The Cotton Patch Version of Matthew and John* (Chicago, Association Press, 1970), p. 25.

8. *The Dagger and the Cross* (Nyack, N.Y., Fellowship Publications, 1950), p. 50. See also the discussion in Ronald J. Sider and Richard K. Taylor, *Nuclear Holocaust and Christian Hope* (Downers Grove, Ill., Intervarsity Press, 1982). pp. 95–119.

9. "Four Modalities of Violence, with Special Reference to the Writings of George Sorel," *Journal of Church and State,* 16 (1974), p. 25.

10. *1 Apology,* 14, 3 (The Ante-Nicene Fathers, Alexander Roberts and James Donaldson, eds. [Grand Rapids, Eerdmans, 1981], vol. 1, p. 167).

11. Glen Stassen, *The Journey into Peacemaking* (Memphis, Brotherhood Commission, 1983), pp. 33–42.

12. *De Corona Militis,* 11 (Ante-Nicene Fathers, vol. 3, pp. 99–100).

13. *Exhortation to the Heathen,* 11 (Ante-Nicene Fathers, vol. 2, p. 204).

14. Peter Brock, *The Roots of War Resistance* (Nyack, N.Y., Fellowship of Reconciliation, 1981), p. 12; Sulpicius Severus, *Vita Martini,* I, i-v, in Migne, PL, vol. 20, col. 161–63.

15. *Origen: Contra Celsum,* Henry Chadwick, tr. (Cambridge University Press, 1953), p. 505.

16. Ibid.

17. Ibid., p. 509. In another place (p. 249) Origen suggested that if wars had to be fought among humans, they should be modeled on the "wars of the bees," which fight with greater order and less cruelty than their human counterparts. Whether Origen can be adduced in support of the just war is a matter of great dispute. See Adolf Harnack, *Militia Christi* (Philadelphia, Fortress Press, 1981); C. J. Cadoux, *The Early Church and the World* (Edinburgh, Clark, 1925); Jean-Michel Hornus, *It Is Not Lawful for Me to Fight: Early Christian Attitudes toward War and Peace* (Scottdale, Pa., Herald Press, 1980).

18. Frederick H. Russell has shown how easily distinctions between crusade and just war were glossed over in the Middle Ages: "In the heat of combat and controversy belligerents forsook the more restrained just war for the holy war. At the moment a just war was deemed necessary, it easily became a holy war that pursued the supreme goals of the belligerents" *(The Just War in the Middle Ages* [Cambridge University Press, 1975],

p. 2). For an analysis of a similar shift in Puritan thought in prerevolutionary England, see Timothy George, "War and Peace in the Puritan Tradition," *Church History,* 53 (1984) pp. 492–503.

19. Orosius, *Historiarum Lib. VIII,* 33. See Roland H. Bainton, *Christian Attitudes toward War and Peace* (Nashville, Abingdon, 1960), p. 89.

20. "First Rule of the Third Order," 5, 16, in *St. Francis of Assisi. Writings and Early Biographies. English Omnibus of the Sources for the Life of St. Francis,* Marion Habig, ed. (Chicago, Franciscan Herald Press, 1973), p. 171.

21. "The First Life of St. Francis," by Thomas of Celano, §99, in *Omnibus,* p. 314.

22. "The Rule of 1221," in *Omnibus,* pp. 43–44. For a fuller discussion of Francis as peacemaker, see Timothy George, "Francis of Assisi: Peace through Suffering Love," *A Cloud of Witnesses: Peacemakers in Profile* (Philadelphia, Westminster, 1986).

23. Cited by Bainton, *Christian Attitudes,* p. 153. On the nuances of the term "Anabaptist," and their varying views on war and peace, see George H. Williams, *The Radical Reformation* (Philadelphia, Westminster, 1962). For an excellent statement of a contemporary "Anabaptist" ethic of peace, see John H. Yoder, *The Original Revolution* (Scottdale, Pa., Herald Press, 1971).

24. Margaret E. Hirst, *The Quakers in Peace and War* (London, Allen and Unwin, 1923), p. 43.

25. *Querela Pacis,* quoted in Bainton, *Christian Attitudes,* pp. 132–33.

26. *A Short Declaration of the Mystery of Iniquity* (London, 1612, pp. 55–56). Also Timothy George, "Between Pacifism and Coercion: The English Baptist Doctrine of Religious Toleration," *Mennonite Quarterly Review,* 58 (1984) 30–49.

27. *Christianity and Power Politics* (New York, Scribner's, 1946), p. 10. See G. H. C. Macgregor's response to Niebuhr in *The New Testament Basis of Pacifism* (Nyack, N.Y., Fellowship Publications, 1954), pp. 117–60.

28. *Stride toward Freedom* (New York, Harper and Row, 1958), p. 224.

29. From *Fellowship,* September 1, 1961. Quoted in *War and the Christian Conscience,* Albert Marrin, ed. (Chicago, H. Regnery, 1971), p. 260.

30. "Baptist Peace Mission in Russia," *Baptist Peacemaker,* 3 (Oct. 1983).

31. Gandhi defined *ahimsa* as "a refusal of all harmful attitudes, even in thought, and even more of harmful actions, in regard to any creature, wherever such refusal can morally be exercised." Quoted in Windlass, *Christianity versus Violence* (London, Sheed and Ward, 1964), p. 156.

6

Ingo Baldermann

The Bible as a Teacher of Peace

Education for peace emerges in the name of a great hope, but it is always on the threshold of despair. Never has there been a greater task for education, nor one so difficult. It requires no less than a complete rethinking of the familiar modes we adopt to make sense of our world; without this complete rethinking, I contend, there is no future for humankind.[1]

This rethinking cannot be limited to the realm of security and military politics. The arms race, which has driven us to the verge of catastrophe, has its roots in fundamental convictions central to our education: *Si vis pacem, para bellum*; the mightly alone can live in peace; a greater threat requires greater armaments. Such basic convictions must be altered.

Hence education for peace cannot confine itself to patient work with individuals and small groups. If the manner of coexistence of nations is to be transformed, public opinion must be educated for peace. Democratic learning processes are necessary for the structures of public opinion to be altered.

CHALLENGING A TRADITION: THE EMERGENCE OF A CHURCH-BASED PEACE MOVEMENT IN EUROPE

Since 1980, such learning processes for peace have gained astonishing breadth in some European countries. Triggered by the 1979 NATO decision to station middle-range rockets and missiles of a new kind in Europe, this pedagogy has reached the point that, since 1981, we can speak of a "peace movement." The roots of this movement reach far back, but only in recent years has there begun to occur a broadly accepted and irreversible change of consciousness.[2]

If public opinion is to change, it is not enough to organize a few protests. A space must be found in which critical discussion will call forth a broad response. This space can be offered only by recognized organizations or by institutions; such is precisely what occurred at first in the churches of Europe—especially among Protestant denominations. It should be recalled that this occurred at a time when parliaments and labor unions in the nations of Europe refused to give space for such discussions, and the media provided very limited coverage of peace activities.

Such a development is rather astonishing when one considers the tradition of European churches. In the past these churches had not only aligned themselves with the prevailing political regime, but to a great extent—with the exception of smaller groups—had identified themselves with that regime. They were willing not only to legitimize the prevailing political regime, but were willing to justify the military endeavors and even the wars of their states; they went so far as to give blessings to warriors and arms. Many churches had developed theological thought patterns that attempted to justify such behavior. Hence the protests of the peace movement questioned not only political beliefs, but also challenged theological convictions whose validity had been accepted as "self-evident" for a long time. The movement challenged basic theological tenets rooted in the Reformation and specifically in the theology of Luther. (It should be noted, however, that modern interpretations of these tenets have often deviated from Luther's original intent.) In what follows I shall review briefly some of these basic tenets.

1. The first tenet to be challenged asserts that faith, the personal relationship to God, takes precedence over action. A concentration on the "inner person" restricts faith to the realm of personal consciousness: what is crucial is what takes place between the individual and God. Impulses for action are of secondary value, and are seen as derivative of the inner relationship to God.

It is admitted that the Bible contains a wealth of commandments relating to the creation of a more humane communal existence. For Protestant Christians, however, unlike Jews, these commandments do not belong to the core of one's religion; rather, they are understood to be utterances with a nonliteral meaning. Hence, humankind should grasp that it is ultimately incapable of performing good and stands in need of redemption. The devaluation of the above-mentioned commandments can be seen in light of the distinction between "law" and "gospel," which Luther strongly emphasized by reference to the Epistles of Paul in the New Testament—but, of course, in an entirely different context and with other intentions.

2. The second tenet to be discussed here is that questions of faith are separate, in principle, from questions of politics. This separation also relies on Martin Luther, specifically to what is called his *Zweireichlehre* or theory of two kingdoms. This interpretation of Luther's thought holds that faith is a matter of the inner person and can determine the personal way of life of the individual. Political action cannot be measured by the standards of faith; it follows its own laws. It is the business of politicians to decide concerning political

necessity; the individual Christian should submit to their decisions and patiently bear the burdens imposed upon subjects.

3. A third basic tenet follows logically from the others and has grave consequences. There is no hope to be obtained for this world through faith. Believers should direct their hope to a personal communion with God beyond death; the world, however, remains a world of injustice, which will ultimately perish for this very reason. This world is ruled by the laws of politics, which may prevent the worst from coming for a limited time, but this holds out no hope for any fundamental amelioration of our lot on earth.

Behind these basic interpretations a bourgeois religion of affluence could entrench itself in an endeavor to meet the challenges of the world political situation.[3] Whoever reads the Bible carefully, however, will discover that this religion is a distortion of biblical faith. But from this self-critical discovery there stretches a long way to an effective change in public opinion.

THE BIBLICAL MESSAGE OF PEACE

Despite these misinterpretations of its central message, the Bible has been able time and again to prove itself a teacher of peace. The authentic biblical teaching on peace has gained for itself a renewed hearing in our time—and despite a massive effort of hostile interests. I shall first sketch the learning process that took place in contemporary European society; I shall then attempt to indicate further steps to be taken along this path.

A saying of Jesus from the Sermon on the Mount has been repeatedly cited in current discussions initiated by European peace movements: "I say unto you, love your enemies" (Matt. 5:44; Luke 6:27). In this saying, we are dealing with an essential part of Jesus' message, supported by all the authority of the man from Nazareth. This is a demand, moreover, that speaks directly to the context of current international tensions. As the East German author, Günter de Bruyn, recently said in Berlin: "The teaching of the Sermon on the Mount in an era characterized by the threat of mass annihilation of Christian and non-Christian alike changes from a commandment of faith to a commandment of reason."[4] This commandment evidences what I contend to be the only possible approach for humanity to escape the catastrophe that would result from a third world war.

Jesus' saying, "Love your enemies," is a call to do what is necessary. He proclaimed it in his time as a way to establish peace in the face of a threatening military catastrophe.[5] Those who follow this way will be called "sons of God" (Matt. 5:45); indeed, already in the introduction to the Sermon on the Mount peacemakers are called "sons of God" (Matt. 5:9).

It is noteworthy that this saying of Jesus did not characterize past attitudes of the major European churches on questions of war and peace. On the contrary, representatives of those churches contended that this commandment of Jesus was unrealizable and hence was destined from the start to reveal to us our incapability to do good. It is only in recent years that we have come to grasp that the survival of humanity depends upon our ability to live in accordance with this mandate. It is no less noteworthy that such a simple saying is currently perceived as capable of shaking age-old convictions. It is as unambiguous as it is demonstrative, and behind it stands the very authority of the Bible.

Here it is necessary to emphasize a point about the unique authority of the Bible. It is not an authority that promotes blind obedience. The Bible does not present a systematically developed doctrine that Christians are obliged to adopt in their thought and action. The Bible is rather a book full of contradictions, a book of dialogue and discussion. At times its words are the record of a desperate struggle for hope and humanity. Whoever wishes to learn from the Bible must engage in dialogue with the text.

Contradictory opinions find support in diverse texts of the Bible. Herein lies the weakness of the Bible. There are Christians who read in the Bible the summons to prepare for the final struggle for the extermination of evil. They want to take part in the battle of Armageddon, of which the last book of the Bible, the Revelation of John (16:16), speaks.[6] For this struggle, they hold necessary rearmament with nuclear weapons. Like-minded groups existed even during New Testament times, perhaps among the Essenes of Qumran, and they have repeatedly emerged in Christian church history. Today such groups (if they come to power) will actually have the means to annihilate the majority of humankind. May we therefore conclude that the Bible is equivocal?

The Bible itself speaks unequivocally, but it is defenseless against such a violation of its meaning, much as Jesus was defenseless against the force of the powerful. The Revelation of John speaks of the impending destruction of the earth through war and starvation, through fire and poison. We grasp these images of holocaust only too well. But they give no one the right to partake actively in this destruction. The Christians of John's Revelation are innocent of such an approach, therefore they can have hope; but those Christians who today discuss the battle of Armageddon are themselves participants in preparing this annihilation.

It cannot be denied that there are wars in the Bible and also words of joy over military victory. Yet whoever engages in dialogue with the Bible will perceive how the criticism of the inhumanity of the exercise of military power becomes gradually stronger. The Bible takes us along a lengthy path of learning; on this path we encounter Jeremiah, Deutero-Isaiah, the Psalms, and Jesus of Nazareth. In the end, it becomes clear that God does not stand on the side of the victors but on the side of the victims: the poor, the powerless, the oppressed.

From the suffering of victims arise the prophetic visions of peace: "For every boot of the tramping warrior in battle tumult and every garment rolled in blood will be burned as fuel for the fire" (Isa. 9:5). "And they shall beat their swords into plowshares, and their spears into pruning hooks; nations shall not lift up sword against nation, neither shall they learn war any more" (Mic. 4:3).[7]

The problem is not that the Bible speaks ambiguously. Whoever identifies with victims can speak only unequivocally concerning the question of war. The words of Jesus are very clear. The problem consists, rather, in that politicians who do not engage seriously in dialogue with the Bible select isolated passages from it in order to promote their reckless policies. We have no other weapon against such distortions of the biblical message but to read more closely what the Bible really says; and we have the hope that the powerless authority of the Bible will prove more powerful in the stuggle for public opinion than the rhetoric of the mighty.

LEARNING PEACE FROM THE BIBLE

Lately in Germany and in other European countries this authority of the Bible, and in particular the authority of the man from Nazareth, has inspired individual Christians and churches to give up traditional thought patterns and to search for new ways to resolve conflicts. The Bible has proved itself once more a "book of learning."[8] Jesus' words from the Sermon on the Mount have found their way into public discussion. Important newspapers have found it necessary to quote the Sermon on the Mount, so that their readers would know what the discussion was all about. This public learning process has been carried out in three clearly recognizable steps:

1. If the saying "love your enemies" is understood not as a "utopian" demand directed to the inner person, but rather as an instruction for action in the realm of politics, it develops its own dynamics: it proceeds to diagnose prevailing political behavior patterns as hopeless. At the same time, it is an impulse that mobilizes the imagination to seek ways for a more humane kind of politics. It begins to become clear how much we are caught up in a language that intensifies hostility instead of overcoming it. The East-West conflict is always presented by both sides as if it represented the unbridgeable contrast between good and evil, between freedom and unfreedom, between humanity and inhumanity. Thus the common image of "enemy" crystalizes into obsessional ideas, which lead to such absurdities as escalation of the arms race.

The politics of deterrence has here trapped itself in a pathological circle: the available weapons of annihilation can bring about such dreadful consequences that they can be justified only by projecting an image of the enemy as absolutely evil. But such an enemy image attains independence and begets the compulsion to make available a much greater potential for annihilation, even though weapons already exist in quantities that are completely senseless. And all this occurs in a worldwide context in which the struggle against hunger alone should lay claim to all the energies of humankind.

It is difficult to discern such a circle as long as we ourselves are snagged within it. A strong, convincing authority is needed in order to break out of it. Jesus' sayings have this authority. The insight that the system of deterrence by the threat of mutual annihilation "contradicts the spirit of Christ" and that therefore we must overcome "the spirit and logic of deterrence" has meanwhile been sincerely expressed by several high-ranking church conferences. This insight can no longer be ignored by Christians.[9]

The demand for a "moratorium of hostile rhetoric" raised by the World

Conference of Religions in 1982 in Moscow constitutes a first step in translating love for one's enemy into political reality. Newscasts show us from day to day how far we still are from living this first step. There is a long road from an undeniable insight to its political realization. Those who seek to practice love encounter strong political resistance. This becomes much clearer in the next steps of the "learning process" referred to above.

2. The love of which the Bible speaks is not a matter of feeling, but mainly a matter of *praxis*. Love for the enemy is meant to change political reality. For this all the powers of imagination and reason are necessary. In this sense, Carl Friedrich von Weizsäcker has urged an "intelligent love of the enemy."

If intelligence is posited in the service of the love of one's enemy, its first demand is that I attempt to see the conflict from the other side, through the eyes of the enemy. There is a German axiom to the effect that in order to initiate peace, one must "walk in the other person's shoes." The Sermon on the Mount makes a similar demand (Matt. 7:12; Luke 6:31) and sees in it a recapitulation of all the demands of the Torah and the prophets.

This demand appears to be such a simple, self-evident rule of humanity that it hardly seems worthy of discussion; but if only a start were made in following it, so-called defensive politics would be fundamentally altered. Disarmament negotiations are regularly accompanied by the warning that only from a position of strength is it possible to negotiate successfully. Time and again this conjuration is uttered in order to forestall a potentially critical attitude. Naturally the strength of one side engenders fear on the other side, and if one side attempts to marshal its own strength against the specific vulnerabilities of the other side, the danger of uncalculable reactions becomes even greater. It becomes much clearer that growth in armaments does not betoken a corresponding growth in security, but rather a growing danger.

One attempt to see "through the eyes of the other" emerged in the endeavor initiated by European church leaders and lay persons to counter the stationing of NATO missiles on their soil. The Pershing II missiles in West Germany have nuclear warheads and a range that enables them to reach targets within the entire western part of the Soviet Union with an extremely short forewarning time; indeed, they can be used to launch a surprise attack. (It is the same area of the Soviet Union that was devastated in the German surprise invasion of 1941 that is now being threatened with even more terrible devastation from the same German soil.) The stationing of these missiles in Germany is the culmination of a process that lacks true political instincts. In such a climate of threat and fear, successful disarmament negotiations are impossible.

3. The Jewish theologian Pinchas Lapide has described the goal and hope of this learning process with the concept "dehostilization."[10] The Sermon on the Mount wants hostility to be overcome by both sides. Hostility grows out of anxiety; hence dehostilization requires the reduction of anxiety. Immoderate power politics cannot achieve such a reduction; even friendly declarations of intention no longer suffice. Only politically unequivocal signals can convince the other side that we are no longer their enemies. When I have once learned to

view things through the eyes of the other, then I will also learn what has to be done to release that one from the compulsion of continuing to regard me as an enemy.

Hence, precisely from the churches the demand arises to begin unilateral steps toward disarmament.[11] That is the way revealed by the Sermon on the Mount. This way, moreover, needs to be characterized by unmistakably definite steps, which cannot be dismissed by the other side as a mere propaganda ploy. Repeatedly rejected by politicians as unrealistic, this demand becomes all the more urgent when one realizes that mutual distrust sabotages productive negotiations from the beginning. Only unequivocal measures can break through a circle of reciprocal distrust. The question is, of course, whether both sides are actually interested in such a breakthrough. Acceding to the demand for a bold and unambiguous advance (toward peace) can be a touchstone of the presence of authentic good will.

CONFRONTING THE ENEMIES OF PEACE: GUIDANCE FROM THE BIBLE

Those who attempt to go the way of loving their enemy will create, by so doing, new enemies. The Bible knows of such experiences. The attempt to throw bridges across the chasms that the official hostility of rhetoric has torn open is considered treasonous. Whoever does this is accused of, willingly or unwillingly, carrying on the work of the enemy.

Peace groups everywhere—in both blocs in the cold war—have undergone this same terrible experience. How should we deal with it? It is another kind of hostility; fundamentally, it does not emanate from one's military opponents, but from one's own ranks. The Old Testament books of the prophets, especially Jeremiah, are full of such experiences.

Here is a hostility that turns emphatically against the demand that one love one's enemy because it holds this demand to be dangerous. To borrow a term from mathematics, hostility is raised to the power of two. There are politicians who need hostility for their political affairs, hence they do not want to overcome it; indeed, they strengthen hostility by all means available to them. The demand of love for the enemy exposes them; they defend themselves against this exposure at first by arousing public suspicion and later by adopting harsh means of repression.

A critical question remains: Is the demand to love one's enemy also valid against those enemies who are implacable promoters of hostility? These persons are leading humanity to the edge of catastrophe by their aggravated incitement to hostility. They are not only my enemies, but, in effect, enemies of all humanity. What they purposefully strive for can only end fatally for humankind. Can the Bible prove itself in this instance also to be a teacher of peace?

In both the Gospels of Matthew and Luke there is a saying by Jesus that answers this question. Matthew 10:34 reads: "Think not that I am come to send peace on earth: I came not to send peace but a sword." And in Luke we read: "Do you suppose that I am come to give peace on earth? I tell you: nay; rather division" (12:51). This statement does not contradict the demand to love one's enemy but belongs to it inseparably. It describes the dialectic of all work for peace: the task of overcoming hostility ignites new hostility. The peacemaker is not allowed to evade this conflict.

In this regard the Psalms gain a new actuality for Christians. On almost every page of this great prayerbook of the Bible the theme of the experience of hostility is expressed. It becomes evident that fear and hostility are inseparably joined; hostility produces fear, and from fear grows new hostility. Yet it is precisely these passages of the Psalms that Christians have been ready to overlook. It was regarded as un-Christian to speak thus about one's enemies. Jesus' mandate to love one's enemies was misinterpreted as a principle that does away with hostility. But hostility and fear could not thus be overcome, merely suppressed, and suppressed hostility unwittingly leads to completely uncontrollable outbursts of aggression. The sustained increase of the means of mass destruction reveals the extent of irrationality to which uncontrolled hostility can lead.

Jesus' demand for love is a long-term program for overcoming hostility. But repression makes the mastering of hostility impossible. Therefore a necessary first step is to resist the repression of hostility—contrary to what Christians have thought for centuries. The Psalms can instruct us. They draw hostility and the fear that arises from it into the light of one's relationship with God; in that light, hostility and fear are exposed to the critical answer of God and can no longer proliferate unchecked to contaminate the soul.

What Jesus says about hostility is his answer to the laments in the Psalms: "I say unto you, love your enemies" and "I come not to send peace, but a sword!" Without the Psalms, both statements are misleading. Here also the New Testament and the Hebrew Bible are closely connected. What Jesus says has grown out of the experience of the Hebrew Bible; the New Testament is indeed incomprehensible without the Hebrew Bible.

Certainly there are outbursts of aggression in the Psalms that will not endure in the face of Jesus' critical response. And there are abysses of hostility that cannot be covered up by supposedly required "love": "When foundations are destroyed, what hath the righteous wrought?" (Ps. 11:3). In any event, one cannot command the righteous to cloak destructive work with what is alleged to be love.

Even more in this regard is to be learned from the Psalms: when we read them in prayer, they allow us to see the world from the perspective of the powerless and oppressed, the miserable and the timorous. In the great biblical dialogues it becomes even clearer that this is God's perspective: God is not impartial, on a sublime height overlooking all of us, but is involved with us and partial to the powerless.[12] God exalted, but looks upon the distressed (Ps. 138:6), listens to the poor (Ps. 69:33), consoles the fearful (Ps. 4:1). To them apply the promise that the Hebrew Bible hears in God's name, "I-am-who-am" (Exod. 3:14).[13]

Thus the Psalms introduce us to the solidarity of the powerless and the timorous. If we have learned this lesson, we can no longer silence their complaints with the commandment of an all-comprehensive love. Jesus' love mandate is not a principle, but rather a depicting of the way of peace; what the meaning of peace is, according to the Bible, will not be decided by the point of view of the powerful, but defined solely from the perspective of the poor and the distressed.

In the Psalms, furthermore, the language of lament is always at the same time a language of hope. The lament is not spoken into a void; it has an addressee: the Creator of heaven and of this precious earth. The Psalms entreat the Creator with the name that recalls the promise: "I-am-who-am."

Only in the light of such hope will it be possible to cope with hostility and fear. Otherwise the grounds for fear are solidified; the powerful insist upon their power, and we are in their hands if they decide upon annihilation. Those who see themselves only as victims are no longer capable of a life of peace. Without hope there is no education for peace.

HOPE AND EDUCATION FOR PEACE

Hope is the innermost theme of the Bible, so much so that the biblical religion as a whole can be defined as hope. The New Testament describes the relationship to God and to Jesus Christ in terms of *pistis*. This Greek word designates trust and fidelity. Accordingly Christians understand their religion as "faith": they articulate this faith in their creeds; they base their life and their major decisions in life on this faith. Hence the crucial question in the political decisions before which we stand: Do we trust in the destructive power of the bomb or in the creative power of love?

According to Christian conviction, faith and declaration belong together. In the discussion about the stationing of new nuclear weapons in western Europe in the fall of 1983, declarations of politicians were heard continually: the declaration for armaments, the declaration for nuclear deterrence, the declaration for military readiness. On the Warsaw Pact side there were similar declarations. It becomes clear that today the question of further armaments becomes a question of faith.

The Bible is acquainted with the fascination that results from faith in the power of destruction. Such is the mortal enemy of faith in the God of the Bible, the God of love and humanity. The Bible describes this counterfaith in multiple images. In the Psalms it appears in the form of *reshaim*, the evil men of violence for whom the life of the poor has no value. But it appears in its most impressive form at the foot of Mount Sinai when Moses, atop the mountain and surrounded by dark clouds, learns the commandments: Thou shalt not kill . . .; Thou shalt not covet . . . anything that is thy neighbor's. The countergod at the foot of the mountain has the shape of a vigorous bull, cast in gold. Faced with its image, the wanderers become intoxicated. This is a god who promises them to run down and stamp out everything that gets in their way. This god is indeed nothing else but the image of the destructive aggression that springs from their uncontrolled fear. They are fascinated by the glitter of gold, but it was the last of their wealth that they contributed; now they are poor. Later generations were willing to sacrifice their children to this god. The unmistakable physiognomy of this god demands, to this day, human victims in sacrifice.[14]

Against this idolatry the biblical faith sets the confession to the one Lord. This is not a confession of blind obedience, but rather an explicit renunciation of the misanthropic gods of power and their worshipers. The Christian confession of Jesus Christ as the *Kyrios* does not compete, in this respect, with the Jewish confession *Adonai echad* (Deut. 6:4: the Lord alone is God); rather, it makes exactly the same point: Whoever expresses this confession can no longer be willing to bring a sacrifice to the gods of power. The confession of this one God is a confession of hope. From this God alone can we expect a life of dignity and the preservation of creation. The powerful of the earth have time and again reacted to this confession with rage and acts of persecution. They can tolerate no other hope except that based on their own power.

Does, then, the hope for the God of humanity and love have a chance against the power of the powerful? Jesus of Nazareth, as the gospels describe him, not only demanded hope; time and again he patiently argued for hope. The strongest arguments are his parables. Jesus speaks to those who set out to change the world into a world of peace and justice and who become disheartened when faced with the enormousness of the task. He speaks to them in a remote corner of the world, in the face of an overwhelming military presence of a world power, and under the threat of a bloody, escalating conflict. In a situation that appears completely hopeless, he tells them about hope and peace:

> It is like a grain of mustard seed, which, when it is sown in the earth is less than all the seeds that be in the earth. But when it is sown, it groweth up, and becometh greater than all herbs, and shooteth out great branches; so that the fowls of the air may lodge under the shadow of it [Mark 4:31-32].

"Yes," we say, "If only our hearers weren't so inaccessible! They simply do not want to grasp what is necessary. What we say bounces off them!" And Jesus answers:

> Hearken; behold, there went out a sower to sow: and it came to pass, as he sowed, some fell by the wayside, and the fowls of the air came and devoured it up. And some fell on the stony ground, where it had not much earth; and immediately it sprang up, because it had no depth of earth: but when the sun was up, it was scorched, and because it had no root it withered away. And some fell among thorns, and the thorns grew

up, and choked it, and it yielded no fruit. And others fell on good ground, and did yield fruit that sprang up and increased; and brought forth some thirty- and some sixty- and some a hundred-fold. [Mark 4:3–8].

His hope is of a contagious certainty. As if he said: it cannot be otherwise; you will see, justice and peace will triumph. "The kingdom of heaven is like unto leaven, which a woman took and hid in three measures of meal, till the whole was leavened" (Matt. 13:33; Luke 13:21).

Translated from the German
by Haim Gordon

NOTES

1. On this "necessity of rethinking," see the Foreword by Willy Brandt to the First Report of the North-South Commission, 1980 (German edition, p. 14).

2. Already in the 1950s in West Germany there was widespread protest against German rearmament, and especially against nuclear armaments. The protest was carried out by church and union groups; it used much the same arguments that the peace movement uses today, but it could not prevail against Adenauer's politics.

3. The Barmen Theological Statement in 1934, which was the first attempt of collective church opposition to Hitler, consistently attacked these basic decisions. Thesis 2 did so specifically: Just as Jesus Christ is God's affirmation of the pardoning of all our sins, thus and with equal seriousness, he is God's powerful *claim on our whole life.*

4. "Protokoll der Berliner Begegnung zur Friedensförderung," Darmstadt and Neuwied, 1982, p. 82.

5. The struggle of the zealot guerillas against the Roman occupying force could at any time turn into open revolt, as happened in the years 66–70, with disastrous results, including the second destruction of Jerusalem.

6. President Reagan has repeatedly expressed himself in accordance with this expectation. After one such occasion, more than a hundred American Jewish and Christian theologians reproached him that such was a "perversion of the Holy Scriptures and a danger for the security of our nation" (Washington, Oct. 24, 1984).

7. This saying of the prophet stands cast in bronze in front of the UN building in New York, a gift of the USSR: it has acquired a special meaning for the work of church peace groups in East Germany.

8. In my work, *Die Bibel—Buch des Lernens* (Göttingen, 1980; East Berlin, 1982), I have tried to describe more in detail the learning process initiated by the Bible.

9. A "renunciation of the spirit and logic of [nuclear] deterrence" was expressed by the Synod of the Federation of Protestant Churches in East Germany. Immediately before the stationing of the new middle-range missiles in West Germany, the synod of the Protestant churches of West Germany stated, "The specter of reciprocal annihilation contradicts the spirit of Christ and is an expression of our sinfulness. Hence the system of nuclear deterrence must be unconditionally dismantled." Thus they incorporated the initiative of the plenary meeting of the World Council of Churches in

Vancouver, which had condemned the "production and stationing of nuclear weapons, as well as their use" as a "crime against humanity."

10. Pinchas Lapide, *Die Bergpredigt—Utopie oder Programm?* (Mainz, 2nd ed., 1982), p. 101 (English translation *The Sermon on the Mount*, Orbis Books, 1986).

11. An excellent compilation and interpretation of ecclesiastical attitudes on this topic is offered in the study, "Möglichkeit and Unmöglichkeit einseitiger Abrüstung. Zum Konzept des Gradualismus—Ein Text der Theologischen Studienabteilung beim Bund der Evangelischen Kirchen in der DDR," East Berlin, 1984.

12. See Luise and Willy Schottroff, eds., *Die Parteilichkeit Gottes* (Munich, 1984).

13. See *Die bibel—Buch des Lernens*, p. 27.

14. I have treated this topic more extensively in *Der Gott des Friedens und die Götter der Macht; Biblische Alternativen* (Neukirchen, 1983), pp. 86ff.

Islam

7

Riffat Hassan

Peace Education: A Muslim Perspective

The concept of peace education is new in the world. Certainly not many Muslims have heard of it or have reflected on whether human beings can, or should, be educated for peace. So far as I am aware, there is no program or project—either academic or social, past or present—in any contemporary Muslim society. The few Muslims in the world who have been willing and able to participate in such an education have done so, almost exclusively, in non-Muslim settings under the guidance or sponsorship of non-Muslims. As one of these few Muslims I consider myself privileged to have had the opportunity to be an evaluator of a pioneer education for peace project at the Ben Gurion University in Beer Sheva, Israel, some years ago.

The fact that I was the only Muslim among all the evaluators and that the project, which involved Israeli Jewish and Arab Muslim students, was set in a far-from-neutral environment where an obvious inequality exists between Jews and Muslims, made my task a difficult and exacting one, not only intellectually but also emotionally and spiritually.[1] But I felt then, and feel now even more strongly, that the experience of observing and participating in the education for peace project at Ben Gurion University was one of the most worthwhile experiences of my life.

This experience, intense and bittersweet, taught me much. Most of all, it showed me that peace education was not a fantasy but an ideal that could be achieved even in conditions that appeared to be inimical to authentic dialogical interaction. More important still, it gave me a glimpse into what could be accomplished even by an experimental peace education project that was struggling continually to review its nature and goals as it moved gropingly from one phase to another in its three-year life span. I believe, both on the basis of my theoretical study as a theologian of Islam and my observation of pragmatic reality, that educating for peace is one of the most compelling religious/ethical imperatives for all persons who believe in the "transcendent" dimension of human life.

In this paper I will endeavor to show that Muslims are called upon by the Qur'ān and the example of the Prophet of Islam to strive for peace through all available means and that, therefore, peace education must have a high priority in Muslim societies and for Muslims generally. Inasmuch as, unfortunately, I have no empirical data relating to actual peace education projects initiated and developed by Muslims, my paper will focus on sources of "normative" Islam and will identify some important theological resources that could be utilized for persuading Muslims not only to participate in peace education programs in non-Muslim societies but also, and more importantly, to establish such programs in their own societies.

As I see it, before one can argue convincingly that Muslims should be educated for peace it is necessary to demonstrate that education and peace are of pivotal significance to the Islamic worldview. This paper is, therefore, divided into two main sections, the first dealing with education and the second with peace, followed by a summation.

THE ISLAMIC VIEW OF EDUCATION

In education, attention must be drawn to an extremely important fact: the overwhelming majority of Muslims in the world are uneducated, the literacy rate of many Muslim countries being among the lowest in the world. Even among those who qualify as "literate," many can barely read or write.[2] Needless to say, the lack of education has an enormous impact upon all human activities in Muslim societies. It is painful—but necessary—to imagine the gap between those who have had the opportunity to develop what the Qur'ān regards as God's greatest gift to humanity—namely, the ability to conceptualize or to think,[3] which makes possible the miracles of our age—and those who have lived in darkness through the centuries, unaware of their own rich heritage, following the way of their forebears blindly, believing it to be the path of life, whereas, in truth, it is a path of death.

I consider it important to keep the general lack of education among Muslims in mind as one begins to reflect on the feasibility of peace education in the Islamic framework, because any scheme or proposal that ignores the facts of life is doomed to failure. Furthermore, it leads to the setting up of unreal expectations and false comparisons. All too often I have seen non-Muslim dialogue partners, including some of the most dedicated ones, throw up their hands in despair and exclaim: "Why are Muslims in general so hard to engage in dialogue?" Or "Why are Muslims who participate in dialogue so 'pre-critical'?"

What these dialogue participants need to realize is that the Muslim world has not gone through the paradigm changes that the Western Judeo-Christian world has, and that it is, therefore, not appropriate to compare either largely uneducated Muslim societies with much better educated Western societies or Muslims who have been educated in the pre-Enlightenment, perhaps even the pre-Reformation, mode, with Westerners who have been educated in the post-Enlightenment, perhaps even the postmodern, mode. It is a sign of insensitivity if not arrogance (or what is sometimes called "cultural imperialism" by Third World persons) to expect Muslims who have not had the opportunity to go through the process of becoming "critical" thinkers to engage in a dialogue that presupposes a "critical" mind-set defined in exclusively non-Muslim (often Western Christian) terms. Such an expectation tends to alienate even those Muslims who are willing to step outside their own "pre-critical" tradition and work toward evolving concepts and categories that are meaningful and acceptable to all dialogue partners. Such alienation can and must be avoided, not only because there are so few Muslims who are dialogue-oriented (out of the almost one billion Muslims in the world), but also because there are so many resources within Islam that can be used to eradicate the ignorance of Muslims as well as to irradiate the hearts and minds and spirits of those "others" who seek to understand Islam and Muslims from within.

The Attitude of "Normative" Islam toward Knowledge

The fact that there are so many illiterate and uneducated Muslims (particularly women) in the world constitutes not only a profound tragedy but also a profound irony in view of the tremendous stress that "normative" Islam puts on the importance of acquiring knowledge. This is clear from many quranic passages and prophetic *hadíth*, "tradition." It is of interest and importance to observe, for instance, that the Qur'ān refers 140 times to God as *alim*: one who has knowledge, and that the very first verse of the Qur'ān revealed to the Prophet Muhammad links to divine bounty the human ability to write and to know:

> Read in the name of thy Sustainer who has created—created man out of a germ-cell! Read—for thy Sustainer is the Most Bountiful One who has taught [man] the use of the pen—taught man what he did not know! [Surah 96.1].[4]

The Qur'ān describes the Prophet of Islam as one taught by God (Surah 4.113) and as an imparter of knowledge to others (Surah 2.151) but commands him, nevertheless, to pray: "O my Sustainer, cause me to grow in knowledge" (Surah 20.114).[5] Further, the Qur'ān exhorts believers not to pursue that of which they have no knowledge, because God will call them to account for actions that reflect a lack of knowledge:

Pursue not that
Of which thou hast
No knowledge; for
Every act of hearing,
Or of seeing
Or of [feeling in] the heart
Will be enquired into
[on the Day of Reckoning]
[Surah 17.36].[6]

Behold, ye rejected it
on your tongues,
And said out of your mouths
Things of which ye had
No knowledge; and ye thought
It a light matter,
While it was most serious
In the sight of God
[Surah 24.15].[7]

About those who have knowledge, the Qur'ān says:

And whoever is given knowledge is given indeed great wealth [Surah 2.269].[8]

God will exalt by [many] degrees those of you who have attained to faith and [above all] such as have been vouchsafed knowledge: for God is fully aware of all that you do [Surah 58.11].[9]

Sayings Attributed to Muhammad

Embodying the spirit of the Qur'ān are some famous sayings attributed to the Prophet of Islam: "The seeking of knowledge is obligatory upon every Muslim" (Baihaqi, *Mishkat*);[10] "Search for knowledge is compulsory for every Muslim male and Muslim female" (Ibn Majah);[11] "He who goes forth in search of knowledge is in the way of Allah till he returns" (Tirmidhi, Darimi);[12] "Search for knowledge though it be in China" (Baihaqi);[13] "Whoever searches after knowledge, it will be expiation for his past sins" (Tirmidhi).[14]

Further:

If anyone travels on a road in search of knowledge, God will cause him to travel on one of the roads of paradise, the angels will lower their wings from good pleasure with one who seeks knowledge, and the inhabitants of the heavens and the earth and the fish in the depth of the water will ask forgiveness for him. The superiority of the learned man over the devout man is like that of the moon on the night when it is full over the rest of the stars. The learned are the heirs of the prophets who leave neither *dinar* nor *dirham* ["neither dollar nor dime"], leaving only knowledge, and he who accepts it accepts an abundant portion [Ahmad, Tirmidhi, Abu Dawud, Ibn Majah, Darimi, *Mishkat*].[15]

Acquire knowledge, because he who acquires it in the way of the Lord performs an act of piety; who speaks of it, praises the Lord; who seeks it, adores God; who dispenses instruction in it, bestows alms; and who imparts it to its fitting objects, performs an act of devotion to God. Knowledge enables its possessor to distinguish what is forbidden from what is not; it lights the way to Heaven; it is our friend in the desert, our society in solitude, our companion when bereft of friend; it serves as an armor against our enemies. With knowledge, the servant of God rises to the heights of goodness and to a noble position, associates with sovereigns in this world, and attains to the perfection of happiness in the next [*Bihar-ul-Anwar, Mustatraf, Kashf uz-Zaman*].[16]

Although it is not possible to say whether any of the above-cited *ahadith* are authentic without a detailed scrutiny of their formal aspect (i.e., the *isnād*, "chain of transmission"), the fact that all of them conform in spirit to the ethos as well as specific teachings of the Qur'ān supports the assumption that they represent, if not the actual words of the Prophet, at least the general attitude of his companions and their successors. There is also historical evidence showing that the Prophet of Islam considered the education of his community a matter of high priority. For instance, Goldziher points out

That Muhammad himself—partly, it may be, on utilitarian grounds— attached considerable importance to the acquisition of the most indispensable elements of knowledge, may be inferred from the conditions on which he released prisoners of war after his victory at Badr. He employed several Quraish captives to teach the boys of Medina to write, and this service counted as their ransom.[17]

Prophet Muhammad's attitude toward the acquisition of knowledge obviously had a strong impact upon the community in which he lived. As Seeman states: "In the realm of education, we may say, Muhammad instituted learning as an incumbent duty upon his people and this established a definite educational policy for Islam."[18] That the obligation to acquire knowledge was "a concept that possessed religious urgency and was ready to play a prominent role in a new religious movement" is testified to by Rosenthal.[19] Gulick expresses the belief that the knowledge-affirming *ahadith* which "have been widely accepted as authentic and . . . have exerted a wide and salutary influence . . . must assuredly have stimulated and encouraged the great thinkers of the golden age of Islamic civilization."[20]

THE CONTENT AND PURPOSE OF KNOWLEDGE ACCORDING TO "NORMATIVE" ISLAM

In Islam the seeking of knowledge includes formal education, but is not confined to such education, nor are academic credentials necessarily the measure of one's knowledge, though they may be regarded as instrumental to learning. To be educated, in Islamic terms, means to possess knowledge, which may be acquired through a variety of sources, particularly revelation, reason, empirical inquiry, history, and intuition. From the quranic perspective, knowledge is obviously not limited to what is learned through the reasoning mind or the senses. Acquisition of knowledge involves the total person in relationship with total reality. To become a "total" or "whole" person, integration of the diverse, often mutually conflicting, aspects of one's outer and inner self is required, as sages through the centuries have taught. To acquire knowledge of total reality, or to become educated ideally in Islamic terms, also requires a process of integration. By identifying and endorsing diverse sources of knowledge often considered to be mutually opposing (as revelation and reason, or reason and intuition), the Qur'ān points toward both the possibility of, and the need for, an integration or synthesis leading to a unity of knowledge that subsumes the multiplicity of the sources of knowledge. That the quranic vision has been internalized by at least some leaders of Muslim thought is clear from the following letter in which Muhammad Iqbāl, the philosopher-poet, describes his own philosophy of education:

Modern India ought to focus on the discovery of man as a personality— as an independent "whole" in an all-embracing synthesis of life. But does our education today tend to awaken in us such a sense of inner wholeness? My answer is no. Our education does not recognise man as a problem, it impresses on us the visible fact of multiplicity without giving us an insight into the inner unity of life, and thus tends to make us more and more universal in our physical environment. The soul of man is left untouched and the result is a superficial knowledge with a mere illusion of culture and freedom. Amidst this predominantly intellectual culture which must accentuate separate centres within the "whole" the duty of higher minds in India is to reveal the inner synthesis of life.[21]

Although knowledge, defined in quranic terms, is the means "to awaken in man the higher consciousness of his manifold relations with God and the universe"[22] its ultimate purpose (as the existentialists would say) is not to see but to be. True believers in God seek to inculcate God's attributes in themselves. God is *alim*: one who has knowledge; hence the seeking of knowledge is obligatory upon all believers. However, the all-knowing God of the Qur'ān is not the Unmoved Mover, Logos, or Absolute of Greek thought, but the dynamic creator and commander of the universe. Hence a Muslim's "essential nature . . . consists in will, not intellect and understanding"[23] and Muslims identify with Ghazzali's statement: "I will, therefore I am," rather than with Descartes' statement: "I think, therefore I am." The will to act is an integral part of the quranic concept of knowledge.

The Qur'ān urges the seeking of knowledge so that through it both inner and outer reality may be transformed. It is of the essence of a river to flow and of the sun to give light. It is of the essence of an *alim* to translate knowledge into objective reality as did the Prophet of Islam and the Qur'ān calls those who know but do not act *jahilun* (ignorant ones) not *alimun* (knowledgeable ones). Understood in these terms, an *alim* is a *mujahid*—that is, one who engages in *jihād*, strives in the cause of God.

THE ISLAMIC VIEW OF PEACE

It is profoundly ironic that stereotypes identify Islam with war and militancy, whereas the very term *islām* is derived from a root, one of whose basic meanings is "peace." Not only is the idea of peace of pivotal significance in the theological worldview of Islam, it also permeates the daily lives of Muslims. Each time two Muslims greet each other, they say *salam alaikum*, "peace be on you," and *alaikum assalam*, "peace be on you (too)." The regularity and fervor with which this greeting is exchanged shows that it is not a mechanical reiteration of words that have little or no meaning but a religious ritual of great importance. The ideal of being at peace with oneself, one's fellow human beings, the world of nature, and God, is deeply cherished by Muslims in general. But if that is the case, why is there such manifest lack of peace, and so much talk of violence, in the present-day world of Islam? In order to answer this question it is necessary to understand what "peace" means according to the perspective of "normative" Islam.

Many, including some who are committed to the ideal of peacemaking, tend, unfortunately, to define peace negatively, as "absence of war" (just as some tend to define "health" as "absence of sickness"). But, in quranic terms, peace is much more than mere absence of war. It is a positive state of safety or security in which one is free from anxiety or fear. It is this state that characterizes both *islām*,[24] self-surrender to God, and *īmān*,[25] true faith in God, and reference is made to it, directly or indirectly, on every page of the Qur'ān through the many derivatives of the roots "s-l-m" and "a-m-n" from which *islām* and *īmān* are derived, respectively. Peace is an integral part not only of the terms used for a believer, "muslim" (i.e., one who professes *islām*) and *mo'min* (i.e., one who possesses *īmān*), but also of God's names *As-Salām* and *Al-Mo'min* mentioned in the Qur'ān:

He is Allāh, beside whom there is no God; the King, the Holy, the Author of Peace [As-Salām], the Granter of Security [Al-Mo'min], Guardian over all, the Mighty, the Supreme, the Possessor of greatness [Surah 59.23].[26]

As pointed out by G.A. Parwez, *As-Salām* is the Being who is the source of peace and concord and who assures peaceful existence to all beings. *Al-Mo'min* is the Being who shelters and protects all and bestows peace in every sphere of life.[27]

That God "invites" humanity to *dār as-salām* (i.e., the abode of peace) is stated by the Qur'ān (Surah 10.25), which also promises the reward of peace to those who live in accordance with God's will:

God guides such as follow His pleasure into the ways of peace, and brings them out of darkness into light by His will, and guides them to the right path [Surah 5.16].[28]

And this is the path of thy Lord, straight. Indeed we have made the message clear for a people who mind. Theirs is the abode of peace with their Lord, and He is their Friend because of what they do [Surah 6.127–128].[29]

Can, then, he who knows that whatever has been bestowed from on high upon thee by thy Sustainer is the truth be deemed equal to one who is blind? Only they who are endowed with insight keep this in mind: they who are true to their bond with God and never break their covenant; and who keep together what God has bidden to be joined, and stand in awe of their Sustainer and fear the most evil reckoning (which awaits such as do not respond to Him); and who are patient in adversity out of a longing for their Sustainer's countenance, and are constantly in prayer, and spend on others, secretly and openly, out of what we provide for them as sustenance, and repel evil with good. It is these that shall find their fulfillment in the hereafter: gardens of perpetual bliss which they shall enter together with the righteous from among their parents, their spouses, and their offspring: and the angels will come unto them from every gate (and will say): "Peace be upon you, because you have persevered!" [Surah 13.19–24].[30]

The verses cited above point the way a believer must follow in order to attain peace in the hereafter. But this way (i.e., of *islām*) is also the way of obtaining peace here and now. In other words, peace on earth (which is a precondition of peace in heaven) is the result of living in accordance with God's will and pleasure. Here it is important to note that Islam conceives of God as *Rabb Al-'Alamīn*: Creator and Sustainer of all the peoples and universes, whose purpose in creating (as stated in Surah 51.56) is that all creatures should engage in God's *'ibādat*. This term, which is commonly understood as "worship," in fact has a much broader meaning and refers to "doing what God approves."[31] In

Isalm "doing what God approves" is not conceived in terms of seeking salvation from the burden of original sin through belief in redemption or a redeemer (none of these ideas/concepts being present in the Qur'ān) or through renunciation of the world (monasticism not being required by God, according to the Qur'ān).[32] Rather, it is conceived in terms of the fulfillment of *Haquq Allāh* (rights of God) and *Haquq al-'ibād* (rights of God's servants—namely, human beings). The Qur'ān considers the two kinds of "rights" to be inseparable as indicated by the constant conjunction of *salāt* (signifying remembrance of, and devotion to, God) and *zakāt* (signifying the sharing of one's possessions with those in need). In fact, as Surah 107 shows, the Qur'ān is severe in its criticism of those who offer their prayers to God but are deficient in performing acts of kindness to those in need:

> Hast thou ever considered [the kind of person] who gives the
> lie to all moral law?
> Behold, it is this [kind of person] who thrusts the orphan
> away,
> and feels no urge to feed the needy.
> Woe, then, unto those praying ones whose hearts from their
> prayers are remote—
> those who want only to be seen and praised,
> and, withal, deny all assistance [to their fellows].[33]

In quranic terms, then, peace is obtained in any human society when human beings, conscious of their duty to God, fulfill their duty to other human beings. In fulfilling this duty they honor what I call the "human rights" of others. These rights are those that all human beings *ought* to possess because they are rooted so deeply in our humanness that their denial or violation is tantamount to negation or degradation of that which makes us human. These rights came into existence when we did; they were created, as we were, by God in order that our human potential could be actualized. These rights not only provide us with an opportunity to develop all our inner resources, but they also hold before us a vision of what God would like us to be: what God wants us to strive for and live for and die for. Rights given by God are rights that ought to be exercised, because everything that God does is for "a just purpose" (Surah 15.85; 16.3; 44.39; 45.22; 46.3). Among these rights, there are some that have an important, perhaps even a crucial, bearing on whether or not a society can realize the ideal of peace; hence a brief account of them follows.

Right to Life

The sanctity and absolute value of human life is upheld by the Qur'ān, which states:

And do not take any human being's life—which God has declared to be sacred—otherwise than in [the pursuit of] justice: this He has enjoined upon you so that you might use your reason [Surah 6.151].[34]

The Qur'ān also points out graphically in Surah 5.35 that in essence the life of each individual is comparable to the life of an entire community, and, therefore, should be treated with utmost care:

> We ordained
> For the Children of Israel
> That if any one slew
> A person—unless it be
> For murder or for spreading
> Mischief in the land—
> It would be as if
> He slew the whole people:
> And if anyone saved a life,
> It would be as if he saved
> The life of the whole people.[35]

Right to Respect

In Surah 17.70, the Qur'ān says: "Verily, we have honored every human being." Human beings are worthy of respect because they have been made "in the best of molds" (Surah 95.4), and possess the faculty of reason, which distinguishes them from all other creatures (Surah 2.30-34) and enables them to accept the "trust" of freedom of will, which no other creature is willing to accept (Surah 33.72). Human beings can acquire knowledge of good and evil, and strive to do the good and avoid the evil. Thus, they have the potential to be God's viceregents on earth. On account of the promise that is contained in being human, the humaneness of all human beings is to be respected and regarded as an end in itself.

Right to Justice

In the Qur'ān, tremendous emphasis is put on the duty to do justice:

O ye who believe, be maintainers of justice, bearers of witness for Allah, even though it be against your own selves or [your] parents or near relatives—whether he be rich or poor, Allah has the better right over them both. So follow not low desires, lest you deviate. And if you distort or turn away from [truth], surely Allah is ever aware of what you do [Surah 4.135].[36]

O ye who believe, be upright for Allah, bearers of witness with justice; and let not hatred of a people incite you not to act equitably. Be just; that is nearer to observance of duty. And keep your duty to Allah. Surely Allah is aware of what you do [Surah 5.8].[37]

In the context of justice, the Qur'ān uses two concepts: *adl* and *ihsan*. Both are enjoined (Surah 16.91) and both are related to the idea of balance, but they are not identical in meaning. A.A.A. Fyzee, a well-known scholar of Islamic law, defined *adl* as "to be equal, neither more nor less," and stated: "in a court of justice the claims of the two parties must be considered evenly, without undue stress being laid upon one side or the other. Justice introduces balance in the form of scales that are evenly balanced."[38] Abu'l Kalam Azad, a noted Muslim scholar, described *adl* in similar terms: "What is justice but the avoiding of excess. There should be neither too much nor too little; hence the use of scales as the emblems of justice."[39] Lest anyone try to do too much or too little, the Qur'ān states that no human being can carry another's burden (Surah 53.38) or have anything without striving for it (ibid., 39).

It is important to note here that, according to the quranic perspective, justice is not to be interpreted as absolute equality of treatment, because human beings are not equal so far as their human potential or their human situation is concerned. Thus, though upholding the principle that the humanness of all human beings is to be respected, the Qur'ān maintains that the recognition of individual "merit" is also a fundamental human right. The Qur'ān teaches that merit is not determined by lineage, sex, wealth, success, or religion—but by righteousness. Righteousness consists not only of *īmān* (just belief) but also of *amal* (just action) as pointed out in the following passage:

True piety does not consist in turning your faces towards the east or the west—but truly pious is he who believes in God, and the Last Day, and the angels, and revelation, and the prophets; and spends his substance— however much he himself may cherish it—upon his near of kin, and the orphans, and the needy, and the wayfarer, and the beggars, and for the freeing of human beings from bondage; and is constant in prayer, and renders the purifying dues; and [truly pious are] they who keep their promises whenever they promise, and are patient in misfortune and hardship and in time of peril: it is they who have proved themselves true, and it is they, they who are conscious of God.[40]

Surah 19.95 testifies to the higher merit of one who strives harder for the cause of God:

Such of the believers as remain passive—other than the disabled—cannot be deemed equal to those who strive hard in God's cause with their possessions and their lives: God has exalted those who strive hard with their possessions and their lives far above those who remain passive.

Although God has promised the ultimate good unto all [believers], yet has God exalted those who strive hard above those who remain passive by [promising them] a mighty reward—[many] degrees thereof—and forgiveness of sins, and His grace; for God is indeed much-forgiving, a dispenser of grace.[41]

Surah 49.13 affirms that "the most honored of you in the sight of God is the most righteous of you."

Just as it is in the spirit of *adl* that special merit be considered in the matter of rewards, so also special circumstances must be considered in the matter of punishments. In the case of punishment for crimes of "unchastity," for instance, the Qur'ān, being nonsexist, prescribes identical punishments for a man or a woman who is proved guilty (Surah 2.2), but it differentiates between different classes of women; for the same crime, a slave woman would receive half, and the Prophet's consort double, the punishment given to a "free" Muslim woman (Surah 4.25; 33.30). Making such a distinction shows compassion for the morally "disadvantaged," while upholding high moral standards for others, particularly those whose actions have a normative significance.

While constantly enjoining *adl*, the Qur'ān goes beyond this concept to *ihsan*, literally "restoring the balance by making up a loss or deficiency."[42] In order to understand this concept, it is necessary to understand the nature of the ideal community or society (*ummah*) envisaged by the Qur'ān. The word *ummah* comes from the term *umm* meaning "mother." The symbols of a mother and motherly love and compassion are also linked with the two attributes most characteristic of God, *Rahmān* and *Rahīm*, both of which are derived from the root r-h-m, meaning "womb." The ideal *ummah* cares about all its members as an ideal mother cares about all her children, knowing that all are not equal and that each has different needs. Although encouraging any one of her children to be parasitical would be injurious and unjust not only to her other children but also to the one who does not fulfill its human potential, she can, with justice, make up the deficiency of any child who, despite its best efforts, still cannot meet the requirements of life. *Ihsan* thus secures what even *adl* cannot; it shows the Qur'ān's sympathy for the downtrodden, oppressed, or weak classes of human beings (such as women, slaves, orphans, the poor, the infirm, minorities, etc.).

Right to Freedom

There is much in the Qur'ān that endorses J.J. Rousseau's famous statement: "Man is born free, and everywhere he is in chains." A large part of the Qur'ān's concern is to free human beings from the chains that bind them: traditionalism, authoritarianism (religious, political, economic), tribalism, racism, sexism, and slavery.

It is obvious that God alone is completely free and not subject to any constraints. The human condition necessitates that limits be set to what human beings may or may not do, so that liberty does not degenerate into license. Recognizing the human propensity toward dictatorship and despotism, the Qur'ān says with startling clarity and emphasis:

> It is not meet for a mortal that Allah should give him the Book and the judgment and the prophethood, then he should say to men: Be my servants besides Allah's; but [he would say]: Be worshippers of the Lord because you teach the Book and because you study [it] [Surah 3.78].[43]

The greatest guarantee of personal freedom for a Muslim lies in the quranic decree that no one other than God can limit human freedom (Surah 42.21) and in the statement that "judgment is only Allah's" (Surah 12.40).

Although it is beyond the scope of this paper to cite quranic pronouncements relating to human freedom in the diverse realms of life, it is important to mention that the Qur'ān abolished slavery (Surah 47.4); that it established the principle of *shura* or government by mutual consultation (Surah 3.159)[44] in order to eliminate the possibility of political authoritarianism; and that it prohibited coercion in matters of religious belief as is clearly stated in Surah 2.256:

> Let there be no compulsion
> In religion: truth stands out
> Clear from error: whoever
> Rejects evil and believes
> In God hath grasped
> The most trustworthy
> Hand-hold, that never breaks.[45]

The same is implied in Surah 18.29:

> The Truth is
> From your Lord:
> Let him who will
> Believe, and let him
> Who will, reject [it].[46]

It is noteworthy that in the matter of religious freedom, the Qur'ān is "liberal" to an amazing degree. Not only does it state quite clearly that the mission of the Prophet (and Muslims) to non-Muslims consists only of a faithful transmission of the message of God and that the Prophet (and Muslims) ought not to feel responsible for the religious and moral choices made by other Muslims or by non-Muslims after they have received the message of God.[47] The Qur'ān also makes it clear that plurality of religions is part of God's plan for humanity:

If it had been God's plan
They would not have taken
False gods: but we
Made thee not one
To watch over their doings,
Nor art thou set
Over them to dispose
Of their affairs
[Surah 6.107].[48]

If it had been thy Lord's will
They would have all believed,
All who are on earth!
Will thou then compel mankind,
Against their will, to believe!
[Surah 10.99].[49]

Going still further, the Qur'ān states:

Those who believe [in the Qur'ān],
And those who follow the Jewish [scriptures],
And the Christians and the Sabians,
Any who believe in God
And the Last Day,
And work righteousness,
Shall have their reward
With their Lord,
Nor shall they grieve
[Surah 2.62].[50]

In other words, not only does the Qur'ān uphold the right of human beings in general to religious freedom, it also recognizes the religious equality of all those who have "iman" and act righteously. Even to those beyond the pale of "right belief," the attitude of the Qur'ān is open-minded and more than merely tolerant, as may be seen from the following verses:

But do not revile those whom they invoke instead of God, lest they revile God out of spite, and in ignorance: for, goodly indeed have we made their own doings appear unto every community. In time, however unto their Sustainer they must return: and then He will make them [truly] understand all that they were doing [Surah 6.108].[51]

And if any of those who ascribe divinity to aught beside God seeks thy protection, grant him protection, so that he might [be able to] hear the word of God [from thee]; and thereupon convey him to a place where he can feel secure: this, because they [may be] people who [sin only because they] do not know [the truth] [Surah 9.6].[52]

In the context of the human right to religious freedom, it is necessary to mention that, according to traditional Islam, the punishment for apostasy is death. There is, however, nothing in the Qur'ān that suggests any punishment at all, let alone the punishment of death. There is absolutely no reason why the quranic imperative that there must be no compulsion in religion should not apply also to the Muslims who wish to renounce Islam. (I believe that the death penalty was not originally for apostasy but for apostasy accompanied by "acts of war" against Muslims. Later, however, this distinction was obliterated by Muslim jurists in order to compel "wavering" Muslims to remain within the fold of Islam.)

Other Rights

Some other rights that may be mentioned in passing are: the right to be protected from defamation, sarcasm, offensive nicknames, and backbiting (Surah 49.11–12) as well as from being maligned on grounds of assumed guilt by scandal-mongers (Surah 24.16–19); the right to a secure place of residence (Surah 2.85); the right to a means of living (Surah 6.156; 11.6); the right to protection of one's personal property or possessions (Surah 2.29); the right to protection of one's covenants/contracts (Surah 3.177; 5.1; 17.34); the right to move freely (Surah 67.15); the right to seek asylum if one is living under oppression (Surah 4.97–100); the right to social and judicial autonomy for minorities (Surah 5.42–48); the right to protection of one's holy places (Surah 9.17); and the right to protection of one's home life from undue intrusion (Surah 24.27–28, 58; 33.53; 49.12).

It is essential in the context of human rights in Islam to mention that there is more quranic legislation pertaining to the regulation of man-woman relationships than on any other subject. The Qur'ān is fully cognizant of the fact that women have been among the most exploited and oppressed groups in the world, and aims, in multifarious ways, to establish their equality with men in terms of their humanness and to secure justice for them in domestic and public matters. An idea of tremendous importance implicit in many teachings of the Qur'ān is that if human beings can learn to order their homes justly so that the rights of all within its jurisdiction are safeguarded, then they can also order their society and the world at large justly. In other words, the Qur'ān regards the home as a microcosm of the *ummah* and the world community, and emphasizes the importance of making it "the abode of peace" through just living.

Even a brief reflection on the "human rights"[53] mentioned above gives one a good idea of the quranic concept of "the good life." This good life, which is made up of many elements and is characterized by peace, is possible only within a just environment. In other words, justice is a prerequisite for peace according to the Qur'ān, which does not understand peace to be a passive state of affairs, a mere absence of war. A peace generated by a thing such as the cold war would, in quranic terms, not only be "unholy" but also unreal because it does not guarantee the existence of the conditions that are required for the actualization of human potentialities or the fulfillment of the total human being who alone is capable of attaining the ideal of peace as the Qur'ān understands it. Without the elimination of the inequities, inequalities, and injustices that pervade the personal and collective lives of human beings, it is not possible to talk of peace in Islamic terms. Such talk makes sense only in a society in which ignorance and oppression have been eliminated, in which the means of sustaining and developing human life and capabilities are accessible to all, in which there is freedom from fear, uncertainty, and anxiety—in short, in a society where justice prevails in every way.

SUMMATION

The central significance of both education and peace in "normative" Islam is clear from the foregoing discussion. There is no question at all that the Qur'ān would wholeheartedly support the idea of educating for peace provided its concepts of "education" and "peace" are properly understood. It is obvious that the quranic ideal is not easy to achieve in a world such as the one in which we live, because it entails not simply the desire to abolish violence and war as means of conflict-resolution but the commitment to "doing what God approves." However, from the quranic perspective, the securing of peace either here and now or in the hereafter is not meant to be easy, as the Qur'ān states in Surah 3.141:

> Did you think that ye
> Would enter *al-jannah*
> [i.e., "the garden": the abode of peace]
> Without God testing
> Those of you who fought hard
> (in His cause) and
> Remained steadfast?[54]

Peace is dependent upon justice and justice is dependent upon *jihād fi sabil Allāh*: striving in the cause of God. It is most unfortunate that *jihād*, which is the means whereby God's vision of a peaceful world can come to be, has become identified in the minds of many non-Muslims and—what is much worse—in the minds of many present-day Muslims, with mere destruction. According to the Qur'ān, Muslims have the right to defend themselves against injustice and the duty to protect the weak from injustice.[55] But they are reminded, over and over, that the "limits set by God" (*hudud Allāh*) are not to be transgressed at any time, and that justice must be done even to an enemy.[56] Furthermore, any initiative toward peace taken by an enemy must be accepted and responded to in good faith and with good will.[57]

The thought with which I should like to conclude this paper is that, in my judgment, the greatest *jihād* for Muslims today lies in the making of war not upon real or assumed enemies of Islam but upon the ignorance and narrowness of heart, mind, and spirit that prevent Muslims from becoming *mo'minum*: those who have attained peace through right knowledge leading to right action. The duty to seek learning even in the midst of war is where the quranic emphasis lies, as pointed out in Surah 9.122:

> With all this, it is not desirable that all of the believers take the field [in time of war]. From within every group in their midst, some shall refrain from going forth to war, and shall devote themselves [instead] to acquiring a deeper knowledge of the faith, and [thus be able to] teach their home-coming brethren, so that these [too] might guard themselves against evil.[58]

NOTES

1. Some of my reactions to the Education for Peace Project at the Ben Gurion University were recorded in "Response to 'Buberian Learning Groups: the Quest for Responsibility in Education for Peace,' by Haim Gordon and Jan Demarest," published in *Teachers College Record*, 84.2 (Fall 1982) 226–31, and in *Education for Peace and Disarmament: Toward a Living World*, Douglas Sloan, ed. (New York, Teachers College Press, 1983).

2. Pakistan is one of the most educated of Muslim countries in the world. The following citations from a government document entitled *Action Plan for Educational Development 1983-88*, published by the Ministry of Education, Islamabad (1984), give an indication of what this means—for it and for the other Muslim nations: "Literacy was estimated at 26.2% in 1981. Behind this unflattering figure, there are large disparities—in terms of rural/urban (17.3% against 47.1%) and male/female (35.1% against 16.0%). Rural female literacy is only 7.3%, the worst case being female literacy in Baluchistan, only 1.8%" (p. 43). "In 1981 the criterion [of literacy] became . . . 'the ability to read a newspaper and write a simple letter in any language' " (p. 43). "The inadequacy of our educational system leaves little scope for debate. . . . Yet, what is heartening is the widespread realization that today we stand at the edge of a precipice, and that our fall is being delayed only because of our tenuous links with the mere semblance of a system, which if precluded of its weaknesses might still prove to be viable. Pakistan as a nation is at the brink of complete educational chaos and disaster" (p. 13). "Today we stand at the crossroads of planning informed by the realization that no meaningful progress can be achieved in Pakistan without a breakthrough in the field of education. The task has forbidding magnitudes. . . . With a literacy rate of 26.2% we mark the borders of the bottom category of countries like Bhutan, Nepal, Afghanistan, Ethiopia, Sudan, Chad, Laos, and Zaire. . . . Of the microscopic minority that manage to get education, the quality is nowhere near the international standards. More and more young men are emerging from the high schools ready neither for college nor for work. The state of higher education is no different. The predicament becomes more

acute as knowledge expands to new frontiers. Obviously, 'all is not well in the state of Denmark' " (p. 32).

3. See Surah 2.30–33.

4. Translation by Muhammad Asad, *The Message of the Qur'ān* (Gibraltar, Dar-Al-Andalus, 1980).

5. Ibid.

6. Translation by Abdullah Yusuf Ali, *The Holy Qur'ān* (Lahore, 1937–38).

7. Ibid.

8. Translation by Muhammad Ali, *A Manual of Hadith* (Lahore, Ahmadiyya Anjuman Ishaat-i-Islam, n.d.), p. 31.

9. Asad, *Message of the Qur'ān*.

10. Ali, *Manual of Hadith*, p. 39.

11. Nisar Ahmed, *The Fundamental Teachings of Qur'ān and Hadith* (Karachi, Jamiyatul Falah Publications, 1973), vol. 3, p. 111.

12. Abdallah al-Khatib at-Tabrizi, *Mishkat al-Masabih*, translated by James Robson (Lahore, Shaikh Muhammad Ashraf, 1975), vol. 1, p. 55.

13. Ahmed, *Fundamental Teachings*, vol. 3, p. 117.

14. Ibid., p. 111.

15. at-Tabrizi, *Mishkat al-Masabih*, vol. 1, p. 53.

16. Cited in *The Spirit of Islam* by Syed Ameer Ali (Karachi, Pakistan Publishing House, 1976), pp. 360–61.

17. I. Goldziher, "Education (Muslim)," in *Encyclopedia of Religion and Ethics*, J. Hastings, ed. (Edinburgh, 1967), vol. 5, p. 198, quoted in *Religious Education in Islam* by J.D. Kraan (Rawalpindi, Christian Study Centre, 1984), p. 14.

18. Seeman K., "Education in Islam, From the Jahiliyyah to Ibn Khaidun," *Muslim World,* 56/3 (1966) 188, quoted in Kraan, *Religious Education*, p. 15.

19. F. Rosenthal, *Knowledge Triumphant: The Concept of Knowledge in Medieval Islam* (Leiden, Brill, 1970), p. 23, quoted in Kraan, *Religious Education*, p. 13.

20. R.L. Gulick, *Muhammad the Educator* (Lahore, Institute of Islamic Culture, 1969), p. 45.

21. Letter dated Dec. 5, 1925, published in *The Indian Review*, Madras, 27/1 (Jan. 1926) 2.

22. Muhammad Iqbāl, *The Reconstruction of Religious Thought in Islam* (Lahore, 1944), pp. 8–9.

23. Vahid, S.A., ed., *Thoughts and Reflections of Iqbal* (Lahore, Shaikh Muhammad Ashraf, 1964), p. 35.

24. G.A. Parwez, *Lughat ul-Qur'ān* (Lahore, Idaru Tulu'-e-Islam, 1960), vol. 2, p. 894.

25. Ibid., vol. 1, p. 263.

26. Muhammad Ali, *The Holy Qur'ān* (Chicago, Specialty Promotions, 1973).

27. G.A. Parwez, *Islam: A Challenge to Religion* (Lahore, Idara Tulu'-e-Islam, 1968), p. 285.

28. M. Ali, *Holy Qur'ān*.

29. Ibid.

30. Asad, *Message of the Qur'ān*.

31. *Arabic-English Lexicon*, book 1, part 5, p. 1936.

32. See Surah 57.27.

33. Asad, *Message of the Qur'ān*.

34. Ibid.

35. A.Y. Ali, *Holy Qur'ān.*

36. M. Ali, *Holy Qur'ān.*

37. Ibid.

38. A.A.A. Fyzee, *A Modern Approach to Islam* (Lahore, Universal Books, 1978), p. 17.

39. Ibid.

40. Asad, *Message of the Qur'ān.*

41. Ibid.

42. G.A. Parwez, *Tabweeb ul-Qur'ān* (Lahore, Idara Tulu'-e-Islam, 1977), vol. 1, p. 78.

43. M. Ali, *Holy Qur'ān.*

44. Of relevance here is the following passage: "The Qur'ān gives to responsible dissent the status of a fundamental right. In exercise of their powers, therefore, neither the legislature nor the executive can demand unquestioning obedience. . . . The Prophet, even though he was the recipient of Divine revelation, was required to consult the Muslims in public affairs. Allah addressing the Prophet says: '. . . consult with them upon the conduct of affairs. And . . . when thou art resolved, then put thy trust in Allah (Surah 3.159)' (K. Ishaque, "Islamic Law—Its Ideals and Principles," in *The Challenge of Islam*, A. Gauher, ed. [London, The Islamic Council of Europe, 1980], pp. 167–69).

45. A.Y. Ali, *Holy Qur'ān.*

46. Ibid.

47. See, e.g., Surah 6.107; 16.82; 42.48.

48. A.Y. Ali, *Holy Qur'ān.*

49. Ibid.

50. Ibid.

51. Asad, *Message of the Qur'ān.*

52. Ibid.

53. For a more detailed discussion of human rights in Islam, see my article, "On Human Rights and the Qur'anic Perspective," in *Human Rights in Religious Traditions*, A. Swidler, ed. (New York, Pilgrim Press, 1982), pp. 51–65; also in *Journal of Ecumenical Studies*, 19/3 (Summer 1982) 51–65.

54. A.Y. Ali, *Holy Qur'ān.*

55. See, e.g., Surah 2.190–93, 217; 4.75–78; 22.39–40, 60; 57.25.

56. See, e.g., Surah 5.8.

57. See, e.g., Surah 8.61.

58. Asad, *Message of the Qur'ān.*

8

Haim Gordon

A Meeting with Naguib Mahfouz

INTRODUCTION

I first met Naguib Mahfouz in the Café Cleopatra on the bank of the Nile in Cairo in the late spring of 1980. Immediately one sensed his warmth and straightforwardness, even before one noticed his twinkling eyes and deep, hearty laugh. It was difficult to believe that this modest soft-spoken man was the most popular and applauded novelist of the Arab world. Later I learned that his popularity defies decrees by various Arab governments that banned some of his books. Arab merchants have learned, together with the hashish that traverses borders illegally, to take along a few volumes of Mahfouz to countries where they are banned—eager buyers will be found for both goods.

Mahfouz was born in 1911 in Cairo and has lived there ever since. He received a degree in philosophy, but he worked as a clerk in governmental ministries, writing in his spare time. His status changed in 1957 when he was awarded the Egyptian State Prize for literature for his autobiographical trilogy on Egypt between the world wars. To date he has published more than two dozen novels and many short stories, which have been read and studied by millions of Arabs from Aswan to Bahrain and from Gaza to Casablanca. Since the 1960s Mahfouz has written regularly for *Al Ahram,* a major Egyptian daily newspaper. At first he published installments of his stories and books; later he began to write a weekly column. In that column he has frequently advocated peace between the Arab nations and Israel; he has also criticized internal Arab and Muslim wars, five of which are currently being waged in various regions of the Arab and Muslim world. His outspokenness on the topic of peace has brought him under severe criticism from many sides, but this criticism does not seem to have diminished the appeal of his novels, or of the various films based on these novels produced by studios in Cairo.

Mahfouz is a devout Muslim. His books frequently criticize official representatives of Islam. In the three books that have been translated into English, *Midaq Alley, Miramar,* and *Children of Gebelawi,* he has repeatedly shown how ruling Muslims are indifferent to the sad plight of adherents to their faith. He believes that Islam must relate to all its adherents, and to their full life; dogma should not be the crux of Islam. When discussing his attitude, as a Muslim, to education for peace, he reminded me of what he had frequently told me in our many meetings over the years: "My books speak for me better than I do; so if after the interview you still have some questions, go read my books." The following interview took place in the spring of 1985 in his office in the *Al Ahram* building.

INTERVIEW

Gordon: How does Islam relate to peace and to peace education?

Mahfouz: If you read the Qur'ān, you will find that the prophet is very friendly to members of other religions. There is no enmity between Islam and other faiths. We Muslims believe that there is only one true religion, much as there is only one God. God cannot give humankind two religions. During long periods of history all religions have thrived in Islamic states. Hence, I see no problem in calling peoples to live in peace with each other on the basis of Islam. Such a calling fully accords with our faith

Gordon: But still there are religious wars and there have been religious wars in which Muslims participated.

Mahfouz: True. But I believe that more often than not, these were reactions to attacks from other religions. If European Christianity had not embarked on the Crusades, religious wars against Islam, there would not have been holy wars between Christianity and Islam. One should also note that in early periods of Islam the rulers were primarily kings, who were often despots, tyrants. There was no free speech and no way to argue with the monarch. Objection to his ruling meant death. If a person acted in some way against the monarch, the response was the sword. But this political way of life did not derive from Islam. The same is true in the Iran-Iraq war. It is not a religious war, but rather a political war. Not only is Iran Shiite, but Iraq also has a majority of Shiites. And Iran states categorically that its purpose in the war is to overthrow Iraq's ruler.

Gordon: But still this is a war between Muslims. How do you explain that soldiers believe in Islam's call for peace—and yet go out to kill?

Mahfouz: I agree, it is terrible. And it is anti-Islamic. But look at what happened in Christian countries during hundreds of years in Europe. They fought each other, often in the name of God, for decades. And we must remember that Christianity defines itself as a religion of love and peace.

Gordon: And yet how would you justify that, of all the monotheistic religions, only Islam believes in a call to *jihād,* "holy war"?

Mahfouz: When he spoke about *jihād* the Prophet meant that one could go to war against atheists. Theoretically Christianity holds that when a person is smitten on one cheek, he must turn the other cheek. The Prophet did not agree. He taught us that one must defend oneself, and especially against atheists who attacked the Prophet and his followers.

Gordon: In your book *The Beggar* we find Muslim-Christian intermarriage accompanied by great suffering. Is Islam tolerant?

Mahfouz: In *The Beggar* the Christian woman's family renounces her when she marries a Muslim. But Islam accepts her.

Gordon: And if a relationship develops in the opposite direction, if a Muslim woman falls in love with a Christian man? What would the Muslim family do?

Mahfouz: They would not allow such a marriage.

Gordon: Why?

Mahfouz: They would probably think that perhaps the woman will be too weak in this relationship, and it might affect her religious convictions.

Gordon: What you have been saying leaves me uncomfortable. It reminds me of the saying: If everything is so good, why is everything so bad?

Mahfouz (laughing): True. When I read the Qur'ān, everything is good. But when I read the book of life—Oh, how different!

Gordon: Do you believe that Qaddafi, the ruler of Libya, is working in the spirit of Islam as you grasp it?

Mahfouz: Qaddafi has convinced himself that he is defending Islam. I disagree.

Gordon: What makes you think you are right?

Mahfouz: According to my reading of Muslim leaders and thinkers throughout the ages, Qaddafi is wrong. Look, you Jews call the period that you lived under Muslim rule "the golden age of Jewish literature and philosophy." That itself contradicts Qaddafi's fanaticism.

Furthermore, from what I remember here in Egypt, before the issue of Palestine divided us, Jews and Arabs lived together peacefully. Jews were not restricted to ghettos; many affluent Jews resided in beautiful suburbs of Cairo. Even when the issue of Palestine arose, of the land the Jews took and settled, even then the imams of Al Azhar [the Muslim theological center] objected to the attacking of Jews as Jews because of what is written in the Qur'ān. They clearly held that there is a difference between Jews who for political reasons are our enemies and Jews of the holy Torah. Even during the Israeli-Arab wars Judaism was not rejected, because that could contradict the Qur'ān.

Gordon: But, if all this is true, why is it that today many Muslims in Egypt are not friendly with us Jews?

Mahfouz: From a Muslim point of view, you Israelis are camping on Muslim land, which was taken from Muslims by force. This point of view has no adverse relationship to your Jewish faith, only to the political act of land-grabbing. Furthermore, after the signing of the peace treaty the religious leaders of Al Azhar agreed to living in peace. Only after your invasion of Lebanon did the imams change their attitude. If you Jews want peace, why did you invade Lebanon?

Gordon: What do you think will happen after we leave Lebanon?

Mahfouz: Then, I hope, we will be able to return to the way of peace.

Gordon: Do you believe that your books educate for peace? If so, how?

Mahfouz: I believe they do educate for peace, primarily because they provide a humanistic outlook. There is no place for fanatics in a humane society; when my books show human beings and members of human society struggling to be human, these writings are working against fanaticism. I believe also that this approach accords with the way of our prophet. Muhammad advises: Don't be extreme in your religion; be honest not extreme. He calls himself the prophet of kindness. And he adds: Any Muslim who does anything bad to other religions will be my enemy in the other world, the world after death.

Gordon: But if all this is true, why does it not appear in your books? In *Miramar,* for instance, the opposite emerges. The hero believes in the Qur'ān and in what you have here been saying, and in his life he fails. There seems to be little place in Egyptian society, as you describe it, for believers in peace, as you see it.

Mahfouz: He fails because of our revolution, which rejected even the good in our former society. The new revolution of Nasser did away with the liberal trends that were fermenting in Egypt. Nasser came to change the entire society, therefore he attacked the liberals, and as a force in Egypt they failed.

Buddhism

9

Manjuvajra

The Buddhist Teaching on Nonviolence

THE ROHINI INCIDENT

In the sixth century before the birth of Jesus of Nazareth, at the time of the defeat of Babylon and the establishment of the Persian empire, the area that now forms the border of Nepal and northern India was a region of city states. Some of these states were republics, governed by an assembly of the elders of the tribe; others were monarchies. It was a period of struggle and intrigues; on occasion diplomatic relations between rival states broke down and war erupted. Eventually the monarchies survived; the kingdoms of Koshala and Magadha were especially powerful, but in the twentieth century they are known only to those with a special interest in the period. Although the names of the great rajas Pasenadi, Bimbisara, and Ajatasattu are now forgotten, the name of one who lived among them is still known and respected throughout the world. Gautama, of the Sakyan clan, became the enlightened one, the Buddha, during this period. Frequently Gautama gave advice to each of the aforementioned kings. He also intervened on at least one occasion to avert a war between two neighboring states; it is the account of this intervention at the Rohini River that will serve as our point of departure for a chapter on the Buddhist teaching of nonviolence.

The Sakyans and the Koliyans shared the river Rohini as a border, using its waters to irrigate their crops. One year there was a drought, and it was clear that there would not be enough water for both states. Both sides in the dispute insisted that they should have the water on the grounds that their crops would ripen with one watering, but they were unable to reach an equitable solution. The negotiations declined to the level of mutual abuse; the Koliyans accused the Sakyans of having cohabited with their sisters like animals, and the Sakyans accused the Koliyans of having lived in hollow trees like animals. Feelings were running high: tribal pride had been wounded. Otherwise peaceable men armed themselves and set out to the battlefield eager for blood.

The Buddha, whose father was a Sakyan and whose mother was of Koliyan descent, was at this moment visiting his home for the second time since his enlightenment. As soon as he heard about the escalation of warlike feelings, he set out for the battlefield and came between the opposing armies. The men set aside their weapons and saluted him. After some lengthy inquiries he managed to determine what the dispute was truly about, although by this time the insults and excitement had all but obscured the original problem. He asked the men gathered there which was more valuable, water or warriors. They replied that warriors were of much more value. He then said, "It is not fitting that because of a little water you should destroy warriors who are beyond price." The assembly was reduced to silence.[1]

The Sakyans and the Koliyans took the Buddha's wisdom to heart and, having realized the supreme value of life, committed themselves to finding a nonviolent solution to their problem. The Sakyans embraced the idea of nonviolence, saying that it was unseemly for the clan of the Buddha to take up arms for any reason.

Some years after the Rohini incident the Sakyans were faced by the forces of the king of Kosala. They offered no resistance and were massacred. The report of the massacre of the Sakyans comes as a profound shock. The description of the incident on the battlefield by the river Rohini strikes chords of familiarity, and the role of the Buddha as peacemaker is also familiar, although one may be surprised by his effectiveness. But the massacre of the Sakyans in the face of their acceptance of nonviolence is stunning. Does it illustrate the naivety of the stance of nonviolence? Does the sense of injustice that it provokes make us question the basic goodness of human existence? Does it provide an argument for the use of violence at least in defense of one's life?

The massacre of the Sakyans drives us to rethink our attitudes toward nonviolence. In this chapter I shall investigate the Buddhist ideal of nonviolence. I shall discuss the ways in which that ideal, and the training in nonviolence that the Buddhist tradition offers, can be realized in the lives of individual men and women. I shall also consider the benefit that peacemakers—those actively involved in the creation of a world freed from war and the threat of nuclear holocaust—can gain from this tradition and its practices.

RADICAL NONVIOLENCE: THE BUDDHIST TEACHING

The Buddha's teaching on the subject of nonviolence *(ahimsa),* and the related sentiments of nonharm *(apanatipata),* compassion *(karuna),* and universal loving kindness *(metta)* is illustrated in the following example, which is taken from a Theravadan text.[2] The Bhiksu Phagguna had been abused by others, and the Buddha said to him:

Wherefore, Phagguna, if anyone to your face should abuse you . . . if
he were to strike you with a fist or hurl clods of earth at you, or beat you
with a stick, or give you a blow with a sword—yet must you set aside all
worldly desires, all worldly considerations, and thus must you train
yourself: "My heart shall be unwavering. No evil word will I send forth. I
will abide compassionate of others' welfare, of kindly heart, without
resentment." Thus must you train yourself, Phagguna.

In this example, and in countless others that could have been used with equal
effectiveness, it becomes clear that Buddhists are exhorted to banish all vestiges
of hatred from their mind. As was explained to Phagguna, even under torture
(by being beaten with a club), or when in danger of being killed (by the blow of
a sword), Buddhists are to train themselves to abide compassionately, lovingly,
and without resentment. Self-protection is not placed above the ideal of
nonviolence. No appeal to an idea of justice along the lines of "an eye for an
eye, a tooth for a tooth" is allowed to interfere with this ideal. Buddhist
teaching does not condone so-called righteous indignation. Love *(metta)*
should even be developed toward those who "destroy or curse [Buddhist]
images and shrines."[3]

Once again, then, we encounter the same uncompromising ideal of nonviolence exhibited by the Sakyans under attack by the king of Kosala. It may
appear that the Buddhist teaching is a naive or romanticized idealism, a
teaching that goes beyond any sensible or balanced view. The Buddhist ideal of
nonviolence is indeed radical; its source is in the very heart of Buddhism. To
understand it properly, we must appreciate the essence of Buddhism itself.

Buddhism is concerned with the psychological and spiritual growth of men
and women from their present level of development to their flowering as true
human beings and—even beyond that—to yet higher levels of being. Eventually the Buddhist spiritual path leads to an altogether different state, a state
that transcends all others: enlightenment or buddhahood. Gautama Siddhartha discovered the route to enlightenment and developed a means *(upaya)* of
communicating his experience to others in such a manner that they, too, could
become established in enlightenment. This communication, and the commentaries on it, makes up the dharma, that essentially untranslatable word that
refers to the totality of the Buddha's teaching.

Psychological and spiritual growth can be seen as the conscious development
of confidence *(saddha)*, wisdom *(panna)*, energy *(viriya)*, concentration *(sa-
madhi)*, and mindfulness *(sati)*. It is achieved by ethical observances, meditation, and the development of wisdom, in both its lower form of intellectual
understanding and its higher form of direct intuitive insight.

Buddhists, therefore, adopt a particular ethical practice so as to stimulate
their growth. They work to develop their state of mind by modifying their
behavior. Practices will help move their mind from a state restricted by selfish
desires and fears for security to a freer state, one characterized by the expansive

sentiments of love and compassion. Ethical observances also prepare their mind for the next stage of spiritual practice, the practice of meditation. Meditators work directly on their mind. They build a connection with their higher nature, preparing themselves for insight into the true nature of reality. In this way they develop a clearer understanding of themselves and evolve to levels of consciousness from which reality can be apprehended ever more deeply.

The enlightened mind exhibits both wisdom and compassion. These two aspects, however, are not essentially different from one another. They are intimately related, two sides of the same coin, as it were. Compassion is the emotional expression of wisdom. An enlightened being, a buddha, sees reality, and, as a result of this seeing, experiences compassion *(karuna)* for all living beings, who suffer because they live under a limited view of what is real. A buddha understands the source of their suffering and is in a position to be able to do something about relieving it. The relief of the sufferings of all beings is the essential work of a buddha. One who engages in this work, on whatever level, is called a bodhisattva.[4]

Ahimsa, nonviolence, is one aspect of this compassion. Nonviolence is thus an aspect of the enlightened mind, an aspect of the higher nature of all human beings. Any act of violence evidences the fact that perpetrators are alienated from their higher nature. Inasmuch as Buddhists have undertaken to overcome this alienation, all acts of violence are proscribed. It is also clear that once they are established in contact with their higher nature, practitioners will not want to sacrifice that contact for the lesser goal of personal survival. Buddhists who maintain their practice of nonviolence and compassion—even though it may cost them their present life—have lost nothing; they have simply held fast to the greater good.

Clearly and uncompromisingly, then, Buddhism teaches that violence in any form causes suffering not only to the recipient of the violence, but also to the perpetrator of such violence as well. Any indulgence in violence serves to both alienate the perpetrator from an awareness of the true nature of reality and to strengthen all the factors that give rise to personal suffering. Thus the practice of nonviolence—and its positive expressions as love and compassion—is the first duty of all those who call themselves Buddhists.

This claim is further strengthened by noting the important position given to the precepts dealing with nonviolence in the various lists of ethical observances within the Buddhist tradition. For example the first precept in the list of five practiced by all Buddhists is "I undertake to abstain from causing harm to living beings," or in its more positive form, "With deeds of loving kindness, I purify my body."[5] The third of the Parajika dharmas, those serious breaches of the monk's discipline that cause him to be expelled from the order of monks, further stresses the centrality of ahimsa in Buddhist practice:

Whatever monk should intentionally, with his own hand, deprive a human or one that has human form of life, supply him with a knife,

search for an assassin for him, instigate him to death, or praise the nature
of death, saying, "O man, what use is this dreadful, impure, sinful life to
you? O man, death is better than life for you"; should [the monk]
purposefully, being of one opinion, instigate him in many ways to death,
or recommend the nature of death to him, and he should die by that
[means], this monk is *parajika,* expelled.[6]

Clearly Buddhism exhorts its followers to live the nonviolent life. In fact,
nonviolence has such an important position in the tradition that it can be said
with confidence that anyone who does not practice nonviolence cannot in truth
be called a Buddhist. Before we consider how this radical ideal and its realization in Buddhist practice can contribute to the peacemaking process, we must
further investigate the lessons to be learned from the Buddha's involvement
with the parties confronting each other on the banks of the Rohini River.

WAR AND PEACE

War appears to be a permanent feature on the human landscape. We also
observe that once the demon of war has been evoked, seemingly peaceful
persons—not excepting those who consider themselves religious—are soon
swept up in collective hysteria, and appear to undergo radical changes of
character. Faced with war, a nation can be spurred to far greater sacrifice than
is ever exhibited in times of peace. As has often been noted, parties to war
appear especially motivated. Why is this, and why is it the case that so often
peace fails to elicit a comparable outflow of energy? Why does the demon of
war find devotees so easily?

To answer this question from the Buddhist perspective, we must delve into
Buddhist cosmology. According to the Buddhist tradition, sentient beings are
born into one of six realms. These realms are usually described as six distinct
levels, but it is perhaps more useful to think of them as six regions on the
continuum of mundane existence. In addition to the human realm, in which
there is an equal balance of suffering and happiness—this realm also provides
the most conducive conditions for development toward enlightenment—there
are the realms of hell, the hungry ghosts, the animals, the asuras, and the gods.
Beings are born into each realm according to their actions in previous births.
Those actions—strictly, the conscious actions that they have performed—set
up a "habit of consciousness." By acting in a particular way, beings support a
view of reality that proceeds to stimulate anew these very actions. This habit of
consciousness is then assumed to be nothing short of the absolute truth.
Because they have acted "unskillfully" in the past, the consciousness of such
beings has been tainted by the "three poisons" of desire, hatred, and ignorance
(of the conditioned nature of our experience). Because we are born into the
human world as a result of past actions motivated by these "poisons," it is not
surprising that our evolution is subject to the momentum of personal and racial
history in which we are predisposed to "unskillful" behavior. According to

Buddhism persons are not innately good. They do, however, possess the choice to evolve or not; they have the potential to overcome the seductive momentum of their lower nature in order to develop their higher being.

In the Tibetan tradition of Buddhism we find a similar idea, expressed even more graphically. The human race is considered to have been born of a monkey and Avalokitesvara, a personification of the highest compassion. Human beings, according to Tibetan mythology, are half animal and half divine. They have one foot in the world of animals, the other in the world of the angels (devas). Their animal nature is easily stimulated, indeed the free flow of their animal energies gives them a keen sense of being alive, of being linked to their roots. However, they are capable of recognizing that energy invested in this part of their nature is badly invested, because it merely regenerates suffering. They must transform this energy, sublimate it to ever higher levels. Often it may seem that such a transformation is going "against the flow," as indeed it is; such evolution, however, is the prize of struggle.

War is the product of and a stimulant to our lower nature. For the Buddhist, war is born of a craving to accumulate power, or to protect our so-called vital interests from a real or imaginary threat. It comes from a need to eliminate any threat to our security. In short, war comes from craving and hatred, which are the very forces that generate our lower nature. War excites that lower, animal part of human nature and consequently stimulates raw, untransformed energy that, if released into action, can do nothing but give birth to pain and suffering. As we have seen in the record of the Rohini incident, the Sakyans had accused the Koliyans of having lived in hollow trees, like animals, and the Koliyans had accused the Sakyans of having cohabited with their sisters, like animals. These accusations drew the two tribes to the battlefield; it is as if their animal nature had drawn them there.

If we consider the genesis of the Rohini incident, we find that we have before us a not unfamiliar picture. It starts with a conflict over the distribution of raw materials deemed essential to the continued well being of both parties. Both the Sakyan and the Koliyan economies, like those of all the city states of the Ganges plain, were agricultural; thus water was a vital raw material. Then, as now, two ways arose to address the difficulty of the short supply of a vital resource. A solution could have been negotiated to produce a relatively equitable distribution. Both tribes would have suffered somewhat, but both would have survived. However, both tribes selfishly laid claim to all of the water, each putting forth elaborate arguments to support its claim. Because there was really no valid argument in favor of either tribe's claim, the process of alienation of the parties from one another began, and the discussions soon descended to what I have called the animal level. Fear of the loss of what appeared to be their "vital interests" stimulated hatred for the "enemy," and such hatred led to violence.

Situations of conflict are certain to arise in human affairs and can, indeed, serve as valuable occasions for spiritual growth. According to Buddhism human beings can respond to conflict in one of two ways. First, if they wish to evolve, they can act from love and compassion. They can recognize their common humanity, and with a commitment to nonviolence, they can cooperate to find a solution. The solution will involve a struggle, which may be vigorous and competititve and may stimulate energy, drawing the best from all concerned. Or, the parties to the conflict can regress, fall under the domination of greed, hatred, and delusion, and allow violence to inhabit their minds and actions. Once love is driven from the human heart, brute force often rises to the fore as a main arbiter of action. In Buddhist terms we have the choice of operating from the love mode or the power mode; the former leads to development, the latter to regression. The Sakyans and the Koliyans had taken the latter path. They had evoked the power mode and devoted themselves to the demon of war. Once it interferes in human affairs, this demon is not easily exorcised. Once activated, these lower energies are overcome only with great difficulty.

What, then, did the Buddha achieve by walking between those two armies on the banks of the Rohini River? The armies were acting from the power mode, the Buddha was acting from the love mode. The combatants relaxed their position and saluted him. Even in their essentially animal state, their own higher nature resonated with that of the Buddha and allowed them to acknowledge him and what he represented. The Buddha questioned both sides and determined the actual source of the conflict. He was able to speak to both tribes because they had a common language, both literally and metaphorically; furthermore, he could speak to them in person. When he discerned the point of conflict, he was able to remind them of the supreme value of human life; they responded accordingly.

What can be learned from this action of the Buddha? First, the Buddha placed himself between the two parties. He did not ally or identify himself with either. In fact he was related to both tribes, but, as one who had "gone forth into the homeless life," he belonged to neither. It is difficult to be committed to peace while holding onto the tribal, national, political, or religious affiliations that provide one with a sense of security and identity. The person who is committed to nonviolence cannot allow that commitment to be compromised by lesser loyalties. This suggests that to be committed to nonviolence one must be prepared to stand alone—to "stand nowhere" as it says in the *Perfection of Wisdom* texts—freed from the need to identify with any group.

Secondly, the Buddha put himself at risk when he walked onto the battlefield. This means that one must be prepared to take comparable risks in order to further the cause of peace. It may even be necessary to risk life or limb to further the ideal of nonviolence. The naive, weakhearted, pseudo-spiritual pacifist finds no place in Buddhism. Rather it is this image of the Buddha, strong and confident, striding into the middle of the battlefield with the determination to effect change that serves as the model of the true peacemaker.

Thirdly, the Buddha engaged in discussions with the warriors on the river bank in order to determine what the original conflict was about and to bring the two sides into communication. Clearly, the conflicts of the twentieth century are more complex than those of twenty-five hundred years ago. Parties to conflict frequently do not speak the same language (literally), and the conflicts often involve more than the simple acquisition of raw materials or an unabashed quest for dominion and power. Today, layer upon layer of rationalization or deliberate distortion frequently hides the deepest source of conflict. And even though we live in a so-called age of communication, it is clear that the parties to various conflicts actually resist communication or actively promote miscommunication.

The Buddha's action suggests that it is not enough simply to call for an end to violent conflict. It will be necessary to investigate the source of a given conflict, expose the root causes, and present viable alternatives to war. It is important to encourage antagonists to remain in communication with one another.

Two and a half thousand years ago, the Buddha succeeded not only by clarifying the issues, but also by appealing to the higher natures of the combatants involved. In addition to so-called conflict management, a reference to spiritual ideals is necessary to address the problems of an economic or social nature that cannot be solved on their own levels. There may be no solution to a problem if looked at in purely socio-economic or political terms. It is of crucial importance that persons relate on the basis of their common humanity rather than on the basis of the tenets of political or even religious ideologies.

Although there are many points of comparison between the Rohini incident and contemporary conflicts, it must, of course, be admitted there there is one outstanding difference. The Sakyan and Koliyan warriors carried swords, bows, and spears. Their chariots were rather crude vehicles drawn by bullocks; even the light and speedy horse-drawn chariots that we associate with the Romans were missing from the scene. If the battle had taken place and many men had been killed, there would have been little effect on the general population in that region of the earth; and the repercussions through time would, probably, have been small. As has so often been noted, if the United States and the Soviet Union of the present time were to engage in a skirmish that used but a hundredth part of their accumulated power, the world would be totally and permanently devastated.

In his discussions about suitable forms of livelihood, the Buddha specifically proscribed the production or sale of arms. In the contemporary world where—at least in democratic states—the government is the alleged servant of the people, Buddhism argues that all available means in harmony with the ideal of nonviolence must be used to stop the production and deployment of nuclear weapons. Without hesitation, the Buddha walked onto the battlefield when the danger was imminent. Today, the arsenals of the East and the West stand facing each other; the danger is imminent and the advocates of nonviolence must take steps now to halt the production of more nuclear weapons and to hasten the dismantling of those already in existence.

Buddhism does not encourage a passive acceptance of fate. Humankind is not subject to any preordained plan, divine or historical; there is no Buddhist equivalent to the myth of Armageddon. Nor are human beings irrevocably to suffer the consequences of their previous actions. Buddhism teaches that we are the author of our own future, both as individuals and as creative members of society. It is thus within our power to create the world in which we live. It can be a world at peace or a world in ruins. The choice is ours.

THE INDIVIDUAL AT PEACE:
THE NONVIOLENT LIFE IN ACTION

Peace is a fine ideal. Most religions agree on this point—at least in theory. Peace in the world will come when national, religious, political, and social groups begin to cooperate with one another on the basis of their common humanity. This, however, will not happen spontaneously. Group values change only when individual members of those groups are prepared to welcome a fresh perspective or to revive forgotten ideals. Initially individuals must make a commitment to nonviolence so that this very commitment can influence the groups with which they are affiliated. The peacemaking process, therefore, starts with the individual man or woman. It is easy to say that we should all love one another and live in cooperation and peace; it is difficult in the extreme to realize such peaceful aims. Buddhism proclaims a radical ideal of nonviolence but—what is more important—it also provides concrete practical methods to achieve this goal.

Buddhists have undertaken to free themselves from the conditioned view of reality created by their past actions. This, as we have seen above, they do both by observing ethical precepts, which train their mind to undo its conditioning, and by meditation. At a minimum, Buddhists practice the five precepts alluded to earlier. A Buddhist "undertakes to abstain from harming living beings" and "with deeds of loving kindness (to) purify (the) body." Buddhism proscribes killing, maiming, torture, and rape. But it also encourages its followers to do nothing that would cause any harm whatsoever to sentient beings. The teachings say that we should not exploit other beings either because of their poverty or their weakness. The dharma thus implies that we should not pollute or destroy the environment upon which so many forms of life, including future generations of human beings, depend. Buddhism clearly teaches that we should not kill animals for food when there are other equally good, if not better, sources of nourishment. Nor should we kill them for their hides or expose them to cruel treatment such as may be the case in the testing of cosmetics or in the development of pharmaceuticals.

Buddhism teaches that small changes lead to bigger changes. It recognizes that without these first steps toward nonviolence, it is unrealistic to think that nonviolence can be established on a broader scale. Vegetarianism helps to develop a respect for life and a sensitivity to the needs of other beings. It is, of course, only a first, small, step. Beyond that, Buddhism teaches that one should abstain from harming any being by any violent act of body, speech, or mind. Harsh speech, speech that discredits or ˜speech that sows the seeds of discord, can be just as harmful as physical acts of violence; yet such acts seldom receive the attention given to more overtly physical deeds. Even thoughts of harming another cannot be the product of a mind that is striving toward enlightenment.

There is also a postive formulation of the precept proscribing violent actions. With deeds of loving kindness *(metta)* Buddhists purify their actions and thereby their mind. This means practicing loving kindness in whatever way presents itself. Loving kindness is universal. It is not love restricted to our own family, friends, or compatriots, nor is it restricted to those of our own race, our social class, or, indeed, our species. *Metta* encompasses the "good," the "bad," and, of course, the "ugly." This is indeed a difficult goal to achieve, but the Buddhist tradition provides useful guidance, encouragement, and, perhaps most importantly, a concrete meditation practice called the *metta bhavana* to help the individual develop what it terms "loving kindness."

In the *metta bhavana* practitioners spend ten minutes or so developing a feeling of goodwill and kindness *(metta)* toward themselves. They begin by recalling occasions when they were feeling at their best; they reflect on their most positive qualities and successes, and seriously consider what they need to do to make these positive states the norm. In this way meditators generate a strong feeling of well-being toward themselves and resolve to sustain this positive state, rather than allow themselves to fall into states of fear, depression, or hatred.

The Buddhist tradition teaches that kindness *(metta)* begins with kindness and concern for oneself. This is not to be understood to mean that one should merely satisfy one's egotistical desires. It indicates that one is oneself a being to whom love and care should be directed; unless one feels content, confident, and energetic within oneself, it is difficult, if not impossible, to feel kindly toward others. Any needless sacrifice of one's own well-being for the supposed well-being of others is discouraged by Buddhism.

After developing loving kindness toward themselves, meditators proceed to develop positive feelings toward a near and dear friend—not a lover, or a family member, but a friend for whom they feel a concern that is devoid of self-interest. In the third stage of meditation, loving kindness is directed toward a person to whom one has no particular feelings, friendly or otherwise. In the fourth stage, the neutral person is replaced by someone to whom one feels antipathy. The fifth, and final, stage witnesses the development of true *metta*. Here the range of feeling is expanded to include not only the four persons of the previous stages, but slowly, by degrees, all persons in the world, all other beings in the world, and finally, all beings throughout the whole of space and time. Loving kindness is directed to all beings in equal measure.

Loving kindness *(metta)*, then, goes well beyond any understanding of "friendliness" as we have come to know it. The Buddhist tradition refers to *metta* as one of the four divine abodes *(Brahma viharas)*. It is, in fact, the place where the Brahmas, the highest of the gods, dwell. The complete absence of any desire to commit an act of violence—the true state of nonviolence—is thus equated by the Buddhist tradition to the level of consciousness of a god. As we read in the *Dhammapada,* one of the best known Buddhist texts:

> O let us live in joy, in love amongst those who hate!
> Among men who hate, let us live in love.
> O let us live in joy, in health amongst those who are ill!
> Among men who are ill, let us live in health.
> O let us live in joy, in peace amongst those who struggle!
> Among men who struggle let us live in peace.
> O let us live in joy, although having nothing!
> In joy let us live like spirits of light!
> Victory brings hate, because the defeated man is unhappy.
> He who surrenders victory and defeat, this man finds joy.[7]

The implication here is that if human beings transform their hate to love—if they take care of their physical, mental, and spiritual health, and if they adopt the love mode over the power mode—they will live as spirits of light (devas). Life will be qualitatively different for those who commit themselves to this nonviolent life. Buddhism teaches that it is not enough to call for peace in this world; the call for peace is nothing short of a call for the transformation of the world. This transformation starts with the individual, and when individuals committed to nonviolence begin to cooperate with one other, their own society and ultimately the world at large will begin to be transformed as well.

Modern secular industrialized society is not founded on ideals of nonviolence, and even though individuals may be committed to peace and living the nonviolent life, they will frequently find themselves in conflict with the prevailing mores of their environment. How does one conduct business in a nonexploitive manner, in the context, for example, of a business community that thrives on the exploitation of others? How does one operate from the love mode in a world that—in so many aspects—insists on operating from the power mode? How difficult it is to maintain a commitment to an ideal when one is surrounded by persons whose views are in conflict with that ideal! For this reason Buddhism has always valued the sangha, the community of those who share the ideal of spiritual growth through the teachings of the Buddha. The community thus acts as a support. It offers an opportunity to practice the ideal on ever deeper levels, as the ramifications of following the teachings begin to affect the many aspects of individual and social life. The community manifests the ideal in a concete form to other persons, who may thus find themselves moved to follow a similar course. In many ways, then, the community assists the development of the individual.

How does the Buddhist community in Western societies help others live a nonviolent life? And what, concretely, can it contribute to the goal of world peace? First, within the community there is encouragement to practice the precepts of nonharm and of loving kindness. In fact, one can be brought to task (in a nonviolent way, of course!) for falling short in this practice. In the secular world violent acts are frequently rationalized away or justified as the necessary means to achieve noble ends. Violent acts by so-called freedom fighters are often condoned; profit, sometimes disguised as "economic necessity," is frequently placed above concern for the well-being of humans or animals exploited in the process. In the nonviolent community rationalizations can be rooted out, and all violent acts—even to the level of unkind jokes—can be discouraged.

Secondly, the community offers the opportunity for individuals to experience the positive advantages of the nonviolent life. It is radically different from, and more satisfying than, a life lived without such a commitment. When mistrust is rooted out of a relationship, it is given the possibility of deepening and thus becoming more rewarding. The sublimation of energies tied up in such negative sentiments as hatred and anxiety releases more energy both for constructive work of a worldly nature and for further spiritual development. In short, the community is the nonviolent world in miniature. Such a community may range from a small group of five or six persons living together and practicing the precepts, meditating, studying, and working together, all the way to a much larger network of persons who come together frequently and have extensive personal contact based on shared ideals.

Buddhism teaches that if we desire peace to be realized in the world, we must first find it within. To find peace within involves nothing short of radical self-transformation. If the call for peace is to be more than merely rhetorical, such transformation must be its path and its goal. The peace movement cannot be built on mere slogans and words; "ordinary" human beings must transform themselves into "beings of light." Buddhism provides many practical methods to facilitate this development; it provides words of encouragement, it provides examples and guidance, and, perhaps most importantly, it provides a network of persons who are actively engaged in living the nonviolent life, as well as a tradition of men and women who have been so engaged for generations.

BEYOND WAR AND PEACE: THE GREAT PEACE

What is it that makes humans waver in their commitment to nonviolence? What is it that shocks us about the massacre of the peaceful Sakyan tribe? An immediate response comes to mind: the fear of death. It is natural for us to cling to life, and it is in protection of this life that even the most ardent lover of peace may resort to "defensive" violence. The truly nonviolent person is the one who has no fear of death, one who can see beyond death to reality. Such a one is a buddha, an enlightened being.

Buddhism teaches that we own nothing that is permanently ours; all conditioned things arise in dependence on causes and will eventually decay. This is true not only for the objects in our possession, but also with regard to our loved ones and even our own bodies. Buddhism denies the existence of a soul, in the sense of a permanent unchanging entity or a core of being. It is the full recognition of this fact that constitutes the essential aspect of the enlightenment of the Buddha. Inasmuch as there is no fixed selfhood, there is, then, no need to hold onto those objects, persons, or beliefs on which we normally base our identity. There is not even the need for attachment to this mortal body. To the extent that persons have ceased to rely on any conditioned object to provide them with a sense of security—including, ideally, a reliance on their own body—they cannot be threatened. If they have nothing to lose, they have nothing to fear: they do not have to resort to violence to protect the allegedly ultimate bastion of security. They simply enjoy the open dimension of being, full of compassion for other beings. The full experience of the truly nonviolent life must therefore issue from enlightenment itself. This realization is the true source of the commitment to nonviolence.

The following story, from the Korean Zen tradition, illustrates a nonviolent action emanating from an enlightened mind enjoying the open dimension of being:

> When a rebel army swept into a town in Korea, all the monks of the Zen temple fled except for the Abbot. The general came into the temple and was annoyed that the Abbot did not receive him with respect. "Don't you know, " he shouted, "that you are looking at a man who can run you through without blinking?" "And you," replied the Abbot strongly, "are looking at a man who can be run through without blinking!" The general stared at him, then made a bow and retired.[8]

The general recognized that the abbot was not acting simply out of bravado. He saw that the strength and the straightforwardness of the abbot came from an altogether different level of being and was thus compelled to recognize the inferiority of his worldy power. The general's power originated from the fear that he inspired in others; the abbot's power originated from the fact that he had no such fear. The abbot was the stronger of the two.

The teaching of the Buddha points to the realization that our true nature goes far beyond our merely human form. On the basis of this realization true peace can be experienced, and the truly nonviolent life can be attained.

NOTES

1. This incident is discussed further in Venerable Sangharakshita's work, *Buddhism, World Peace, and Nuclear War* (London, Windhorse Publications, 1984).

2. I. B. Horner, trans., *Majjhima-Nikaya* (London, Pali Text Society, 1970), vol.1, p. 124.

3. M. L. Matics, trans., *Bodhicaryavatara* (London, Allen & Unwin, 1970), chap. 6, verse 64.

4. Bodhisattvas have dedicated their life to the attainment of enlightenment for the sake of all beings. They are not just interested in their own salvation. In fact, they recognize that this is a meaningless ideal: their suffering is linked to the suffering of all beings. Bodhisattvas live and work in the world, although their motivations are not

worldly. The bodhisattva ideal is discussed at length in Sangharakshita's *The Bodhisattva: Evolution and Self-transcendence* (London, Windhorse Publications, 1983).

5. The precept quoted is the first in two well-known lists. The complete lists, and their positive expressions are:

a) The Five Precepts
   I undertake to abstain from harming living beings.
   I undertake to abstain from taking the not given.
   I undertake to abstain from sexual misconduct.
   I undertake to abstain from false speech.
   I undertake to abstain from taking intoxicants.

   With deeds of loving kindness, I purify my body.
   With open-handed generosity, I purify my body.
   With stillness, simplicity, and contentment, I purify my body.
   With truthful communication, I purify my speech.
   With mindfulness clear and radiant, I purify my body.

b) The Ten Precepts
   I undertake to abstain from harming living beings.
   I undertake to abstain from taking the not given.
   I undertake to abstain from sexual misconduct.
   I undertake to abstain from false speech.
   I undertake to abstain from harsh speech.
   I undertake to abstain from useless speech.
   I undertake to abstain from slanderous speech.
   I undertake to abstain from covetousness.
   I undertake to abstain from animosity.
   I undertake to abstain from false views.

   With deeds of loving kindness, I purify my body.
   With open-handed generosity, I purify my body.
   With stillness, simplicity, and contentment, I purify my body.
   With truthful communication, I purify my speech.
   With words kindly and gracious, I purify my speech.
   With utterance helpful and harmonious, I purify my speech.
   Abandoning covetousness for generosity, I purify my mind.
   Changing hatred into love, I purify my mind.
   Transforming ignorance into wisdom, I purify my body.

6. From "The Pratimoksa Sutra of the Mulasarvastivadins," translated by Charles Prebish in *Buddhist Monastic Discipline* (New York, Institute for Advanced Studies of World Religions, 1975).

7. Juan Mascaro, trans., *The Dhammapada* (London, Penguin Books, 1973), vv. 197–201.

8. Trevor Leggett, *The Tiger's Cave* (London, Routledge & Kegan Paul, 1977).

10

Ichiro Moritaki

Peace Education:
A Personal Buddhist Odyssey

The atomic bomb, dropped on Hiroshima on August 6, 1945, robbed me of the eyesight of my right eye. Fortunately, however, I have managed to live to be eighty-three. The experience of the unspeakable disaster of the bomb has led me to devote the rest of my life to the movement for the abolition of nuclear weapons and for the aid of atomic-bomb victims.

I was born of a farming family in the mountain area to the north of Hiroshima, where Buddhism had permeated every way of life and every custom. In the course of my upbringing, I was severely admonished against playing with matches, an act that might cause a forest fire. "If you cause a forest fire," I was told, "you will be doomed to live in hell for seven generations." I asked my grandmother, "Why should we be doomed for as long as seven generations if we cause a forest fire?" She said:

Well, you can imagine how many thousands or millions of insects and small beings live in the forest, can't you? If you cause a forest fire, you will burn all of them alive. Can't you understand that if you take their lives by causing a forest fire, it is quite an appropriate consequence of your sin that you should be punished for seven generations?

This lesson reached even a child's understanding easily.

In my district, we used the expression *sesshō-suru* to describe the act of

This article has been translated from the Japanese by the author, assisted by Professors Matsumoto and Katsura and by Mr. Nakamura, all of Hiroshima University.

killing living beings. So great is the influence of Buddhism in my home environs that the term for the Buddhist precept against killing is used in ordinary parlance. It was quite natural for a grandmother to teach her grand-child the evil of causing a forest fire by employing Buddhist precepts.

If it violates the Buddhist precept against killing to deprive insects and small animals of their lives by a forest fire, needless to say the dropping of an atomic bomb, which destroyed a whole city almost instantaneously and killed two hundred thousand of its citizens, was one of the most heinous sins ever committed by humankind. I was in an ophthalmic hospital in the countryside for half a year throughout the fall and winter of the year 1945, receiving treatment that led to the saving of sight in my left eye. I had never devoted myself to Buddhist meditation as exclusively as I did in that half year in the hospital. Many questions came into my mind during that period, among them: Is it permissible for modern civilization, which has given birth to the atomic bomb, to keep developing in the same direction as before? Won't our civiliza-tion inevitably destroy itself if we advance in this direction? Aroused by these questions—which have probably arisen in the minds of many—I began to survey aspects of the origins of modern scientific and industrial civilization in whose midst the atomic bomb was born.

Francis Bacon discovered a new way of learning to interpret the "great book of nature," a new way to know the physical laws in nature by observation, experiment, and induction. He insisted that by making use of the laws, we could make nature conform to our will and the advancement of our material happiness. The Industrial Revolution later took up the use of steam power, thus furthering the process of mass production. Still later, the forces of colonization, often backed by the military, succeeded in acquiring materials for mass production in the underdeveloped world; such colonies also served as markets for the products of industrialized nations. Colonial wars broke out one after another. In the meantime, electrical power had been discovered and used; finally, atomic power was developed, the power released by the bomb dropped on Hiroshima. It was this event that opened my mind's eye to the centrality of "power" in the rise of modern industrialized society. I could find no other way to define modern civilization, as it had thus far developed, than as "a civilization of power." Nor could I help criticizing it.

This "civilization of power" is in danger of following a course to destruction at its own apex. We must seek another course, another direction, for our civilization. I cannot think of any other direction than that provided by the ideal of a "civilization of love." For neither Buddha nor Christ nor Confucius, whom many regard as timeless teachers of humankind, approves of "the principle of power"; on the contrary, each puts great emphasis on "the princi-ple of love." Is it not an urgent necessity that human beings have wholehearted recourse to these teachers if they are to survive? It is time that we, situated on the verge of destruction at the apex of the "civilization of power," hearken to the teachings of some of the world's great religions: Buddhism, which teaches "great compassion is in the heart of the Buddha"; Christianity, which teaches

"God is love"; and Confucianism, which teaches the golden rule of perfect virtue in opposition to the rule of military government. We have to seek a new way for the survival of humankind.

THE BEGINNINGS OF BUDDHISM

Buddhism began when Gautama Siddhartha became the Buddha, "the Awakened." Buddhism consists in practicing the teachings of the Buddha; it shows the way to become awakened. Its essence lies, I was taught, in a well-known legend. When Siddhartha, at the age of seven, saw a bird spear a worm on a leaf in a garden, he asked himself with deep sorrow why living beings must feed on each other. As a prince of the king of Kapila, married to Yasodhara and having a son named Rahula, Gautama seemed to be leading a happy life. But the sensitive and meditative prince contemplated birth, aging, sickness, and death, as is told in a narrative called "Sights at the Four City Gates"; Gautama decided that he would renounce the world to seek truth.

At first, he engaged in traditional Indian ascetical practices believed conducive to mental equilibrium. After five years of ascetical life in the woods, he was physically worn out but saw no hope of acquiring the mental equilibrium he sought. It was a song accompanied by a *koto* (a kind of harp) sung by a country girl that made him realize the so-called middle way. The *koto* does not make a sound if its strings are either too tight or too loose; only when its strings are strained to take the middle way can it make an exquisite sound.

Gautama had experienced two extreme ways of life: the sensual life of pleasure in his royal palace, and the life of ascetical practices in the woods. He rejected both extremes. After he left the ascetical life, Gautama bathed in the river Nairanjana to purify himself, and regained his strength by drinking cow's milk that a girl gave him. Then he sat in meditation under a big *bodhi* tree at Buddhagaya, making a firm resolution that he would never end his meditation—even if it led to his death—until he had acquired enlightenment and had become one who was awake. A story tells on a grand scale how the devil allured Gautama with every means imaginable to make him give up his meditation. This struggle with temptation, I suppose, represents Gautama's final battle with worldy thought. He won this battle with "the army of the devil," and it was at the sight of the morning star on December 8th that he was finally awakened to the truth: he became the Buddha, the Awakened.

The Buddha first preached the path to enlightenment to his former five companions of ascetical practices, later admitted by him as monks at Deer Park. This is what is known as the "Turning of the Wheel of Truth" in which the Buddha preached "the Four Noble Truths" and "the Holy Eightfold Path." The Four Noble Truths are the truth of suffering, the truth of the origins of suffering, the truth of the cessation of suffering, and the truth of the path that leads to the cessation of suffering. The first truth, the truth of suffering, teaches that life is transient and changes rapidly, and that it is filled with the four major "sufferings" of birth, aging, sickness, and death. Moreover, life, it teaches, is filled with the sufferings of not acquiring what one desires, of separation from what one likes, and of meeting what one hates—not to mention the sufferings of grudges, envy, revenge, anger, strife, and struggles. Indeed, this first truth proclaims, in general, that life itself is identified with suffering.

The second of the four truths is the truth of the origins of suffering. The Buddha identified *bonno*s (worldly passions) with the primal origin of our sufferings, which assume various aspects in our lives. There are one hundred eight *bonno*s, such as gluttony, covetousness, greed, anger, hatred, arrogance, envy, and jealousy. When these worldly passions accumulate in our minds, a state of suffering arises. The Buddha defined the primal cause of all worldly passions as ignorance (*avidyā* or spiritual darkness). This is ignorance about life and the world. We caress and cling to our physical body as if it were ourselves. But the flesh is nothing more than an "integration," a result of the combination of such so-called causes and conditions as father, mother, ancestors, rice, salt, vegetables, sunlight, air, water, fire, and so on, so that there is nothing that we can claim as our own. The body, in other words, is the integration in time and space of such elements. Wisdom appears when persons feel that they are one with the cosmic existence; ignorance is the state of mind in which they cling to their flesh as if it were themselves. Worldly passions are called "ignorance" with regard to intellect; with regard to emotion and volition, they are called "love-thirst." When ignorance and love-thirst arise as the primal causes of sufferings, then aging, sickness, and death appear.

Thirdly, what is the truth of the cessation of suffering? Cessation is a state of mind in which both ignorance and love-thirst *bonno*s are annulled, so that the threefold karma of behavior, language, and mind can be freed from the bondage of ego-attachment and can work with perfect freedom. Cessation is the ideal state of human life. Cessation is also called peaceful nirvana (or supreme enlightenment), which is likened to the condition of a lamp being blown out. Life embodying nirvana may at first seem to connote something negative, but life freed from ignorance and love-thirst, as well as from ego-attachment, is not life lived in a deathlike silence. Freed from ignorance, wisdom arises; freed from love-thirst, mercy appears. Wisdom and mercy constitute the essence of nirvana. Nirvana is the state in which wisdom and mercy are lived harmoniously. One attains buddhahood, therefore, through the active working of wisdom that lets one realize the truth of the universe, as well as through mercy, which is so expansive as to allow for an identification of oneself with all living beings. A buddha is, first of all, one who is completely freed from the concerns of self. We can easily understand how active is the working of wisdom and mercy in the Buddha himself if we survey his forty-five-year mission following enlightenment.

Fourthly, what is the truth of the path to cessation? It is the right path to attain nirvana, and is elaborated as the Holy Eightfold Path: right comprehension, right resolution, right speech, right action, right mode of life, right effort, right thought, and right peaceful-mindedness. These all express the idea of the Middle Path, which, as has been noted, the Buddha finally realized after he had meditated on the extreme modes of pleasure and asceticism.

The truth of the path to cessation is elaborated with regard to behavior, language, and mind. The Holy Eightfold Path, in other words, consists of the Threefold Learning—namely, discipline, meditation, and wisdom: discipline shows how the life of a Buddhist monk should be lived; monks can enter meditation when they observe discipline; and wisdom will arise in their mind when they enter meditation. It is the duty of a Buddhist monk to appropriate this Threefold Learning of discipline, meditation, and wisdom.

BUDDHISM IN JAPAN

It was, first of all, due to the efforts of Prince Shotoku that Mahayana Buddhism spread in Japan. It is no exaggeration to say that without this prince there would be neither Japanese Buddhism nor Japanese culture. He was prince regent to Emperor Suiko, and administered affairs in Japan for thirty-nine years approximately one thousand three hundred years ago. He was also the first devotee of Buddhism, and thus can be hailed as the common father of the many Buddhist sects that appeared in Japan afterward. The prince's work constitutes the mainstream from which much of Japanese culture has flowed; this is evident if we think of Horyuji and Shitennoji, the greatest monuments of Japanese Buddhist architecture, which he built. Prince Shotoku also wrote *Sangyōgisho,* commentaries on the three scriptures of Buddhism, which showed his profound understanding of the sutras of Mahayana Buddhism, such as the lotus sutra, the Srimala sutra, and *Vimalakírti-nirdeśa.*

In addition to the above, the prince wrote the "Seventeen Articles Constitution," the first Japanese constitution. In so doing, he hoped to bring peace to a woeful and suffering nation, a nation caught up in the struggles between the Mononobe and the Soga clans for national hegemony. The prince advocated peace as the ideal for Japan in the first article of his constitution, saying *"Wa* [peace and harmony] shall be the first principle that is to be respected." For the purpose of the realization of a peaceful country, he also authored "Respect the Triple Jewel" as the second article of his constitution. (The "Triple Jewel" refers to the Buddha [the teacher of truth], dharma [truth], and sangha [community]. The other articles in the constitution solemnly and minutely prescribe instructions so that the bureaucrats of the emperor could administer the affairs of Japan diligently for the realization of peace and the general good of the people. No other constitution in the Buddhist tradition prescribes objectives for peace education as clearly as does the "Seventeen Articles Constitution." The prince was a peerless genius.

I should have liked to detail further achievements in peace education by Prince Shotoku in this article. But in the space allotted me I can mention only the titles of the masterpieces written by my mentor, Professor Shirai, on the subject: "Lectures on the Seventeen Articles Constitution" and "Ethical Study of *Sangyōgisho* of the Shotoku."

The work of Shotoku in fostering the Buddhist ideal of peace was continued in the Tokugawa period (1603–1887) by the high Buddhist priest Jiun, called by some the "present-day Buddha." Jiun began an active preaching life, and set forth "True Disciple" with the view of reviving Buddhism. He expounded the so-called ten moral actions and preached them plainly, so that both Buddhist monks and lay worshipers might understand the Buddha's mind and acts, and live in accordance with them. "The Teaching of the Ten Moral Actions" or "The Way to be Human," written by Jiun with a view to the enlightenment of his people, elaborates the concept of discipline as clearly as is to be found within the canons of Mahayana Buddhism. The ten moral actions are put into the three categories of behavior, language, and mind, by which they are to be practiced by Buddhists. The three disciplines concerning behavior are abstaining from killing, stealing, and unchastity; the four disciplines concerning language are abstaining from lying, idle talk, slandering, and harsh language; the three disciplines concerning the mind are avoiding anger, covetousness, and false views. The aim of establishing these disciplines in Buddhism is not only to encourage an individual to pursue the ideal life with respect to behavior, language, and mind, but also to foster the realization of a peaceful society on the earth.

When I think of peace education, I cannot help recalling these "ten moral actions" as set forth by Jiun. Jiun's work contains valuable instructions for both monks and the laity, regardless of religious affiliation, and is probably the best single text in Buddhism for educating others in the way of peace. To our relief, sound-minded persons, though not as yet in great numbers, are absorbing it and imparting its teachings to others.

BUDDHISM AND PEACE EDUCATION

Where can we detect the origins of the Buddhist contribution to peace education? I believe that such a contribution begins to manifest itself at the starting point of Buddhism itself. When Gautama Siddhartha became the Buddha, the Awakened—having found the truth after rigorous practice of the right paths—he said, "Ah! Every sentient being possesses the buddhahood," thus realizing that everybody can be a buddha. Having discovered and overcome the causes of sufferings, of false worldly views, and of discord, Gautama could attain the invaluable peace of nirvana. Nevertheless, he could not rest there in some self-satisfied manner. For once he realized the possibility that all human beings can be buddhas, as he himself had become, he thought it his duty to teach them the truth, and to thus emancipate them from the illusion of sufferings.

The Awakened is said to have treated everybody as one's only child *(isshiji);* in other words, he had the unfathomable mercy to love every sentient being as if it were his only offspring. Mercy prompted the Buddha to emancipate others from ego-attachment, false views, and strife in this world, thus bringing them to the pure peace of nirvana. Thus the Buddha began his tireless, relentless preaching activities to awaken persons to their inborn buddhahood by every means available. What peace education should truly be is embodied in the eighty-year life of the Buddha, who devoted his whole existence to the enlightenment of humankind.

Thus it may be said that the path of the bodhisattva serves in Mahayana Buddhism as the most appropriate model for peace education. Bodhisattvas are the magnanimous of mind, who, having set their mind upon enlightenment, devote their whole life to practicing the six perfections *(pāramitā):* charity, morality, perseverance, diligence, meditation, and wisdom. These constitute the bodhisattva's way to attain nirvana as taught in many Mahayana texts. Yet the essential character of bodhisattvas lies in their efforts to awaken others, rather than to remain satisfied with the attainment of their own self-awareness. In short, the bodhisattva is one who diligently proceeds on the path to the enlightenment of *others.* The ultimate goal of the bodhisattva is to lead others to the land of Buddha, the world of peace—doing the same things as others do in their everyday lives, yet enlightening them at the same time by the unique quality of their everyday practice.

Although the Buddhist sects founded in the Kamakura period (1192–1333) have survived until today, many of them, regrettably, have been reduced to sects advocating the practice of mere conventions. Nevertheless, the striving for mercy and the avoidance of killing, both of which lie at the core of Buddhism, are deeply rooted in the mind of the Japanese people. Besides, as we have seen, the essence of Buddhism through the ages has been the teaching that strives to emancipate us from the illusion of ego-attachment. Here seems to be the key to the Buddhist teaching on peace, a core teaching that can never be completely covered over by mere conventions.

What is the current situation with regard to peace education as advocated by contemporary Buddhist sects? The sect established by Nichiren, who adhered to the lotus sutra and worked as an ascetic devotee, has become the most active sect in Japan today. Nichiren's "Discourse on the Establishment of Righteousness and the Security of the Country" seeks nothing short of bringing about peace through "True Doctrine." The essence of the teachings of Nichiren is most faithfully followed by Nihonzan-myohoji, a religious order led by a high priest, Nichidatsu Fujii. He not only built many pagodas both in Japan and elsewhere for the worship of the Buddha, but also devoted himself to saving humankind in the nuclear age from fatal catastrophe through the propagation and practices of the teachings of Nichiren, especially those of mercy and the precept against killing. He died in January 1985 at the age of ninety-nine.

The Pure Land Buddhism sects set forth by Honen and Shinran have come to acquire the largest number of followers in Japan. They have finally initiated an antinuclear movement; indeed, it would hardly be possible for those who meditate on merciful Amida Buddha—and who deeply care for living beings— to remain idle when the life of humankind is exposed to great peril in a nuclear age. Egyoku Hata, chief abbot of Daihonzan-Eiheiji (a Sōtō Zen sect that has faithfully followed the teachings of Zen set forth by Dogen), is now also diligently engaged in promoting the ideal of world peace.

I myself learned Zen under the direction of Settei Maruyama (high priest of Rinzai Zen) when I was a student, and later studied it under Gikō Inoue (high priest of Sōtō Zen). I personally believe that it is wholly thanks to the wisdom of Zen that I have been able to help atomic-bomb victims and to work for the movement to abolish nuclear weapons during these forty years since I suffered from the bomb in Hiroshima. In my case, Zen has succeeded in educating for peace.

A SIT-IN FOR WORLD PEACE

Finally, I want to give some account of a peace movement in which I, as a Zen-Buddhist, participated—and still participate. This movement has sponsored sit-in actions against the testing of nuclear weapons. In 1962 the U.S. government announced that it would carry out a large-scale nuclear test in the Pacific Ocean. Although it was clear that this was designed to counter the large-scale test that the U.S.S.R. had carried out the year before, we realized that it would lead to an era of nuclear competition. Thus a sit-in action began on April 20 in Hiroshima in front of the Peace Memorial Monument; it demanded nothing short of a total suspension of the proposed nuclear test.

For twelve days I and Kiyoski Kikkawa, another atomic-bomb victim, maintained our sit-in action. I was sitting as if I were fighting, with my back to the sea, for I had submitted my resignation to Hiroshima University. A *juzu* (a kind of rosary), a symbol of Buddhism, hung on my hand. At night we took a brief nap in a tent, but basically we decided to maintain a day-and-night sit-in for an indefinite period. (I suffered from sunstroke on the third day and could not help taking a rest on that day; for the remainder of the period I sat throughout.)

This sit-in action rapidly grew in size. It reached other atomic-bomb victims, religious persons, workers, students, ordinary citizens, young and old, male and female, so that the number of participants increased from day to day. In response to our movement, sit-in movements broke out in various places all over Japan. An old woman of the Pure Land Buddhists prayed to Amida Buddha, chanting his name; Nichiren women devotees beat drums and chanted the title of the lotus sutra all around me and alongside many Christians. An old Christian doctor with his wife and several nurses came to us every morning with hot black tea, and prayed that peace and health would be with us during the sit-in. Many adherents of different religions gathered there, but I never felt a sense of strangeness. It seemed to me that everybody present was of one mind.

But one day a small girl passing by me several times spoke the following words to herself: "Can they stop anything just by sitting?" These words came home to me. The question resounded in my ear as to whether you could stop nuclear tests merely by sitting in protest. The small girl had put a cutting question to a man who thought he was sitting to realize his raison d'être at the risk of his very life.

I thought about the meaning of a sit-in through and through and about alternative actions. Even if I were to succeed in breaking into the test center, like a guerrilla—even if I were to destroy the equipment for the nuclear test— this very act would still be an act of war, accomplished through "power," rather than the act of a true peace movement. There is no other path for a peace movement than that of appealing to public opinion without having recourse to any violent action. The sit-in is typical of a nonviolent action. It is so basic an act as to be called primitive. Nevertheless, it is a universal mode of nonviolent demonstration in which young and old in both West and East can participate at any time in history.

While sitting in front of the Peace Memorial Monument, I unexpectedly found myself to be different from what I was used to being in everday life. I wondered if the others sitting around me also felt different from their usual selves. Customarily, we do everything either for our advantage or to our liking. After all, do we not do everything for our own selves? Yet while we were sitting in front of the Peace Memorial Monument,we were neither sitting "for ourselves" nor "using an hour" to our benefit. We were doing something that was not merely for our good. Having nothing to do with our egocentric, customary selves, we seemed to have become different persons.

There is nothing so difficult to overcome as "the nucleus of self" (ego-attachment). It is almost beyond our power to get out of this attachment to self. Nobody can imagine what feats could be achieved if persons could only break through "the nucleus of self." The persons sitting in front of the Peace Memorial Monument had indeed become different selves. Persons who had broken through their "nucleus of self," even if only to a small degree, were sitting in an atmosphere clearly different from the usual. It was as if "a chain reaction of mind" were under way in that atmosphere.

It is said that when a neutron is introduced into a uranium nucleus, it splits the nucleus releasing another neutron, which splits, in turn, into another nucleus. Thus the chain reaction of the fission of uranium breaks out at an extremely high speed. What enormous power would be gained if we could break through "the nucleus of self" and initiate a chain reaction of mind!

While I sat in front of the Peace Memorial Monument, I felt the thrust of the sit-in action reaching many others day after day, forming just this kind of chain reaction of human minds. I cried to myself, "Eureka!" I put the feeling of the moment into words:

> A chain reaction of spiritual atoms
> Must overcome
> The chain reaction of material atoms.

This was the answer that I finally gave to the question put by the small girl; but it also was my manifesto of a kind of satori or enlightenment that I gained through the peace movement in an era of nuclear weapons. I have made these words my motto for life, convinced that they show us a new path for our present civilization, which seems to be seeking its destruction. On this "right path," we must create a civilization of the peace-loving mind, instead of a civilization rooted in nuclear power.

Persons who join peace movements against nuclear weapons are those who have broken through their own egoism, even if only to a limited degree, and who devote themselves to the noble obligation of humankind to ensure its own survival. There can be no other means to meet the challenges of the present critical moment than for a worldwide grassroots peace movement to take shape. As a spiritual tradition that teaches the "breakthrough of the nucleus of self," Buddhism is a most valuable source for the birth of such a movement.

Hinduism

11

Ramakrishna Puligandla

The Hindu Quest for Peace

TWO CONCEPTIONS OF NONVIOLENCE

To the modern mind, Hinduism has come to be so closely associated with peace and nonviolence that one might mistakenly believe that war and violence were rare in the history of Hindus. Let it be noted that, to the contrary, war and violence were not uncommon in the long and complex history of Hindu civilization, and were never categorically ruled out by the tradition as a means of settling collective human conflicts and of obtaining conquest, power, and glory:

> In any case war was generally accepted as a normal activity of the state, even by the Buddhist kings. The doctrine of nonviolence, which in medieval India had become very influential, and had made most of the respectable classes vegetarian, was never at this time taken to forbid war or capital punishment. It was only in modern times that Mahatma Gandhi reinterpreted it in this sense.[1]

As in all other civilizations, there has been an evolution of the concept of nonviolence in Hindu civilization.[2]

The best Sanskrit equivalent of "violence" is *hiṁsā,* which means not only killing a living being but even inflicting upon it any form of pain, harm, injury, and suffering.[3] In short, *hiṁsā* is any act that is not only not conducive to the well-being of a living thing but also results in its ill-being. By contrast, the term *ahiṁsā* connotes refraining from killing a living being as well as from inflicting on it any form of pain or suffering.

Broadly speaking, we can distinguish in the Indian context two original

139

conceptions of nonviolence: the Vedic (Aryan) and the non-Vedic (ascetic, pre-Aryan). The vedic conception is to be found in the Vedas, *Dharmasāstras,* and *Purānas.* The ascetic conception is traceable to the pre-Aryan indigenous civilization of India. In the subsequent history of India these two conceptions influenced each other. In the course of time, Jainism and Buddhism became the primary vehicles of the ascetic conception of nonviolence and engaged in severe criticism of sanctioned violence in the Vedic religion. The mutual influence of the Vedic and non-Vedic conceptions of nonviolence over a long history constitutes the evolution of the Hindu conception of nonviolence.

The Vedic conception of nonviolence is founded in a system of values central to the Vedic goals of life. These values are dharma, *artha,* and *kāma,* collectively known as *trivarga.* Dharma may be roughly understood as ethical values (such as duties and obligations); *artha* as economic values (such as material wealth and prosperity); and *kāma* as hedonistic values (such as pleasure, happiness, and fulfillment of desire in general). Accordingly, the dominant goals of vedic life are longevity, prosperity, and happiness, for obtaining which various gods were worshiped and propitiated through sacrificial rites. The Vedas thus sanctioned the killing of animals as ritual offerings to gods. According to the Vedic conception of nonviolence, such killing—ritual violence—was to be regarded as nonviolence, and violence not sanctioned by the Vedas was not to be engaged in. The Vedic conception of nonviolence, then, is qualified nonviolence.

In sharp contrast, the ascetic (non-Vedic) conception of nonviolence is rigorous, uncompromising, and unqualified. Under no circumstances should one kill a living being or inflict pain and suffering on it through thought, word, or deed. One should totally renounce violence and not employ it under any circumstances.

What is the reason behind the Vedic sanction of certain forms of violence— for example, the ritual killing of animals? The answer sheds light on factors leading to the evolution of the Vedic concept of nonviolence. The chief values and goals of the Vedic way of life were essentially concerned with life in this world: health, wealth, and happiness; and even when one attains to heaven— the abode of the gods—one is still in the grip of death. Thus the Vedic conception of nonviolence was dictated by the three goals and values that dominated the Vedic conception of life itself. There was no need here for asceticism and renouncing the world in order to attain immortality.

In sharp contrast, the ascetic conception of nonviolence was dictated by what the pre-Aryan ascetic tradition regarded as the ultimate goal of life— namely, absolute freedom and ultimate release from births and deaths (*moksha*). In other words, the overarching goal and value of the ascetic tradition is the ultimate spiritual goal and value; whereas the *trivarga* of the Vedic religion is essentially nonspiritual and nonultimate. In the later Vedic period, "the Upanishadic period," *moksha,* ultimate release and absolute freedom from the fetters of time and death, was added to the *trivarga,* and consequently the earlier Vedic hierarchy of goals and values, as well as the associated conception of nonviolence, was modified.

Opposition to violence thus began as opposition to institutionalized—sanctioned—killing of animals (ritual slaughter) and culminated in opposition to all forms of violence against any living being, including plants. The role of the ascetic conception in bringing about the gradual change in the Vedic conception of nonviolence cannot be overemphasized.

The single factor that exercised the greatest influence on the transformation of the Vedic conception of nonviolence is the yogic, Jaina, and Buddhist teaching that all violence is rooted in ignorance (*avidyā*) and all nonviolence in knowledge. The influence of the ascetic tradition can easily be seen in declarations from the *Dharmasāstras* and *Purāṇas:* (1) Immortality is the gift of nonviolence.[4] (2) Freedom from rebirth is to be attained through nonviolence.[5] (3) Through the practice of nonviolence one grasps reality.[6] (4) One gains the merit of the *vājapeya* sacrifice through the practice at all times of nonviolence, truthfulness, and control of the senses.[7] (5) Nonviolence is the supreme sacrifice, the best possible fruit, the best friend, and the highest form of happiness.[8] (6) There is no dharma superior to nonviolence toward all living beings.[9] (7) *Ahiṁsā* toward all living beings is greater than all other virtues.[10]

Thus the early Vedic conception of nonviolence, which justified sanctioned violence and regarded it as nonviolence, changed under the influence of the ascetic tradition. The concept of nonviolence emerging from such an evolution became "the Hindu concept of nonviolence." The philosophical foundations of this conception of nonviolence were formulated with increasing clarity in the later Upanishads.[11]

BRAHMA AND ATMAN

The central insights of the Upanishadic teaching can be summed up in two concepts—Brahma and Atman—and one proposition—that they are identical.

Brahma (Sanskrit, *brahman*) is the unborn, uncreated, eternal, unchanging reality underlying the myriad worlds of phenomena—of the senses and mind. Brahma is formless and nameless and hence imperceivable and unthinkable. Brahma pervades all existence—smaller than the smallest and greater than the greatest. Brahma is neither a he nor a she but the That. Brahma can be realized only in nonperceptual, nonconceptual intuition.

Atman (Sanskirt, *ātman*) is the unchanging, abiding silent witness, *sakshin*. Like Brahma, Atman is unborn, uncreated, eternal, formless, nameless, and pervades all existence. Atman is single and unitary and is not to be identified with body, mind, ego (*jīva*). Atman is pure, objectless consciousness. Atman, like Brahma, cannot be captured by the senses and mind, but can be realized only in nonperceptual, nonconceptual intuition.

Brahma and Atman are *not* two numerically distinguishable realities; rather, they are one and the same. Hence the Upanishadic proposition declaring the identity of Atman and Brahma.

Moksha—ultimate release and absolute freedom—is to be attained through one's own existential realization of the identity of Atman and Brahma, the identity of one's true being with Brahma, the ultimate reality. Such realization brings one freedom, wisdom, and peace. Because *moksha* is the attainment of the *knowledge* of the identity of Atman and Brahma, *moksha* is not a state to be looked forward to after death; rather, it is to be realized here and now, in one's bodily existence.

Many claimed that with the teaching of the identity of Atman and Brahma the Vedic conception of nonviolence culminated in the exclusion of all forms of violence toward living beings. They argued that the realization of the identity of Atman and Brahma is at once the realization of the identity of oneself with all beings. It therefore results in the dissolution of all forms of selfishness and therewith all forms of violence. Put differently, nonviolence is a logical consequence of the Upanishadic teaching of the identity of Atman and Brahma.

It is certainly true that by this declaration of the identity of Atman and Brahma the Upanishads acknowledge the ascetic insight that all violence is rooted in ignorance and can be eliminated only by knowledge, but it must be admitted that, although the term *ahiṁsā* was used many times in the Upanishads, nonviolence was not dealt with in any detailed ethical context. It was only with the rise of Jainism and Buddhism that nonviolence acquired greater scope and significance in Hindu thought and practice. Hence the exhortation of the *Gītā*[12] that yogins should look upon all beings as one by analogy with their own self, and the exhortation of the *Anuśāsana-Parva* that one should never do unto another what one does not wish done unto oneself.[13]

Has the Hindu tradition categorically ruled out all forms of violence? The answer is clearly negative, and the reason is to be sought in the Hindu caste system. The king, the ruler, and the warrior were never required to totally renounce violence;[14] and it is only rarely that a ruler—for example, the Emperor Asoka—outlawed war and violence, and prohibited the sacrifice of animals at religious rites and ceremonies: no living being should be sacrificed.[15]

Even the *Gītā* does not condemn or reject war and violence by the ruling class. It is the dharma of the ruler to engage in war and violence to protect his subjects and ensure their well-being. Hence although nonviolence toward all living beings became in time the common ethical ideal of Hindus, and inspired and influenced the lives of many, violence was used throughout history by the ruling class. There were elaborate codes of conduct for warriors requiring them not to kill or harm the enemy who surrenders, or soldiers whose weapons are broken or lost and flee in fear, and to treat them and conquered subjects humanely and kindly.

That war and violence as essential ingredients of statecraft were never categorically rejected by Hinduism should not surprise us. Hinduism is not alone in this. The Buddhist and Christian civilizations also engaged in violence at the level of the state. Thus we have a common problem: how to avert war and violence at the state level. No civilization has yet succeeded in outlawing war as a means of settling collective human conflicts. A source Hindus can call upon in addressing this problem is that they are the inheritors of a living tradition, to which nonviolence toward and reverence for all life is central.

But, alas, recent (as well as not-so-recent) events in India send contrary signals. The wars with China and Pakistan and the Punjab crisis show that violence is often resorted to. The violence witnessed in the Punjab crisis, the subsequent assassination of the prime minister, the mass killings that followed the assassination, and the unabated terrorism on land and in the skies all make one wonder whether lasting peace is achievable.

GANDHI AND NONVIOLENCE

Gandhi was the first Hindu in modern times to categorically reject war and violence. His rejection of violence, unlike that of Sri Aurobindo,[16] is total (it is to be noted, however, that his nonviolence was anything but cowardly).[17] It is worth bearing in mind that in the Hindu tradition yogins, renunciates, and *sannyāsins*—ascetics in general—have long subscribed to and practiced total nonviolence. Gandhi was not an ascetic in the standard, widespread sense of the term, although his lifestyle certainly exemplified many ascetic qualities. Gandhi rejected violence early in his public life; his commitment to *ahiṁsā* was complete and categorical.[18] Gandhi's life was a demonstration that, contrary to the general view that only ascetics can totally renounce violence, nonascetic members of society can wholly renounce violence and employ only nonviolent means for a just management of the state.

Although born and raised a Hindu, Gandhi grew up in a predominantly Jaina environment; and we have already noted that the Jaina conception of nonviolence is essentially ascetic. Gandhi's own ideal of nonviolence fundamentally derives from the ascetic tradition, and his great merit is that of not only interpreting the Hindu tradition, particularly as articulated in the *Gītā*, in light of his own inspiration from the ascetic tradition, but also showing that unremitting commitment to nonviolence can be effectively practiced in dealing with the most complex and explosive of human conflicts. His accomplishments through nonviolence convinced many, within and without India, that unqualified nonviolence is a practicable and powerful means toward the establishment of a just social and political order, and therewith to peace. Thus Martin Luther King, Jr., employed Gandhian techniques of nonviolence in his struggle for equal rights.

Can nonviolence be successful in preventing war and violence among nations? Can it serve as adequate means to halt nuclear confrontations and nuclear war itself? These are not easy questions. Many believe that nonviolence is the only viable means for the prevention of the utter destruction of this planet by nuclear weapons. As such, there can be no better way to begin our task than by a study of the Gandhian theory and practice of nonviolence and devise means for their application to the resolution of intranational and international conflicts.

NONVIOLENCE AND THE NUCLEAR THREAT

Such a study will bear fruit, however, only when our commitment to nonviolence is absolute and unqualified—that is, we should commit ourselves to nonviolence with all our heart, mind, and soul.

Hinduism deals not only with violence among human beings but also with violence against the environment. In the Hindu tradition, in contrast to the Western tradition, there are two ethical ideals: (1) the good (well-being) of humanity—*lokahita*, and (2) the good (well-being) of all living beings—*sarva-bhūta-hita*.

Lokahita, as Radhakrishnan pointed out, is parallel to humanism in the Western tradition. But, to the best of my knowledge, the well-being of all creatures was not a matter of great concern in the mainstream Western tradition. If anything, nonhuman creatures are regarded as radically different from human, and humankind has not many specific duties or obligations toward them.

The Hindu tradition emphasizes the well-being of *all* creatures as much as it does the well-being of humanity. Thus, Manu, the progenitor of the human race, calls for expiation on the part of one who destroys plants, whether wild or cultivated.[19] In the *Mahābhārata*, we are told that it is our highest duty to ensure the well-being of all creatures.[20] Concerning the need to kill animals for food, it has been taught that the warrior class incurs some demerit from hunting, and hunters are exhorted, as they are in Amerindian traditions, not to eat the flesh of the hunted animal without first offering it to God.[21] And inasmuch as even the tilling of land and raising of crops involves the killing of many organisms invisible to the naked eye, the farmer is exhorted to make an offering of the harvest before eating of it.[22]

It is well known that vegetarianism has long been an integral component of the Hindu tradition. Eating meat is forbidden by the *Dharmasāstras*. Manu condemns meat-eating.[23] According to the *Mahābhārata*, the flesh of animals is like that of one's own children; those who eat meat are the most contemptible of human beings.[24]

Thus, reverence for all life and therewith the obligation to secure the well-being of all living things is a fundamental tenet of the Hindu tradition of nonviolence. Killing animals for pleasure and profit, destroying rivers and forests, and polluting the atmosphere and the interior of the earth are harmful to living beings and will eventually result in the destruction of humankind itself. Plants and animals are not beings wholly different from us; on the contrary, there is an essential kinship that binds us all; harm and injury done to any creature is harm and injury to ourselves. Our management of natural resources therefore requires utmost sensitivity, care, concern, and skill; in a word, it calls for wisdom.

In preparation for my conclusions, three propositions, as crystalized in Shankara's Advaita Vedanta Hinduism, the most influential form of Hinduism, are significant. These propositions are important for peace education because they are the expressions of insights most conducive to the cultivation of a vision of humankind and of the world essential for achieving unity, harmony, and peace, not only among human beings but also between human beings and the nonhuman environment.

1. All beings are manifestations of the nondual reality, Brahma (Atman); all differences are differences in forms and names only; experiential realization of the identity of oneself with all beings is the highest goal and value of human life. Such a realization is indeed the attainment of *moksha*—ultimate and absolute freedom.

2. All beings are but different manifestations of the nondual Brahma means that phenomena are not isolated entities radically different from one another; rather, they are all of one essence—namely, Brahma. This essential unity of all phenomena is discernible in the interconnectedness of all phenomena.

3. There are two kinds of knowledge and truth: the lower, perceptual-conceptual, relative, conditioned truth (*vyava-hārika-satya*) and the higher, nonperceptual, nonconceptual, absolute, and unconditioned truth (*paramārthika-satya*).[25] Just as there are many phenomena, so also there are many lower truths; and because there is but the nondual reality (Brahma), there is one, and only one, higher truth. All lower truths, without exception, are the product of perceptual-conceptual activities; in contrast, the higher truth, transcending all perceptions and conceptions, can be realized only in direct, nondual intuition (*prajña*). Conflict and opposition are the result of mistaking some lower truth for the higher truth and thereby advancing absolute claims on its behalf. "Lower truth" does not mean falsehood; rather, it means truth certifiable by all beings constituted alike and operating with a given perceptual-conceptual—categorical—framework. Lower truths are valid and efficacious in limited domains of experience but can never capture the higher truth, which is none other than the nondual Brahma itself.

CONCLUSIONS

1. I have shown that there were originally two conceptions of nonviolence in the Indian context: the Vedic and the non-Vedic (ascetic). The Vedic conception regarded ritual violence as nonviolence. In contrast, the ascetic conception was one of total, unqualified nonviolence and was best exemplified by yogins, Jainas, and Buddhists. These two conceptions influenced each other over centuries. Under the influence of the ascetic tradition on the one hand and of internal criticism and objections against sanctioned violence on the other, the Vedic conception evolved into the "Hindu conception of nonviolence." With increasing rejection of all forms of violence, the Hindu conception more or less coincided with the ascetic. "More or less" because, although the Hindu conception became highly refined and approached that of unqualified nonviolence, war and violence were never categorically condemned and renounced by the Hindu tradition, and continued to be an integral part of statecraft.

The reason for the nonrejection of violence as part of statecraft is twofold.

(1) It is the dharma of the ruler to protect his subjects and secure their well-being; and because it is morally wrong not to live in accordance with one's dharma, the ruling class is not to renounce war and violence. (2) There is the question of the practicability of total nonviolence in the conduct of the business of the state and of life. This is not a question peculiar to the Hindu tradition but one that confronts all traditions. Even in a tradition to which nonviolence is central and has long been practiced at various levels of society, categorical rejection of war and violence at the state level is indeed difficult. The Hindu tradition had not yet discovered a means of implementing unqualified nonviolence at all levels of society, in particular at that of government.

2. Gandhi was the first Hindu in modern times to attempt to realize the ideal of nonviolence in all spheres of life—the social, the political, the economic, and so on. Gandhi was well aware that the ideal cannot be fully realized in the empirical world. Nevertheless, the ideal served him as the source of inspiration to realize it in increasing degree and range. It is with Gandhi that the Hindu conception of nonviolence attained a greater clarity in theory and practice than ever before. For this reason, his life can be a fountainhead of inspiration in the arduous task of ridding the world of war and violence.

3. There is the question whether nonviolence can serve as adequate means to prevent nuclear proliferation and colossal destruction of our common abode by a nuclear war. It is important to realize that we have no choice in this matter, for it is the height of unwisdom to think that the possibility of a nuclear war can be eliminated by violence. Although we do not know how Gandhi himself may have approached this problem, one thing is clear: we have much to learn by a careful study of the Gandhian theory and practice of nonviolence.

4. Through its teaching of the identity of Atman and Brahma, and thereby of the fundamental interconnectedness of all existence, Hinduism can inspire us to a wise and compassionate ecological management that secures the well-being of all creatures, human and nonhuman alike.

5. The principle of two truths of Hinduism fosters understanding and appreciation of traditions and cultures other than one's own. Thus a study of Hinduism can help promote the spirit of unity in diversity.

6. There is no suggestion here that Hindus themselves, either individually or collectively, have been successful in totally renouncing violence; quite the contrary, they, like all other peoples, have yet a long way to go. The only factor in their favor in their struggle against violence is that the spirit of *ahiṁsā* has long permeated their tradition and is exemplified by persons like Gandhi in our own day.

NOTES

1. A.L. Basham, *The Wonder that was India* (New York, Grove Press, 1959), p. 123.

2. For an excellent study of the evolution of the concept of nonviolence in the Indian tradition, see Unto Tähtinen, *Ahimsa: Non-violence in Indian Tradition* (London, Rider, 1976).

3. Ibid., Appendix, pp. 131–33.

4. *Manusmṛti*, 6.60.

5. *Varāha-Purāṇa*, 121.24.

6. *Viṣṇu-Purāṇa*, 6.7.36.

7. *Anuśāsana-Parva*, 106.42.

8. Ibid., 116.39.

9. *Śānti-Parva*, 262.30.

10. Ibid., 265.6.

11. All the fundamental concepts and principles of the major schools of Indian philosophy can be found in *A Sourcebook in Indian Philosophy*, S. Radhakrishnan and Charles A. Moore, eds. (Princeton University Press, 1967).

12. *Bhagavad-Gītā*, 6.32.

13. *Anuśāsana-Parva*, 113.8.

14. For a thorough treatment of the duties and obligations of the ruling class of the Indian tradition, see Basham, *Wonder*, "The State: Political Life and Thought," pp. 78–136.

15. *Rock Edicit I*, Girnar versions; see also Tähtinen, *Ahimsa*, p. 37.

16. Sri Aurobindo (Arabinda Ghose, 1872–1950), regarded as one of the great mystic-philosophers of twentieth-century India, was a powerful thinker and a superb literary stylist. A prolific author, Sri Aurobindo expounded his philosophy in many works. Among his most well-known writings is *The Life Divine*. He also founded the Integral Yoga, an elaborate and complex practical discipline by which to transform man into an enlightened being. His āshram in Pondicherry, India, is known throughout the civilized world. His views on nonviolence, contrasted here with those of Gandhi's, are from his *Letters on Yoga, Part 1* (Pondicherry, 1971), p. 49.

17. For a fine discussion of this point, as well as an unusually sensitive, scholarly, and comprehensive study of various aspects of Gandhi's philosophy in general, see Glyn Richards, *The Philosophy of Ghandhi* (New York, Barnes & Noble, 1982).

18. Ibid.

19. *Manusmṛti*, 11.145.

20. *Śānti-Parva*, 215.7–8.

21. *Bhāgavata-Purāṇa*, 10.51.63.

22. *Varāha-Purāṇa*, 8.26–30.33.

23. *Manusmṛti*, 5.51.

24. *Anuśāsana-Parva*, 114.11.

25. For a detailed discussion of the principle of the two truths, see R. Puligandla, *Jñāna-yoga: The Way of Knowledge. An Analytical Interpretation* (Lanham, Md., University Press of America, 1985).

12

Maya Chadda

Satyagraha: Gandhi's Approach to Peacemaking

Most religious traditions seek to answer questions about the nature of the human being and society, the causes of conflict, and the conditions of peace. Over its 3,000-year history, Hinduism has also developed a rich and unique repertoire of ideas about, and approaches to, these questions. The Hindu quest for the meaning and purpose of existence and correct human conduct has resulted in distinctive answers that perceive the self (Atman) to be the only true instrument for realizing the nature of universal and divine reality (Brahma) and selfless action to be the true path of salvation. Drawing on these well springs of religious tradition, many nineteenth- and twentieth-century Indian philoso-phers and social reformers have developed theories of collective action for social advancement and avoidance of conflict. M. K. Gandhi's theory of nonviolent action—satyagraha, often referred to as a moral alternative to war—is the latest and perhaps the most significant contribution by such reformers.

As a major figure of peace in our century, Mohandas Gandhi warrants serious attention, both for his ideas of nonviolence and for his courageous translation of these ideas into action. As Martin Luther King, Jr., so aptly said, "If humanity is to progress, Gandhi is inescapable—we may ignore him at our own risk."[1] In this chapter, I shall discuss the Gandhian perspective on peace and examine the applicability of his thesis of nonviolent action to contempo-rary conflict situations.

It is important to bear in mind at the very outset that Gandhi was not interested in constructing an abstract theory of nonviolence and peace; rather, his was a practical quest. Similarly, although he searched for ways to resolve social conflict in the context of Hindu philosophical ideas, the defense of Hinduism in itself was never his primary goal. In fact, the Gandhian thesis of nonviolent action (satyagraha) has paradoxical connections with the main currents of Hindu thought. The Gandhian satyagraha is undeniably rooted in Hindu metaphysics, but it rejects the main preoccupation of Hindu religion— the quest for individual salvation.

Similarly, Gandhi based his thesis of satyagraha on the scriptural notion of suffering, but instead of accepting suffering as a consequence of past actions (karma), he turned it into a formidable force to eliminate social injustice—an idea that has found no expression in Hindu scriptures. In other words, although the Gandhian thesis cannot be appreciated without reference to Hindu religious tradition, it can never be understood fully within the exclusive confines of that tradition.

Indeed, the real value of the Gandhian thesis lies in Gandhi's creative application of the Hindu spiritual tradition. His ideas transcended that tradition, and spoke to the universal concerns of oppression and violence in its most authentic voice. Gandhi did this by evolving a theory that was a practical recommendation on what to do and how to act under conflict conditions. For Gandhi, what was practical had to be moral, and all morality had to be true to the spiritual quest in the human heart. In this sense, then, those who practiced satyagraha were not merely engaged in endorsing the desirability of high moral values; they were, as Gandhi insisted, obliged to act upon them.

Gandhi stood alongside all the great teachers of the world religions in urging others to reach into their spiritual traditions to overcome violence. He was, however, unique in placing his emphasis on action and making action a major test for the validity of his thesis. Nevertheless, it is in this regard that satyagraha has been most severely criticized. Many have charged that the Gandhian thesis of nonviolent action is naive, utopian, and impractical in the real world. In the following pages, I shall take account of these charges and assess whether satyagraha is an adequate strategy for conflict resolution. To do this, I shall first discuss the concepts that contribute the main thrust of the Gandhian thesis; secondly, outline the operational logic of satyagraha; and thirdly, examine its application to and practicability in the modern world.

FUNDAMENTAL CONCEPTS

1. According to Gandhi, the supreme human endeavor should be the pursuit of *satyā,* truth. Gandhi often quoted the core philosophical assertion from the *Bhagavad Gita, satyanasti paro* dharma, "there is no higher duty than adherence to truth." This was the Upanishadic concept of the ultimate, eternal truth that is akin to self-realization, transcending barriers of history, time, and culture. However, it was not the eternal truth that guided Gandhi's thought and action, but the idea of relative truth. The quest for ultimate truth offered an overall conceptual umbrella for his thesis and provided the necessary moorings in Hindu epistemology; however, the operational relevance of this quest to the

Gandhian strategy of action remained minimal. Gandhi argued that he had not found the absolute truth, saying, "Thus I must hold to the relative truth as I have conceived it."[2] Implicit in this statement was his belief that all actions contained an element of error. Therefore, all positions, that of opponents as well as one's own, should be treated with equal consideration.

Such a belief could, however, confront one with a nasty problem of ethical relativism. How does one know what is the relative truth in a given instance, if that truth is bound to vary from person to person and from one situation to another? Gandhi sought a way out of this dilemma by insisting that relative truth was not simply one's beliefs about the physical world; instead, it had to be a step toward self-realization, a move in the direction of expanded consciousness where egocentric distinction between the self and others will eventually collapse.[3] In addition, he insisted that the just position in any situation can be discovered by applying the criterion of collective social advancement and fulfillment of human needs. As Joan Bondurant points out, for Gandhi, "man was the measure," and the way to justice had to lead through the progressive testing of relative truths.[4] Yet, it was apparent to Gandhi that there could be serious disagreements about what was in the common interest. He therefore insisted on strict adherence to ahimsa, nonviolence, or, literally, the refusal to injure others.

2. The basic operative assumption that Gandhi makes is that nonviolence constitutes a positive procedure for promoting worthwhile social change. It is not merely that one should refrain from violence, because it is wrong; sometimes violence is not wrong.[5] There can be conditions in which one is justified in inflicting violence—for instance, if the only other choice is acting in a cowardly manner. Violence is also justified for the protection of those under one's care, or under the care of the larger community. In Gandhi's view, the best response was based on nonviolence; the second best was violent defense. The worst form of response was submission to a tyrant or running away out of fear of consequences. In Gandhi's words:

> I would rather have India resort to arms in order to defend her honour than that she should, in a cowardly manner, become or remain a helpless witness to her own dishonour.[6]

Thus, for Gandhi, the question was not one of establishing on philosophical grounds the absolute disvalue of violence and therefore the desirability of nonviolence; rather, it was a question of discovering what to do under specific circumstances.

Such a method required discipline of mind and body. Gandhi advocated practicing austerity, restraint over one's manifold desires, and detachment, arguing that these would impart to the practitioner the strength to undertake satyagraha.

3. This, then, brings us to the central idea in his thesis, satyagraha, which literally means "clinging to truth" or "holding fast to truth." The notion of

satyagraha combines the ideas of truth and nonviolence. As a concept, satyagraha gave expression to Gandhi's religious and ethical ideas; as a technique, it put these ideas into practice; and as a philosophy, it mobilized Hindu philosophical traditions to eliminate contemporary social injustice. Thus applied, the traditional precepts of *satyā* and ahimsa were extended beyond their original meanings and beyond the problem of individual salvation to become an important part of a technique of practical action for solving contemporary social and political conflicts.

Gandhi had evoked tradition for essentially revolutionary purposes. As it was eventually applied, satyagraha was used not only to attain India's independence from the British, but also as a potent instrument against all manner of unjust practices within Hindu society, particularly the caste system, the segregation of the untouchables, and discrimination against women. As a result, it challenged age-old practices of Hindu orthodoxy that had become so entrenched in the social fabric of India.[7]

The purpose of satyagraha was persuasion and conversion, never coercion. "It aims at winning over a man by the power of love and gentle persuasion and by arousing in him a sense of injustice rather than forcing him to submit out of fear and embarrassment."[8] Therefore, satyagraha could not be launched without first fully exploring the usual avenues of reconciliation.

For Gandhi, satyagraha was not a passive procedure; it was meant to be an active method of resisting injustice through deliberate noncooperation. Nor did Gandhi think that merely appealing to the adversary would ever be sufficient to remove injustice. He said:

> I have found that mere appeal to reason does not answer where prejudices are age-long and based on supposed religious authority. Reason has to be strengthened by suffering and suffering opens the eyes of the understanding.[9]

In other words, reasoning had to be backed by firm action and refusal to compromise on one's basic position. It was not enough merely to bear witness to an injustice; one had to actively struggle against it. Such a struggle could not be initiated without a careful analysis of the situation, and until the "truth" (relative) of a given injustice had been determined.

Satyagraha, then, had to be about a true and substantial issue. Many have argued that there may not be any agreement on how such an issue is defined. It is true that one cannot arrive at a general criterion for identifying a true and substantial issue in the abstract: the possibilities may be infinite. However, in concrete, empirical instances, it is possible to narrow the choices to a few. All philosophical discourse about conflict resolution has to be settled in concrete circumstances, taking into full account all relevant socio-historical information. This is all that Gandhi claims satyagraha must attempt to do. Thus we see that satyagraha, as Gandhi conceived it, was not an ideology of protest. It was not to be limited to demonstrations, shouting of slogans, fasting, strikes, or boycotts. Each of these instruments might be used at one time or another, but only as part of a ladder of escalation that in turn had to fit into the methodology of satyagraha.

It was also clear that satyagraha could not be practiced without sufficient training for a clear understanding of what it involved. Was it, then, an instrument only for a few who were well versed in its technique? Clearly, Gandhi did not think so. Satyagraha had been applied by him to resist a variety of social injustices; with the passing of time, it had gained larger and larger numbers of participants drawn from the average citizenry.

Beginning in South Africa, Gandhi launched satyagraha against the laws of the Transvaal government, which required every Indian to procure a certificate of registration or face deportation. Another set of South African laws declared Hindu, Muslim, and Parsee marriages illegal. Opposition through satyagraha involved the imprisonment of thousands of Indians and eventually led to the nullification of those laws. After arriving in India, Gandhi implemented satyagraha in 1916–17 against the British indigo planters at Champaran in Bihar, where peasant cultivators were unfairly treated and taxed. In 1918 satyagraha was also brought to bear on the dispute between the textile mill owners and laborers in Ahemedabad and involved a strike by workers. The technique of satyagraha was subsequently practiced in 1924 on behalf of the untouchables, who had been forbidden to use the roads in the vicinity of the Vykom temple in Travancore, South India. Having refined his strategy on relatively smaller stages, Gandhi launched a series of satyagraha, beginning in 1930, which involved mass participation in civil resistance and noncooperation aimed at the British. In the majority of these campaigns Gandhi achieved remarkable success, gaining ever growing popular participation and support for his declared objectives.

Clearly, the masses who responded in these instances had undergone neither training nor education in Gandhi's theories of nonviolent struggle . Those who would lead had to approximate the ideal of satyagraha and set an example for the rest. As for the masses, it was enough if they could faithfully follow their leaders and try to understand the core principles of the struggle; it was not necessary that they subscribe to it as an ideology.[10] In this respect, writes Bandhopadyaya:

> Gandhi likened the discipline of the nonviolent army of satyagraha to that of a violent army in the battlefield, where the general takes the basic decision and the ordinary soldiers obey his orders under certain rules of discipline.[11]

Implicit in satyagraha was Gandhi's assumption that all rulers are dependent for their position and power upon the obedience and cooperation of the ruled. Their power therefore comes from outside themselves. If subjects withdraw cooperation and refuse to submit, a regime will become seriously weakened. If the withdrawal is maintained in the face of various sanctions, an end to the regime is in sight. According to Gandhi, power does not flow from acquisition and possession of arms, but from a relationship in which one side concedes to the other the right to dominate. Gandhi sought to turn the logic of political dependency against oppression and injustice. Theoretically, he was on solid ground in postulating power as a dynamic relationship rather than a possession. Gene Sharp writes:

> War and violence can be ended when the satyagraha strategy is fully grasped and the associated corollaries such as nonviolent discipline, the necessity of wise choice of methods, preparation and training, development of internal strength, and persistence in face of repression are properly understood.[12]

Indeed Gandhi himself and others who subsequently studied his technique of nonviolent struggle have viewed it as a "moral equivalent of war" or a "functional alternative to war" or as a "novel mode of solving group and national conflicts."[13] No one was naive enough to suggest that conflict could be eliminated from human affairs, but Gandhi claimed that satyagraha was superior for the resolution of apparently irreconcilable differences.

THE OPERATIONAL LOGIC OF SATYAGRAHA

As a strategy, satyagraha was based on a sound understanding of the adversary relationship and sought to maximize the strengths of the protagonists while exposing to full attack the psychological weakness of the antagonists. It required strict adherence to several rules and laid down a well-thought-out ladder of conflict escalation that would culminate in a resolution. In all conflicts, it was meant to transform the situation and to result, not in a victory of one side and defeat of the other, but in a new consensus in which both parties to the dispute could claim victory.

If, for a moment, we isolate Gandhi's strategy of action from his moral imperatives, it becomes clear that the rules implicit in satyagraha actions closely follow the rules of any conventional conflict. First was the rule of self-reliance, a necessary strategem if the practitioners of satyagraha want to maintain their freedom of action. Also, self-reliance will impose realistic limits on the goals of conflict by preventing overambitious actions, and will thus keep conflict from escalating out of control. The second rule was that satyagraha followers had always to keep the initiative in their hands. This required continuous assessment of the conflict situation and pressing forward with the next step in the satyagraha strategy. The third rule dealt with the correct means for propagation of objectives—the strategy and tactics of the campaign. This rule was important to mobilize mass support, to educate participants in the ways of satyagraha, and to convey one's demands to the opponent in the clearest terms possible. Reduction of demands to a minimum consistent with truth was the fourth rule. Exaggerated demands were contrary to the philosophy of satyagraha, as well as counterproductive. Reason and the clearly understood willingness to negotiate in reasonable terms were to be the weapons for persuading the opponent.

The fifth rule called for the advancement of the movement through steps and stages determined by the dynamics of a given situation. This rule directly related to the goal of preserving the initiative in the hands of the satyagraha followers. The sixth rule stated that self-examination was needed to weed out weakness within the satyagraha group. As in any battle, morale and discipline were critical to the success of a campaign. It was believed that self-analysis would boost courage and provide an incentive to go on. The seventh rule emphasized persistent search for avenues of cooperation with the adversary on honorable terms. The opponent had to be fully convinced of the sincerity of the protagonist's desire for peace, rather than for triumph of one adversary over the other. Refusal to surrender essentials in negotiations was the final rule. Exponents of satyagraha must admit no compromise with the "essential portions of valid objectives. Care must be exercised not to engage in bargaining or barter."

In addition to these rules, satyagraha practitioners were required to adhere to a code of conduct that stressed determined action, refusal to submit despite punishment, protection of the opponent from insult or attack, protection of property, and exemplary conduct even under pressure of abuse, insult, or punishment.[14]

After an analysis of five major satyagraha campaigns launched by Gandhi during the struggle for national independence, Joan Bondurant concludes: "In examining satyagraha in action, it becomes clear that satyagraha operates as a force to effect change." To succeed, it required "a comprehensive program of planning, preparation, and studied execution," and not simply a spontaneous upsurge of mass protest. Satyagraha failed whenever "one or more of the stages of the campaign was slighted."[15]

PRACTICABILITY AND APPLICATION

As has been noted earlier, two sets of questions need to be addressed in our examination of Gandhian strategies: First, can this strategy work outside India, or does it require a Hindu milieu for its mass acceptance and application?

Joan Bondurant maintains that religious or philosophical compatibilities alone do not explain Gandhi's success in India. In fact, the theory of conflict underlying satyagraha and the strategy it yields have wider applications that go well beyond India. She cites the Khudai Khidmatgar (Servants of God) movement among Pathan Muslims in the Northwest Frontier Province of British India, in which Khan Abdul Gafar Khan, the leader, recruited thousands of Muslim supporters and carried out a successful nonviolent struggle.[16] The Muslim Pathans are known for their bravery, and their general population lives by the creed of military honor and valor in battle. Indeed, in one rather touching episode described by the author, Muslim Pathan women, who are traditionally wont to hide behind a veil, faced well-armed British soldiers and refused to move; when forced, they lay down with copies of the Qur'ān clutched to their hearts.

Gene Sharp, in his book, *Ghandi as a Political Strategist,* cites several more instances of satyagraha and persuasively argues that since Gandhi's use of it in India, the technique has been implemented far more widely than is generally believed. Among the most important instances he cites is its adoption by Martin Luther King, Jr., against racist practices in the United States. Even in totalitarian systems, there have been instances of similar resistance, although nowhere has it led to the overthrow of such regimes. The Norwegian resistance during the Nazi occupation is one of the most significant examples. Other cases include:

> Major aspects of the Danish resistance, 1940–45, including the successful general strike in Copenhagen in 1944; major parts of the Dutch resistance, 1940–45; the East German rising of June 1953, in which there was massive nonviolent defiance which included women in Jena sitting down in front of Russian tanks; strikes in political prisoners' camps in the Soviet Union in 1953, which are credited with being a major influence for improving the lot of prisoners; and the major aspects of the Hungarian revolution, 1956–57, in which in addition to the military battles there was demonstrated the power of the general strike, and large-scale popular nonviolent defiance.[17]

Sharp further points out that the degree of "success and failure" varies in each case. None of these movements was undertaken as a conscious application of Gandhian principles of satyagraha; nevertheless, they offer ample proof that nonviolent action is possible, not only beyond a Hindu cultural context but also against totalitarian systems that pay little heed to the niceties of democratic procedures. In fact, in one of the first critical examinations of the Gandhian strategy, Krishnalal Shridharani states:

> My contact with the Western world has led me to think that, contrary to popular belief, satyagraha, once consciously and deliberately adopted, has more fertile fields in which to grow and flourish in the West than in the Orient. Likewise, satyagraha demands public spirit, self-sacrifice, organization, endurance, and discipline for its successful operation, and I have found these qualities in Western communities more than in my own.[18]

In conclusion, one might point out that satyagraha is not based on elements peculiar to Hindu society, but rather on insights into the psychological interdependence that is common to all human conflict. It is true that certain political cultures might be more compatible than others with the satyagraha philosophy, but such political compatibility is not limited to India.

SATYAGRAHA AND CONFLICT TODAY

The second question: Is satyagraha an adequate substitute for violent conflict, and under what conditions would this be true?

In the postwar world, peace is threatened generally by three kinds of national or international conflict. The first and most destructive is the arms race, carrying with it the possiblity of nuclear confrontation; the second is that of conventional wars between states for territory, resources, honor, or ideological supremacy; the third is a consequence of totalitarian or authoritarian rule resulting in oppression and denial of equality, freedom, and justice to the whole population of a state or to distinguishable groups within it.

The wars of national liberation in Latin America and Africa are instances of the third type. The second and third kinds of threats can become intertwined, as evidenced in such wars as the one between Ethiopia and Somalia in the late 1970s (in which Somalia put forward claims to the Ogaden region based on traditional movements of tribes within its own jurisdiction), or the disputes between India and Pakistan over the territory of Kashmir. The war between Iran and Iraq is at once ideological conflict (where the Shī'ah fundamentalist Islam of Iran has set itself against the more secularist, traditional Sunni Islam of the Arabs) and a dispute over boundaries separating the two states. The conflict between Arab states and Israel is similarly multilayered. It is about territory, the rights of the Palestinians for a homeland, and Israel's right to exist as a state.

There is very little possibility that in the foreseeable future any state will replace arms with nonviolent means to deter aggression. Indeed, almost all governments believe that nonviolence is irrelevant to the problem of defense, and that therefore armed force must be the ultimate arbiter in human affairs. Against this unqualified faith in the efficacy of force, one must point out that wars do not always obtain their desired ends, nor does oppression ensure true and enduring control over peoples and nations. Indeed, Adolph Hitler did not obtain his objective through force, nor did various imperial nations such as Great Britain and France gain their ends by employing force in their colonies. The wars of national independence have time and again proven the impotency of superior force when matched against massive grassroots violent and nonviolent resistance. Thus, there is no reason to believe that force and violence will invariably intimidate others and achieve the ends desired of them. By the same token, nonviolence is not applicable in every situation of potential conflict, although Gandhi and his supporters claimed that it was.

Let us take the case of ultimate violence first. Ever since the advent of nuclear weapons, the world has lived in terror of annihilation. The means of destruction are so lethal that they have rendered largely irrelevant the objectives for which a war could be waged. There is no real purpose in waging a war if the conflict spells certain mutual destruction within a few minutes and if very little of either adversary's national substance would be left to dominate the other.

Horsburg, however, argues that although satyagraha is no substitute for deterrence, the spread of nuclear weapons to a large number of states will create a situation in which nonviolent means of resolving conflict will become increasingly relevant. He admits that disagreement and hostilities will persist: "There are bound to be many cases in which negotiations will end in a deadlock." However, he claims that "it does not seem wildly speculative to predict that in these circumstances an increasing interest will come to be taken in the possibilities of noviolent action." He defends his position:

> If it is said that those optimistic speculations are absurd, I must insist that they are soundly based on the logic of deterrence. If the risks that deterrent policies involve must continue to increase, the use of armed force in the international sphere must become progressively more dangerous and hence it must eventually become too hazardous to use in the most extreme national emergencies.[19]

Unfortunately, the logic of deterrence does not quite work in the way Horsburg describes. Nuclear states often engage in conventional wars and by a tacit agreement refrain from using their most lethal weapons. For instance, in the conflict over the Falkland Islands between England and Argentina, England certainly had the capacity to wage a nuclear war. Similarly, in the 1979 conflict between China and Vietnam, China had an independent nuclear capacity and Vietnam was under the Soviet nuclear umbrella. Indeed, one might point out that the rough parity in nuclear weapons has aggravated the competition for the Third World between the U.S.A. and the U.S.S.R.

If satyagraha is impractical in a situation of nuclear war, does it have any relevance in negotiations for nuclear disarmament? In other words, can it act as a preventive? Can the Gandhian principles of steps and stages, sympathetic undersanding for one's adversary, formulation of minimal demands consistent with truth, refusal to threaten or intimidate the enemy, and open diplomacy be meaningfully applied to fashion a strategy for gradual nuclear disarmament?

In principle, the Gandhian framework can be an important guide for negotiations on disarmament. Indeed, even conventional diplomacy recognizes the need for confidence-building measures and reciprocity. Nor can negotiations be successful unless both sides are convinced of the sincerity of their opponents. However, today such settlements are seldom arrived at by open diplomacy or via adherence to the idea that mutual demands should be consistent with truth. More often than not, open diplomacy is used to score points with critics at home, to pressure the adversary, or worse still, to camouflage reluctance to negotiate. The usual practice in arms negotiations is to demand the maximum, in the hope that the final agreement will ensure more than what is required for defense.

It is difficult to imagine a situation in which a nuclear power would unilaterally disarm without an effective substitute strategically equivalent to armed strength. Although some scholars have postulated the adoption of nonviolence and gradual phasing out of dependence on arms, it is clear that a nation would have to undergo fundamental structural changes in its society and politics to accept the Gandhian view of human nature and forego the sense of security offered by weapons.

There are, however, elements in satyagraha that have an important bearing on the question of how to engage constructively in bargaining for disarmament. Let us look at some of the causes of the arms race between superpowers. According to several scholars, the arms race is a result of certain attitudes common to both the U.S.A. and the U.S.S.R. Each country has dehumanized the other, discounting the fears and concerns of the other's population and characterizing the other's leaders as war mongers. This attitude was evident in Dulles's characterization of the Soviet Union as the "diabolical enemy," as it is in the Reagan administration's view of the U.S.S.R. as the "evil empire." And yet, scholars and practitioners of international diplomacy have pointed out that the situation leading to war or peace is one of mutual dependencies. For instance, analyzing U.S.-Soviet relationships, Henry Kissinger contended that "both sides had to be aware of this dependency if mutually damaging wars and costly arms were to be avoided."[20] SALT I was based on a successful identification of such dependencies.

Schelling, in his work on the theory of interdependent decisions, has pointed out that in negotiations "the best course of action for any nation depends upon what it expects another nation to do, and strategy involves influencing the other nation's choices by working on its expectations of one's own behavior."[21] Kegley and Wittkopf, in their study of American foreign policy, have similarly maintained that the cold war was a "conflict over reciprocal anxieties bred by the way officials of both sides elected to interpret the actions of the other. Its origin may be seen as mutual mistrust of motives."[22]

In the realpolitik view of the world, parties to a conflict must be regarded as mutually exclusive: "we" and "they," the oppressed and the oppressor, the ruler and the ruled, are perceived as separate entities. It is then reasonable to assume that international tensions would diminish, and progress on arms reduction might be possible, if the United States and the Soviet Union rejected the realpolitik perspective and conceded the same human fears and hopes to each other that they each claim for themselves. This is the central premise of satyagraha.

The theory of power and politics implicit in Gandhian thought rejects this separation and stresses instead a fundamental continuity between two seemingly opposite entities. The Gandhian strategy of action requires that the protagonist attribute an irreducible minimum humanity to the enemy; to do otherwise is to betray one's own humanity. The significance of this premise for reconciliation of conflict and for the process of negotiations can hardly be overstressed.

There is one more possibility of applying the Gandhian technique to the problem of disarmament. This is in mobilizing mass movement against the arms race and building grassroots support for negotiations. The methodology of mass mobilization in this situation, however, would be no different from that for other issues. Critics might argue, and with justification, that peaceful protest would not solve the basic strategic dilemma and might in fact threaten national security by forcing democratic societies to negotiate away their advantages. Against this argument, one may point out that acquisition of arms beyond a certain point is useless, and a peace movement can raise awareness among the masses as well as generate pressures on governments to devote more money to social advancement rather than to defense.

This brings us to our question under consideration. Can massive nonviolent resistance be an adequate means of nonnuclear defense? Several scholars have examined the nonviolent method of defense and concluded that, at least theoretically, it is a plausible alternative, although widespread ignorance and prejudice against its methodology have often prevented its being considered seriously.

One supporter of nonviolence, Gene Sharp, points out that military power today does not have the real capacity to defend in conflict the people and society relying upon it. Often it only threatens mutual annihilation. He goes on to say that although nonviolent civilian defense will not stop the aggressor at the borders, military aggression does not give the invader political control of the country. He suggests that in civilian defense, military aggression can be resisted by the population as a whole, making it impossible for the enemy to establish and maintain political control. Enemy control can be prevented by massive and selective refusal to cooperate:

> For instance, police would refuse to locate and arrest patriotic opponents of the invader. Teachers would refuse to introduce his propaganda into the schools, as happened in Norway under the Nazis. Workers and managers would use strikes, delays, and obstructionism to impede exploitation of the country. . . . Politicians, civil servants, and judges, by ignoring or defying the enemy's illegal orders, would keep the normal machinery of government and courts out of his control. . . as happened in the German resistance to the Kapp Putsch in 1920. . . . Newspapers could refuse to submit to censorship . . . as it happened in the Russian 1905 revolution and several Nazi-occupied countries.[23]

Moreover, Sharp argues, civilian defense would set in motion restraining influences by stimulating dissension in the invader country and splits within the regime and the international community. This would only further weaken the aggressor's desire for occupation. Sharp cites numerous instances of effective nonviolent actions, although he admits there are as yet no cases in which prepared civilian defense has become official defense policy.

Gandhi's solution to external invasion would be to convert the conflict from one at the borders to one against occupation within the country. This is quite consistent with his philosophy as well as his strategy.[24] It is unlikely that fighting at the borders can persuade the enemy to admit the legitimacy of the protagonist's position. Inasmuch as Gandhian goals are to win over and persuade the antagonist, exponents of satyagraha require time, contact, and opportunity to drive their point home. Occupation, not armed confrontation, is more likely to offer these conditions.

A struggle against occupation, rather than defense at the borders, will shift the conflict to the turf where satyagraha has a decided advantage and where the enemy must depend on popular cooperation. However, there are cases where satyagraha will not be feasible. For instance, the enemy may be interested merely in inflicting military humiliation and may withdraw promptly after armed intervention. In some situations, the national population may be too small in numbers to mount effective nonviolent resistance. In other situations, the invader may be interested merely in extracting raw materials, and may not require cooperation of the civilian population to do so. In most other instances, however, the Gandhian theory of power will become operational and give civilian defense a powerful means to foil the ambitions of an aggressor.

It has been suggested that satyagraha can be a reasonable alternative to violent conflict where: (1) the socio-political system is relatively liberal with the minimum democractic freedoms of speech, press, and assembly guaranteed; (2) the adversary is not a thoroughly ruthless, heartless person, group or government; (3) there is general support for satyagraha among the people; (4) well-known national leaders are associated with it; and (5) external assistance or support can be depended upon. But satyagraha can succeed even where not all of these conditions are available.

The Norwegian resistance to Nazi rule, the Indian community satyagraha against the Transvaal government, the Chinese boycotts of 1905, and the revolutionary change in Russia were not conducted in a liberal socio-political environment. Draconian laws were in effect, and in each case the government had the means to stamp out opposition promptly. It must be pointed out that, with the exception of South African involvement, protestors resorted to satyagraha without fully understanding its principles or techniques, mainly because arms were not available. Even in South Africa, Gandhi was still experimenting with satyagraha, and it had not as yet attained the fullness of a strategy for conflict resolution. This was to happen much later and in India, where satyagraha succeeded, not because British rule was democratic and liberal—the massacre of innocent women and men at Jalianwala Bagh pointed to the opposite—but because the British had ignored Gandhi's early calls for satyagraha, thinking it to be an entirely eccentric and unworkable idea. The movement gathered force in the meantime, until it became too late to control the nationalists' fervor or the moral élan among the masses.

Indeed, even in the late 1980s there is persuasive evidence that satyagraha would be the appropriate alternative for conflict as a means of change. As one looks at Central American upheavals, such as those in Nicaragua and El Salvador, a certain similarity of underlying causes becomes apparent. There is not much dispute even among policy-makers in Washington that in each case the conflict is a result of long years of oppression, misery, and denial of freedom to the majority. However, in the oppressive environment, tightly-knit violent revolutionary movements spring up, plunging the country into civil war. The masses want neither communism nor the semifeudal oligarchies that have been the rule in Central America, and certainly they do not want civil war. In fact, when the revolutionaries succeed, as they did in Nicaragua in 1979, the results may be different only in degree from the oppression of the past. Born in violence, and threatened by great powers like the United States and its surrogates, a revolutionary government has no choice but to enforce austerity and strict rule.

However, in each case the guerilla movement could not have succeeded without mass support. Indeed, in the classic strategy enacted in Cuba and elsewhere in Latin America, the guerillas first fight for control of the countryside and slowly tighten the noose around the capital. As a final blow, the capital or major metropolis then goes on strike, and government comes to a halt. In other words, noncooperation and mass support could not be obtained without organization and publicity. And in every successful case these are quite effectively employed, even when clandestine operations are necessary.

Satyagraha is a better functional alternative to guerilla warfare in the classic strategy scenario, because here Gandhi's theory of power can be operationalized with stunning effect. The ruling oligarchies cannot remain in power unless they deliver a large portion of the wealth of the country to external powers on whose support they depend for their own survival. In other words, such regimes represent the interests, not of the masses within, but of exploiting forces outside their country. This is the regime's strength; however, if viewed from the perspective of satyagraha strategy, it is also its major weakness.

A great power like America may intervene on behalf of ruling interests on the pretext that the revolutionary movement is aided and abetted by America's enemies. Because self-reliance and nonviolent persuasion are the cardinal rules in satyagraha, there would be no need for arms from abroad; thus, the United States would look foolish sending an army against unarmed citizens who were simply agitating for human rights, and demanding liberty and democracy. What is more, if satyagraha were to succeed and political change be brought about, the resulting government, founded as it would be on peace and popular legitimacy without ill will, should be able to maintain internal as well as external peace.

Indeed, one of the most critical revolutions of recent times, the revolution in Iran, has many lessons for us in this respect. Admittedly, Islamic fundamentalism has nothing in common with Gandhian satyagraha; however, we should note several elements that this movement holds in common with other revolutions. First, the masses in Iran were imbued with moral and religious fervor; secondly, they were willing to accept enormous suffering, punishment, and even death for the success of their cause; and thirdly, they bravely faced the shah's troops, displayed enormous courage in face of superior arms (often only meagerly armed themselves), and staged massive demonstrations, strikes, and rallies despite express warning not to do so. The Islamic Revolutionary Party that came to power was certainly not imbued with ahimsa; indeed, it proceeded to eliminate all opposition. Nevertheless, it is significant that it had used noncooperation and civil resistance to topple the shah. It should be noted that the shah saw only two choices before him: to plunge the country into a bloodbath or to abdicate. He chose the second, not because he was particularly compassionate and liberal, but because he saw little purpose in pursuing the path of civil war.

Gandhi would have abhorred the goals and methods of the Islamic revolution, but that is not the point here. The point is that moral determination, willingness to sacrifice, and mass resistance can succeed, even in an environment where there is no liberty to organize and no freedom to rally enthusiasts openly around a cause. The Islamic revolutionary used the mosques just as the Solidarity movement in Poland has used the Catholic Church. "People power" succeeded in the Philippines.

There are, however, important limits to satyagraha. It cannot be used in a situation where the invader is bent on exterminating leadership of the conquered group, or where violence is seen not as a regrettable necessity but as a glorious affirmation of group identity. Satyagraha might not have been effective against the Nazi terror in Germany, although Gandhi believed it to be the only method that could work against the overwhelming military power of the Third Reich. His advocacy of satyagraha in this instance flowed from the fact that for Gandhi, satyagraha was a creed, a fundamental philosophical tenet, and not merely a policy that could be used with discretion. At other times, however, he did claim to have presented it as a policy and forcefully argued for its adoption because of its strategic advantages.

As the foregoing discussion indicates, one need not accept satyagraha as a creed to appreciate its feasibility in certain circumstances. As a national liberation ideology it will be effective if numbers are on the side of satyagraha supporters and oppression is not total. On the other hand, one does not need a liberal democracy for it to be operationalized.

CONCLUSIONS

To sum up, Gandhi's greatest contributions have been threefold. First, he insisted upon the principle of proportionality in human affairs. This dimension is often missed in discussions on satyagraha. The criterion of substantial issue, the insistence that demands should be consistent with truth, and the requirement that consideration be given to diverse points of view, including that of the adversary—all stress Gandhi's firm refusal to succumb to the conventional procedures of settling conflicts by bargaining for peace. Restraint is a great public virtue; Gandhi made it into a critical norm of politics.

Secondly, Gandhi devised a technique of conflict resolution that articulated in action a critical perspective on the human condition. This is the axiom that I and my adversary are not separate. In this, as in other ideas (truth and nonviolence), he had subscribed to the Hindu view of the eventual identity of the self and the material world. As the Upanishads insist, the doctrine of separation is a falsehood and prevents an individual from reaching Brahma, the ultimate truth. Gandhi extended this insight to the social realm and insisted on the essential continuity of victim and oppressor. Thus, Gandhi united religion to politics and evolved a vision of human society that would not differentiate between what was spiritually desirable and what was merely politically expedient. His was a holistic view that sought harmony in all aspects of life. As he observed:

A person cannot do right in one department of life while he is occupied in doing wrong in any other department. Life is one indivisible whole.[25]

Gandhi's third contribution was in restoring power and autonomy to the individual and in investing his actions with social significance. Gandhi insisted that knowledge of injustice imposed on individuals an obligation to act. One could not be merely a witness to injustice, however indignant. To be fully human, one had to act according to one's conscience. Gandhi therefore made the individual the focal point of his theory. Lone individuals may not force someone else to comply, but they are certainly free to suffer for others, and in the process are able to set themselves free from social and emotional bondage.

This exaltation of sacrifice to an operational principle, and the evolution of a step-by-step strategy of action based on suffering, constitute Gandhi's unique achievement. In evolving this method of nonviolent action, he merged theory and practice into one unified whole. Gandhian satyagraha was at once the end and the means of social action. As a strategy, then, it went well beyond a Hindu setting, but in its fundamentals it remained true to core values of Hinduism. Yet even here his sights were on common human concerns:

Religions are different roads converging upon the same point. What does it matter that we take different roads so long as we reach the same goal?[26]

Gandhi advocated satyagraha not as a new religion but as a superior means for attaining social harmony and human advancement for peace. This alliance of a pragmatic quest for solutions and a deep spiritual conviction also point to the way in which future generations may be educated in the task of struggling for peace.

NOTES

1. "Gandhi and America," *Focus on Asian Studies,* 4 (Fall 1984) 9.
2. M. K. Gandhi, *An Autobiography or the Story of My Experiments with Truth* (Ahmadabed, India, Navajivan Publishing House, 1948), p. 6.

3. For a succinct discussion of this point, see H. J. H. Horsburg, *Nonviolence and Aggression: A Study of Gandhi's Moral Equivalent of War* (London, Oxford University Press, 1968), p. 35.

4. Joan Bondurant, *Conquest of Violence: The Gandhian Philosophy of Conflict* (Berkeley and Los Angeles, University of California Press, 1965), p. 21.

5. Raghavan Iyer, *The Moral and Political Thought of Mahatma Gandhi* (London, Oxford University Press, 1973), pp. 196–97.

6. Quoted in Iyer, ibid., p. 201.

7. Glyn Richards, *The Philosophy of Gandhi* (London, Curron Press, 1972), pp. 80–96.

8. In *Young India* (Oct. 8, 1925) Gandhi said: "Nonviolence is 'not a resignation from all fighting against wickedness'; on the contrary, the nonviolence of my conception is a more active and real fight against wickedness than retaliation whose very nature is to increase wickedness. I seek entirely to blunt the edge of the tyrant's sword, not by putting against it a sharper-edged weapon, but by disappointing his expectation that I would be offering physical resistance."

9. N. K. Bose, *Selections from Gandhi* (Ahmadabed, India, Navajivan Publishing House, 1957), p. 222.

10. In this regard, paraphrasing Gandhi's letter of March 1922, Iyer writes: "Gandhi recognized that it would be difficult to get large masses of men to be nonviolent . . . but he was convinced that if even a band of intelligent and honest men with an abiding faith in ahimsa could be formed and trained, it could ensure the nonviolent atmosphere required for the working of civil disobedience in accord with ahimsa." *(Moral and Political Thought,* p. 191).

11. Jayantanuja Bandopadyaya, *Social and Political Thought of Gandhi* (India, Allied Publishers, 1969), p. 47.

12. Gene Sharp, *Gandhi as a Political Strategist* (Boston, Porter Sargent, 1979), p. 38.

13. Krishnalal Shridharani, *War without Violence* (New York, Harcourt and Brace, 1939), p. 27.

14. For a discussion of rules and steps in the proper conduct of satyagraha, see Bose, *Selections,* p. 175; D. G. Tendulkar, *Mahatma,* vol. 3 (Bombay, Jhaveri and Tendulkar, 1952), and Shridharani, *War,* pp. 5–42.

15. Bondurant, *Conquest,* p. 104.

16. See ibid., pp. 131–44.

17. For a detailed analysis of these events, see essays by Arthur Griffith, "The Resurrection of Hungary"; A. K. Jameson and Gene Sharp, "Nonviolent Resistance and the Nazis: The Case of Norway"; Joseph Scholmer, "Vortkuta: Strike in a Concentration Camp"; Leo Kuper and Albert Luthuli, "South Africa: The Beginning of Nonviolent Resistance"; C. Erik Lincoln and Martin Luther King, Jr., "Nonviolence and the American Negro"; in Mulford Sibbley, ed., *The Quiet Battle* (Boston, Beacon Press, 1963).

18. Shridharani, *War,* pp. 35–36.

19. Horsburg, *Nonviolence,* p. 196.

20. Albert Eldridge, *Images of Conflict* (New York, St. Martin's Press, 1979), p. 198.

21. Thomas Schelling, *The Strategy of Conflict* (New York, Oxford University 1963), p. 16.

22. Charles Kegley, Jr., and Eugene Wittkopf, *American Foreign Policy: Pattern and Process* (New York, St. Martin's Press, 1982), p. 56.

23. Gene Sharp, *Exploring Nonviolent Alternatives* (Boston, Porter Sargent, 1970), p. 51.

24. When Hitler invaded Czechoslovakia, Gandhi wrote: "The Czechs could not have done anything else, when they found themselves deserted by their two powerful allies. And yet . . . if they had known the use of nonviolence as a weapon for the defense of national honour, they would have faced the whole might of Germany with that of Italy thrown in" (*Harijan,* Oct. 8, 1939). And again: "Even if Hitler was able to build a vast empire through the force of arms he would not be able to digest so much power" (*Harijan,* Oct. 13, 1940).

25. "The Words of Gandhi," *Focus on Asian Studies,* 4 (Fall 1984) 10.

26. Ibid.

PART THREE

PEACEMAKING IN ACTION

Leah Goldberg

Songs from the End of the Road

I.
The road is quite beautiful—said the lad.
The road is quite difficult—said the young man.
The road was quite long—said the man.
The old man stopped to rest by the road.

Sunset paints his white hair golden red;
Grass, wet with evening dew, glows at his feet,
Above him the last bird of day is singing:
—Do you remember how beautiful, how difficult, how long
    was the road?

II.
You said: day chases day and night—night.
There is still time—you've said in your heart.
And you saw evenings and mornings pass your windows,
And you said: you see, there's nothing new under the sun.

And one morning you wake up old and gray,
And your days are numbered and very dear, each one,
And you knew: today is a last one under the sun,
And you knew: today is a new one under the sun.

III.
Teach me, my God, to bless and to pray
For the mystery of withered leaf, for the glow of ripe fruit,
For the freedom of just this: to see, to sense, to breathe,
To know, to hope, to fail.

Teach my lips blessing and song of praise,
As You recreate each fresh morning, each fresh evening,
Lest my day today be the same as yesterday and the day before,
Lest I throw on my day like a habit.

translated by Myra Shapiro

169

13

Betty Cannon

The "Demonic Double" and Early Education for Peace

In pure reciprocity, that which is Other is also the same. *But in reciprocity as modified by scarcity, the same appears to us as antihuman insofar as* this same man *appears as radically Other—that is to say, as threatening us with death. Or, to put it another way, we have a rough understanding of his ends (for they are the same as ours), and his means (we have the same ones), as well as of the dialectical structures of his acts; but we understand them as if they belonged to* another species, *our demonic double* [*Jean-Paul Sartre,* Critique of Dialectical Reason].[1]

INTRODUCTION

This passage, in which Sartre defines the difference between positive and negative reciprocity, is part of a growing dialogue that indicates the concern of serious modern thinkers about intergroup hostilities. For Sartre, viewing others as "Demonic Doubles"—that is, as evil, alien antihuman beings unworthy of sympathy and concern—is the source of much of this intergroup hostility. Sartre goes on to say that this vision of the Other as antihuman in a context of scarcity is the "abstract matrix of every reification of human relations in any society."[2] It is the source of our need to regard and treat human beings as if they were *things.*

Obviously, war and other forms of aggression (defined as hostile actions or behavior) would be a probable outcome of viewing another nation as our Demonic Double, a view chillingly apparent in the propaganda of the United

States and the Soviet governments.[3] Because the potential for violence on the international scene seems to threaten the survival of life on this planet, more and more psychologists are turning their attention to questions of human aggression and the psychology of war. The passage quoted above indicates how psychological issues connect intimately with economic, sociological, and political issues—with issues concerning scarcity and oppression, for example.

In this essay, I shall attempt to explore the interpersonal origins of aggression in the habit of viewing other persons as radically Other—as my Demonic Double—as this contributes to the mass psychology of war. I believe that persons might be more willing to make war on scarcity, rather than on each other, if war or the kind of thinking that leads to war did not serve a psychological purpose for many. I should like to try to discover what that purpose is. I believe that Sartre's "existential psychoanalysis," a technique for looking at contemporary lives in terms of their interpersonal histories, is a fruitful way of investigating the origins of aggression and of that aggressive life stance that makes good warmongers and good soldiers.[4]

The reader may ask, "Why existential psychoanalysis?" After all, the universal prevalence of war would seem to be one situation where innate aggressionists score a solid point.[5] But I am firmly convinced that neither of the traditional psychological metatheories—innate aggression or behavioral conditioning—adequately explains war as an *interpersonal* phenomenon. Existentialist theory does. In addition, existentialist theory holds some hope for changing the interpersonal scene in a positive direction, which innate aggression does not offer, and it does so without borrowing from the social technology and human manipulation advocated by behaviorists like B.F. Skinner.[6] If one's way of being with others is ultimately chosen as the best path one could develop in childhood for dealing with the ubiquitous alternation between subject and object in human relationships, then it should be possible for persons to change their ways of relating to others. Existentialist theory assumes that persons act as they do, not because they have been conditioned to do so or because they are obeying powerful biological or unconscious forces, but because that is the way they perceive reality. To show them another reality would, then, help to change negatively aggressive ways of relating to others. Existentialist theory could thus be expected to yield some positive principles on which to base the practice of peace education.

The ontological category of the Demonic Double, which is at the heart of this approach, is Sartre's answer to the problem of evil. Although Sartre did not use the term "Demonic Double" before *Critique of Dialectical Reason* and although he does not even there emphasize this term, he had investigated the kind of dualistic thinking about others that leads to conceiving of certain individuals as the repository of all evil as early as *Anti-Semite and Jew* (1946). I refer to this as an "ontological category" because Sartre derives his concept of evil from an understanding of the basic structures of *being human* rather than, say, drive theory or environmental conditioning.

I believe that Sartre's answer to the problem of evil throughout his work has serious implications for the developing field of peace education. At first glance, it might appear that this answer involves "psychologizing" evil out of existence. After all, Sartre unequivocally states that "evil is projection."[7] Indeed evil as the kind of "motiveless malignity" that Coleridge attributed to Shakespeare's Iago and that is usually meant when one views the Other as a devil, clearly does not exist for Sartre. Yet Sartre does not let evildoers—the anti-Semites, child abusers and neglecters, cowardly bourgeoisie, blind Stalinists, colonialists, racists, and others whom he condemns throughout his work—off quite so easily. Comprehended from within their own worldviews, these persons do not commit gratuitous evil. They do what they consider to be *their* good, despite the structures of "bad faith" that the existential psychoanalyst may discover in their projects.[8] Yet Sartre does not hesitate to judge their effects on others as "evil." Ironically, it is through viewing the Other as my Demonic Double—as an evil, alien, absolute Other—that Sartre claims I come to do objectively (but not subjectively) evil deeds. Hence evil, including war and all forms of oppression, springs from the perception—and projection—of absolute evil onto the Other. It comes from my failure to comprehend the Other as a human being like myself. To the extent that I thus exchange the possibility of positive for negative reciprocity, I become the Demonic Double that I fear. I become evil.

Needless to say, Sartre's position differs radically from most philosophical and religious views of the problem of evil. My essay will discuss the implications of accepting Sartre's radical premise for peace education. Inasmuch as the Demonic Double has a long history in religious and mythical thinking before Sartre, I must first trace its presence in two contrary religious strains in order to understand very clearly how Sartre's ontological category of the Demonic Double differs from—and explains—the Demonic Double of traditional religions. A Sartrian approach would reject both traditional religious views—one because its dualism leads to inhumanity and the other because its quietism leads to a failure in active resistance to evil deeds. This discussion will take up the first section of my essay.

In the next section, I shall briefly trace the development of Sartre's concept of the Demonic Double through his writings—not as an academic exercise, but because I believe that a look at Sartre's own ideas and examples can give a more thorough understanding of the relevance of this category to peace education.

Having thus firmly established who the Demonic Double is, I shall in the third section apply the technique of existential psychoanalysis to a concrete situation involving speculations on early childhood education for war and peace. Here I shall attempt an existential analysis of interviews with Green Berets and war resisters from the Vietnam war reported by David Mantell in his book, *True Americanism: Green Berets and War Resisters.*[9] My contention is that the childhood history of the war resisters, seen in existentialist terms, can provide the opportunity to formulate certain principles for early childhood education for peace that might lead to "true world citizenship" without the necessity for war. As for the Green Berets, I believe that we can, by investigating the way in which the stage is set in the bosom of the family for a propensity toward war and dehumanization, begin to show how it might be otherwise—how we might educate our children for positive reciprocity, for full human relationships with others, and for peace.

Finally, I shall use all of the above discussion as a basis for proposing some educational principles and exercises that might aid parents and teachers interested in early childhood education for peace.

Throughout this essay, I want to emphasize the significance of theory for practice. I believe that a comprehensive ontology of aggression, such as the one Sartre presents in his treatment of the Demonic Double, is necessary to any authentic and rigorous attempt at education for peace.

SARTRE'S IDEA OF THE DEMONIC DOUBLE VERSUS TWO TRADITIONAL RELIGIOUS VIEWS

The theme of the Demonic Double has illuminated many novels and stories. Among the best known are Robert Louis Stevenson's *The Strange Case of Dr. Jekyll and Mr. Hyde*, Oscar Wilde's *The Picture of Dorian Grey*, and Dostoevsky's *The Double*. Even more significant is the long history of the Demonic Double in religious thinking, folklore and myth, East and West. I distinguish Sartre's concept of the Demonic Double from two traditional religous views of the problem of evil. These two views are the orthodox Christian view of good and evil as irreconcilable opposites, which is also the view of many other religions, and the less well-known view of good and evil as manifestations of the *coincidentia oppositorum*, the union that must take place between opposites to form a greater whole. The Demonic Double appears in the mythologies of both religious views, but to a different end. Sartre has categorically rejected the first view. For different reasons, I believe he would reject the second as well. Neither, according to Sartre's own position, is equipped to change the kind of reality perception that leads to oppression and violence—and Manicheism positively promotes inhumanity in many forms.

Sartre refers to all dualistic religious and ethical views as Manicheism, after the dualistic religion founded by the Persian Mani (or Manes) in the third century A.D. Claiming that he was the Paraclete (Holy Spirit) promised by Jesus Christ, Mani proposed a doctrine of antagonism between the realm of God, represented by light and spiritual enlightenment, and the realm of Satan, symbolized by darkness and the world of material things. In Mani's system, women were considered to be part of the forces of Satan, seducing men in order to prevent the day of emancipation from matter and darkness.

Although Manicheism was considered a heresy, there is a similar dualistic view of good and evil in Christianity itself. In the Judeo-Christian tradition, such dualism is for the most part an invention of the Jewish Apocrypha and the New Testament. Satan, despite Christian attempts to identify him with the serpent in the Garden of Eden and thereby to claim that his machinations had been present from the beginning of time, had simply not been an important figure in the Old Testament.

By way of contrast to the many references to Satan, Beelzebub, and the Prince of Darkness or the prince of this world in the New Testament, the Old Testament contains only four direct references to Satan as a supernatural being and all four are found in postexilic books (later than 597 B.C.).[10] The most well-known is in the Book of Job, where Satan appears to be one of the sons of God dwelling in God's court. Satan and God carry on a very civilized conversation about Job, as though Satan were God's doubting side. Indeed there are other places in the Old Testament where God is referred to as a "satan"—that is, an adversary or interferer. In the story of Balaam's ass in Numbers 22, the Hebrew says that when Balaam attempted to pass through the mountain to deliver a curse on the Hebrews, Yahweh stood in Balaam's way as a *satan* unto him.[11] (English translations speak of "the angel of the Lord" who came to hinder Balaam.) Possibly, Satan is not a prominent figure in the Old Testament for the simple reason that Yahweh, as a fierce and jealous God, incorporates some of the supposedly "evil" characteristics later ascribed to the Devil. Yahweh is, like the ancient Greek gods, perhaps not yet "good" enough to merit a counter-force representing pure evil.

If Satan plays an insignificant role in the Old Testament, he is given a prominent one in the New Testament. According to scholarly speculations, the Jews may have been influenced by the Babylonians during the period of the exile to adopt a more dualistic view of good and evil. In any case, the highly developed demonology and angelology of the Jewish Apocrypha are reflected in the teachings of Jesus in the New Testament. There Satan and a host of demons are made responsible for all kinds of evils—from insanity and physical ailments to the temptation of Christ and his apostles. The culmination of all this is in the Book of Revelation, where an enormous battle is waged between God and Christ on the one hand and Satan and the Antichrist on the other with the aim of obliterating evil forever. This view of Satan as the mighty Prince of Evil has captured popular imagination more deeply than the more philosophi-cal definition by Augustine and other church fathers of evil as the *privatio boni*, deprivation of good.

Many of the world religions have been even more dualistic than Christianity, where one might suppose that the Devil is under the ultimate domination of God. Such religions present good and evil gods who are brothers, even though the eventual outcome of their struggle usually presents the good brother as winning. Zoroastrianism, which probably influenced both Christianity and Manicheism, is the most obvious example. In the Persian myth of Ahura-Mazda and Ahriman, Ahura-Mazda is responsible for life, light, truth, and the blessings of humankind whereas Ahriman is the source of death, darkness, lies, and the ills of humankind. The world where human beings live is the battle-ground of these two gods, human souls their prize. Ahriman, like Satan in the New Testament and Christian folklore, commands a host of demons or devas, who try to draw humankind away from Ahura-Mazda and into evil ways. Other Demonic-Double brother gods include the good Osiris and the evil Set in ancient Egyptian mythology, the good Baldur and the evil Loki in Norse mythology (the one example of a prediction of the ultimate triumph of evil), and the trickster gods with their good brothers in Amerindian folklore.

Reinterpreted in Sartrian terms, such cosmic dualism reflects a human dualism. And indeed persons are divided into the good and the bad, the sheep and the goats, in most of these religions. (The situation in Amerindian religion is more ambiguous, because cultural taboos rest on a sense of shame rather than sin.) I believe that Sartre's ontological category of the Demonic Double will provide us with an explanation for this need for dualism on the cosmic and human levels.

In addition to the Manicheistic outlook of the religions discussed above, there is a second traditional religious view of the relationship between good and evil. This view, which insists on a reconciliation of opposites in a higher synthesis, is more prevalent in Eastern than in Western religions. Psychologist Carl Jung, who studied the *coincidentia oppositorum* in many cultures and religions, believes that this view is superior to the traditional Christian view.[12] According to Jung, it would only be by incorporating the Devil into the Trinity, thereby making of it the mystical Quaternity, that Christianity could become a truly mature religion. In fact, the early Christian philosopher Origen, who is considered heretical, did propose just such an eventual reconciliation. According to Origen, when the perfection toward which all of creation is struggling has been achieved, the Devil will be saved and evil will cease to exist.

Such a view suggests that God allows evil to exist for God's own purposes, which is just the view of Hindu theology. But Hindu theology goes even further: both good and evil are illusions, which will be dispelled as an individual moves toward enlightenment. Not only this, most Indian divinities have a gracious and kindly form *and* a "terrible form." They achieve in themselves a unity of opposites. At the same time, they can also appear as Demonic Doubles, as is demonstrated in the Vedic struggle between Vritra, who symbolizes darkness, inertia, immobility, and chaos, and Indra, the solar hero. Yet the ultimate truth in Hindu theology is that all is one in Brahma (God), and Vedic doctrine insists on the brotherhood of the devas and the asuras, the powers of light and the powers of darkness. The transcendence of opposites is a constant theme of Indian spirituality.

Nor is such a conjunction of opposites always absent from Christian myth and folklore. Mircea Eliade has investigated the union of the Demonic Double with his good brother in many religious texts, folktales, and myths from many cultures in his book *The Two and the One*. In doing so, he notes the way in which the theme of the Demonic Double in the Christian folk tales of southeastern Europe is really a thin disguise for the *coincidentia oppositorum*. In these tales, God and the Devil are presented as blood brothers, or as co-eternal, or as needing each other to complete the creation of the world.[13] Indeed in all of these accounts from a variety of relgious traditions, it is the union of good and evil, rather than their irreconcilable disparity, that is emphasized.

How, then, would Sartre view these two traditional religious views of the problem of evil? He has already told us what he thinks of Manicheism. In its human form of casting the Other as my Demonic Double, it is the impetus for persecution, war, and inhumanity in many forms. Aside from wars, there is no doubt that the Jewish persecutions throughout the centuries and the great witchhunts culminating in the sixteenth and seventeenth centuries in Europe are the most obvious fruits of this categorization of others as an evil antihuman species in league with the Devil. Through regarding other individuals or groups as Demonic Doubles, an individual or group will find itself committing the evil that it fears in the Other—as when a war is started out of the perception of the necessity for self-defense. As Sartre says, "Violence always presents itself as *counter-violence*, that is to say, as retaliation against the violence of the Other."[14]

What, then, would Sartre think of the *coincidentia oppositorum?* Certainly it is a more benign religious doctrine than Manicheism; it does not provoke evil deeds. Yet the *coincidentia oppositorum* is a mystical doctrine that gives evil its due as really existing—at least in time and in the world of sense objects, which some traditions deem illusory. Sartre's point is that gratuitous evil does not really exist except as a projection. Once a denied impulse or an "evil" action becomes *my* impulse or *my* action, it becomes my *good*. It is only as the action of my Demonic Double that it is perceived as pure evil. Yet real evil, in a social sense, does result from Manicheistic thinking about the Other. It causes persons, for instance, to burn witches, to fight wars, to indulge in racism, colonialism, and class snobbery, and to create a despised or criminal group of those others who are regarded as Demonic Doubles. Such real social evil does not receive its due in the *coincidentia oppositorum*. Sartre, in addition to philosophical differences, would therefore have to reject the quietism implicit in this view. Sartre's own position, I believe, will become clearer as we examine further the evolution of this idea of the Demonic Double in his thinking.

THE DEVELOPMENT OF SARTRE'S IDEA
OF THE DEMONIC DOUBLE

Though not identified by this name, the concept of the Demonic Double has a long history in Sartre's work. Its ontological foundation is Sartre's description of the subject-object alternation involved in the conflict of consciousnesses described in *Being and Nothingness* (1943).[15] This subject-object alternation causes me to recognize that I have an outside for the Other—an outside that I can neither grasp nor control. Masochism, the attempt to recapture that outside by making myself a degraded object before the Other, is one response to this discovery. Sadism, the attempt to seize and control the Other's consciousness, is another. Yet even sadists, as Sartre describes them in "Concrete Relations with Others," do not exactly make of the Other a Demonic Double—they merely try to dominate and control the Other's consciousness as a way of escaping the degradation involved in being made an object by the Other.

On the other hand, in the sadist's motives one can find the beginning of an evolution toward perceiving others as Demonic Doubles. Hence children who are objectified in a dehumanizing manner will, as we shall see, be motivated to reify others in a similar manner. In addition to denying the common humanity of their Demonic Doubles, they will see in their Demonic Doubles the rejected impulses that they will not claim for themselves. In other words, one does not simply attempt to control or outmaneuver the Demonic Double. One also makes of him or her the receptacle for one's own projections.

In *Anti-Semite and Jew* (1946) Sartre first investigated the damage done to a despised group cast in the role of the Demonic Double. His observations there suggest that the Jew performs a necessary psychological function for the anti-Semite. "If the Jew did not exist," Sartre says flatly, "the anti-Semite would invent him."[16] The function that the Jew performs allows anti-Semites to enter an elite community (those who are not Jews, but true Frenchmen) and to escape their freedom. Anti-Semites, Sartre says, use the Jew to make of themselves an impenetrable *this*—that is, to further a life project that is in bad faith because it involves an escape from freedom. Refusing to live with the tentativeness and uncertainty that necessarily accompany authenticity, anti-Semites live instead with a kind of blind faith in themselves inspired by the hatred they feel for Jews and the fear they themselves inspire in others. In other words, anti-Semites reify the Jew in order to objectify themselves as a certain kind of person. As such, Sartre says, anti-Semitism becomes a kind of "poor man's snobbery." Yet anti-Semites need the Jew at the same time that they wish to destroy the Jew, because without the Jew anti-Semites would be forced to examine themselves and provide another explanation for their frustrations, failures, and mediocrity. They thus define the Jew as the absolute evil that explains all their own misfortunes. The Jew, according to anti-Semites, is both totally free and yet chained to evil. Thus anti-Semites believe that Jews, like Satan, will an evil that is also their nature. Hence it is that anti-Semitism is "at bottom a form of Manichaeism": anti-Semites and their fellows are good; the Jew is evil.[17]

It need hardly be added, though Sartre does add it, that psychology reveals that such Manicheism conceals a deep-seated attraction toward evil—an attraction that often leans toward sexual sadism, as when the anti-Semite finds himself drawn toward the "beautiful Jewess." In other words, the anti-Semite projects his own rejected impulses onto Jews. This identification of the Jew with the powers of evil and with Satan has a long history in Christian thinking, as Joshua Trachtenberg has shown in his book *The Devil and the Jews*.[18] In this respect, then, the Nazi movement was the culmination of centuries of the kind of dualistic moralism that Sartre condemns from *Anti-Semite and Jew* to *Critique of Dialectical Reason*. The Jew had become the Demonic Double.

Sartre again considered the effects of Manicheism on one of its unfortunate targets in *Saint Genet: Actor and Martyr* (1952). He says there of Genet, as he had said of the Jew, that he fulfills a certain function for the "decent folk" who condemn him to a life of crime. Just as the Jew creates a sense of community among anti-Semites, so the child Genet creates a sense of community among the "good persons" who look with horror at the young thief:

> Even before he emerged from his mother's womb, they had already reserved beds for him in all the prisons of Europe and places for him in all shipments of criminals. He had only to go to the trouble of being born; the gentle, inexorable hands of the Law will conduct him from the National Foundling Society to the penal colony.[19]

Like the Jew for the anti-Semite, Genet lives out the worst fears of law-abiding citizens for their own freedom. In order to regard themselves as good, they need him to embody all evil. Evil, Sartre says, "springs from the right-thinking man's fear of his own freedom."[20] Society's treatment of Genet is a form of bad faith:

> Evil is a projection. I would go as far as to say that it is both the basis and aim of all projective activity. As for the evildoer, we all have our own: he is a man whose situation makes it possible for him to present to us in broad daylight and in objective form the obscure temptations of our freedom. If you want to know a decent man, look for the vices he hates most in others.[21]

To reclaim the projection, right-thinking persons would have to recognize the potentiality for crime in themselves: "to understand the misfortune of a young thief would be to recognize that I too can steal."[22] Hence, although Sartre (with a certain twist of St. Augustine's doctrine of the *privatio boni*) defines "evil" as a deprivation of being, he at the same time equates freedom with the capacity for negation. In other words, such a definition of evil is really a myth: good is placed on the side of order and fullness, evil on the side of disorder and lack. Yet all progress, all projection of oneself toward a different future, all acts of imagination, and all revolt in the direction of a better future require negation. Hence "the respectable" fool themselves into believing that the status quo, themselves as "good" persons, and static order are positive and real.

In fact, Sartre concludes, it is in the name of such "good" that a multitude of real evils comes into existence. This is why Sartre insists that his readers "use Genet properly." As Sartre says at the end of the book, Genet in his solitude, his opposition reduced to impotence, his defeats, and his failures, is "our fellow man, our brother." "Genet holds the mirror up to us: we must look at it and see ourselves."[23]

Part of the reason we must accept Genet in this way is that, failing this, we are likely to fall into the self-righteous attitude that promotes regarding others as our Demonic Doubles. Even in *Saint Genet* Sartre had concluded that this is the kind of thinking that leads to war:

Thus, the evildoer is the Other. Evil—fleeting, artful, marginal Evil—can be seen only out of the corner of one's eye and in others. Never is it more perceptible than in wartime. We know the enemy only by comparison with ourselves; we imagine his intentions according to ours; we set traps for him into which we know we would fall if we were in his place and we avoid those which we would have set. The enemy is our twin brother, our image in the mirror. Yet the same conduct which we consider good when it is ours seems to us detestable when it is his. He is the evildoer par excellence. It is therefore during a war that a Good man has the clearest conscience. It is in time of war that there are the fewest lunatics. Unfortunately, one cannot always be fighting. From time to time there must be peace.[24]

In a time of peace society recruits the racially or culturally different, the oppressed, the exploited, and the purely wretched as its evildoers. But it is war that offers the prime opportunity for Manicheism. In order to overcome the tendency to need war, a society would have to move toward a form of childrearing that reduced the need to create Demonic Doubles in peacetime or in war. It would also, as Sartre points out in *Critique of Dialectical Reason*, need to overcome the scarcity of resources that reinforces such thinking. Yet I believe that a movement toward positive reciprocity, my regarding the Other as another self, is also necessary to overcome scarcity. Otherwise, the world spends its resources on the frightening buildup of arms rather than on overcoming hunger and disease. This is a circle, and one must begin to counter this pernicious form of perceiving/creating reality. Existential psychoanalysis begins with an investigation of the childrearing policies that promote thinking of the Other as my Demonic Double, rather than simply as a fellow human being like myself.

We now know who my Demonic Double is: he is the projection onto the Other of all those evil deeds I fear that I in my freedom might commit. He is the reification in an evil, alien, absolute Other of all my own disowned impulses and desires and fears about what I might do or be. He therefore reassures me of my own goodness. Not only this, my Demonic Double provides me with the occasion to release all the pent-up hatred, resulting from my own objectification and reification by others, that it would never be possible to direct at another who is conceived to be like myself. My Demonic Double thus provides me with the opportunity, at the same time that I deny my freedom and identify myself as the "good person," to make of some outcast person or enemy group an object with no chance of becoming a subject. In the presence of my Demonic Double, I escape the danger of being judged, because I reserve all judgment to myself.

Sartre's concept of the Demonic Double, in the passage quoted from *Critique of Dialectical Reason* at the beginning of this essay, thus suggests an ontological/social basis for understanding the very human need to scapegoat and dehumanize others. In *Anti-Semite and Jew* and *Saint Genet* Sartre has presented the devastating effects of such thinking on its targets. In *Saint Genet* he has traced its effects on a child who became one of society's chosen scapegoats. What Sartre has not done, and what I should like to attempt in the fourth section of this essay, is to describe the kind of childhood that predisposes one to see other individuals and other groups as Demonic Doubles. By providing a phenomenological description of such a childhood and its opposite, I believe that existential psychoanalysis can contribute some sound psychological principles to the enterprise of early childhood education for peace.

GREEN BERETS AND WAR RESISTERS:
TOWARD AN ONTOLOGY OF AGGRESSION

Existential psychoanalysis, like traditional psychoanalysis, relies for its data on individual case histories and concrete individual experience.[25] In order to explore the childhood origins of the inclination to think of others as Demonic Doubles, I decided to look at the childhood experiences of individuals who seemed more warlike in contrast with those who were more inclined toward peace. What I wanted for this investigation were unbiased self-reports. Unfortunately, such material is very scarce, and most of the time I found that researchers had failed to tell me what I really wanted to know, whereas eyewitnesses had an axe to grind.

One book, David Mantell's comparison of twenty-five Vietnam-era Green Berets with twenty-five war resisters in *True Americanism: Green Berets and War Resisters*, did give me what I wanted. Mantell provides copious quotes from interviews both with seemingly ideal soldiers and their opposites on a variety of topics ranging from war experiences to childhood and adolescence to relationships with women and significant others. Although my conclusions are not necessarily the same as those of Mantell, they in no way contradict his findings and I do appreciate the fidelity with which he reported the exact data on which he based his conclusions. This enabled me to make my own interpretations from another theoretical orientation.

Obviously, to be fully verified even from an existentialist perspective, these interpretations would need to be correlated with interpretations of interviews with soldiers and others in other wars and other cultures. I would have little opportunity to do this in a short essay. Still I think we may begin to formulate an ontology of aggression by questioning these men's experiences in order to understand what makes a good soldier and his opposite.

Surely, the Green Berets in Mantell's study would be considered good soldiers in almost any kind of war: they enjoyed and took pride in their work. They were good at what they did. They worked well with a team. And they experienced few if any harmful aftereffects of engaging in warfare. Inasmuch as they volunteered for active duty, we may assume that something in them wished to see combat. How, we ask, do their histories, their relationships with others, and their needs differ from those of young men who do not have an inclination for war—from those of the war resisters in Mantell's study, for example?

Basically, it seems to me that the Special Forces soldiers tended to view others, not only the enemy but also comrades, possible role models, and women with whom they had been intimate, as objects rather than subjects. Not that they did not attribute human plans, motivations, and manipulations to them, but that, in a manner reminiscent of Sartre's discussion of the Demonic Double, they failed to regard others as human like themselves. In other words, their failure included a failure of empathy. For this reason, perhaps, they were not usually very disturbed at the sight of the death of either their comrades or enemy soldiers. That this was not a learned response from battle is indicated by the fact that many Green Berets, as teenagers, had apparently reacted with a similar imperviousness to violent accidental death, even of persons close to them.[26] Often they compared the excitement of battle to the excitement of hunting, indicating further their dehumanization of the enemy.

As might be expected, the Green Berets in Mantell's study did not report the flashbacks and nightmares that plagued many draftees and other soldiers in Vietnam. In this respect, they were perhaps perfect soldiers, and the experiences that influenced them to be so might be investigated by any country wishing to educate its children for war. In fact, Mantell found to his surprise—because he had expected more patriotism from the Special Forces—that many of these men were open to the possibility of joining the military of another nation if the United States should make peace in Vietnam. They positively enjoyed the excitement of war and took pride in their proficiency at it.

The war resisters, by contrast, did not tend to view others as mere objects. Unlike the Green Berets, they reported many others since childhood whom they had allowed to have a profound influence on their lives. Not that they wavered with every wind, but they were open to role models and deep friendships. They also reported that women, as well as men, had sometimes profoundly influenced them. As for their romantic relationships, they tended to regard them more seriously than the Green Berets and to report being attracted to more human, rather than merely physical, qualities in their partners. For the most part the war resisters had not experienced violent death, did not enjoy hunting, and often reported having kept menageries of various sorts of animals.

Although I would not hypothesize that war resistance per se would be a sign of psychological health,[27] and indeed some war resisters reported psychological difficulties of various kinds, I do think that resistance to this particular war might be an indication that a young man had the ability to think through his government's objectification of a nation of peasants as a dangerous communist threat. It does seem from their self-reports that the war resisters, who remained to face prosecution for their beliefs, rather than flee to Canada or Europe, were personally less well-equipped for war and more well-equipped for peace than the Green Berets. This may be one reason why they chose the moral ambiguities surrounding the Vietnam war as an opportunity to refuse to participate, whereas the Green Berets used this same war as an opportunity to indulge their need for aggression and excitement.

Our question concerning the contrasting attitudes toward other persons displayed by the Green Berets and war resisters is this: Was there anything in their early experience that predisposed each group to one position or the other? In other words, does childhood experience educate for war or for peace, and if so, how? What I noted in the self-reports of the soldiers, unlike those of the resisters, was that they came from families where they had experienced themselves as helpless objects. The resisters, on the other hand, came from families that were not always happy, but their parents respected them as subjects.

This is not necessarily a matter of violence or the lack of violence, because the war resisters also experienced physical punishment—though much less frequently than the Green Berets. Nor does it have anything to do with whether or not members of each group felt loyalty to their families. As every therapist knows, persons will usually present themselves as coming from good families, only later to reveal the most unusual aberrations. Most persons feel a loyalty to their families, and most feel that, because it is the only family they have known, it must be "normal." What we need, then, is reports concerning concrete relationships between parents and children. Mantell, fortunately, gives us this.

Here is one Green Beret's account of his mother's habitual way of punishing him as a child, an account that is fairly typical of this group except that it is more often the father than the mother who acts the total autocrat:

[Green Beret]: She was, uh, the type of person who said something once and she was stern. When she said, move, you moved then and there or you got killed. She'd take us and beat us half to death . . . with anything . . . yeah, with a chair too [laughs]. . . .

[Interviewer]: You actually bled?

[Green Beret]: Hell, yes. My mother didn't play.

[Interviewer]: Did she hit you on the head too?

[Green Beret]: Shit, yes. Anywhere, wherever she connected, that's where you got it. . . . Hell, it would hurt like hell, you know. You'd cry and then she would continue beating you until you stopped crying and shit, you know. And she had a thing, that you didn't look at her while she was beating you, you know. You wouldn't dare look up at her. I never understood it. She called it, rollin' your eyes. I mean, if you looked up at her she would beat the hell out of you. The last time I told her I wasn't going to cry, I told her, shit, I wasn't going to cry anymore, you know, and if she beat me to death I wasn't going to cry. She continued beating me and, hell, I wouldn't cry.[28]

It is true that the Green Beret parents as a group were much more likely to beat their children severely than the draft resister parents, and Mantell concludes that this has something to do with their adult personalities. No doubt it does. But I am going to guess that there is something even more important in the above passage than the severity of the pain inflicted on the child: the attitude that the Green Beret's mother displayed toward him in the course of the beating. In other words, perhaps it was not just his mother's violence but the human meaning of the violence that influenced him to become a professional soldier. The heart of that meaning, I believe, lies in her injunction not to *look* at her while she was beating him.

Let us place this injunction within the context of Sartre's discussion of relationships with others in *Being and Nothingness*. Sartre tells us that it is through the *look* of others that we come to know the humiliation of having an "object side." It is this gaze of the Other that dethrones each of us from the position of sovereign subject to shameful object.

Sartre's example is a man who, out of curiosity or vice, is bent over a keyhole intent on the scene within a room. So long as he is alone, he is all subject. But suddenly he hears footsteps. There is an abrupt shift in awareness: he is a shameful voyeur, an object of someone else's consciousness. In one way or another, Sartre says, we all originally experience this alternation between subject and object in shame and fear, although later we may also come to experience it in pride.[29]

I would add that so long as a boy's first experiences of himself as an object are experiences of his parents' acceptance and delight, and also so long as he learns that he can assert himself as a subject and not remain merely a delightful toy, this experience of one's object side can be benign. But what of those childhood experiences where the object self, which one presents for the parents' gaze, is made to seem distasteful or wrong? And what of those situations where the assertion of one's own subjectivity is strictly forbidden? In fact, this appears to be just the case in the example of our Green Beret's relationship with his mother as described above. She is only subject; he is the forever degraded and abused object. She will not even allow him to look at her.

Interestingly, Sartre points out that one of the dangers that sadists run is that their victims, like the dying Joe Christmas in Faulkner's novel *Light in August*, will cast a look that reasserts their power as subject over their oppressor as object.[30] It is just such a reassertion of subjectivity that our Green Beret's mother forbids him.

That this interpretation is correct is further borne out by other case histories and by the fact that Mantell himself describes the parents of Green Berets as generally lacking sensitivity to their children as subjects. Their arbitrary assumption of power was their chief common characteristic. Mantell writes:

> They used physical measures to punish their children and simultaneously declared violence to be bad. They scolded, nagged, and screamed at the children, but prohibited their emotional release. While unleashing the

full fury of their anger they ignored and trampled their children's feelings and demanded courtesy and consideration in return. The parents regarded their own behavior and its acceptance by their children as self-evidently correct.[31]

The fathers in these families tended to be even more arbitrary than the mothers. As Mantell puts it, "Perhaps the one prohibition which best exemplifies [the Green Beret] family system is the father's prohibition against personal inconvenience. . . . The family existed to satisfy him."[32]

By contrast, the war resisters' accounts of their families were striking for "the sensitivity they indicated toward family members and the relationships between them."[33] War resister father-son relationships, although the amount of contact varied, were generally marked by "helpfulness, mutual respect for each other's rights and individuality, patience, affectionate expression, understanding, acceptance, and freedom of movement and expression."[34] In other words, the chief difference between the two kinds of families was the degree to which the parents were willing to respect their children as subjects or to arbitrarily treat them as objects.

Nor does attributing the Green Berets' later need to objectify others to some mechanical process, like "identification with the aggressor,"[35] really do justice to the experiential side of the process involved. We can see that by the end of the scenes described above between the Green Beret and his mother, he had *decided* to reassert himself as a subject by refusing to submit. One does not need to resort to a mechanical explanation to understand this, because it is perfectly understandable in human terms. One can always conjecture that just maybe he could have decided otherwise—perhaps, in fact, another child in the same family made a different decision.

On the other hand, such a response is comprehensible in terms of Sartre's ontology. Sartre points out that the need to objectify the Other is a response to finding oneself objectified by the Other. Perhaps, like the sadists in Sartre's description of the conflict of consciousnesses, these Green Berets had developed a particularly rigid need to maintain the Other in the position of object because of their own harsh early experiences. The Other had proved far too dangerous as subject.

The problem, then, seems to be the refusal of the Green Berets' parents to recognize their children as subjects, rather than, per se, the physical punishment that they administered—although I would assume it is easier to brutalize a person with whose subjectivity one refuses to acknowledge. This supposition is further substantiated by the following description of a situation between a war resister and his mother, chosen because of its superficial resemblance to the situation between the Green Beret and his mother analyzed above. Both the text of this account and the family assumptions that we can read between the lines indicate a vast difference between the rights of children as subjects in this family system as contrasted with the Green Beret family system portrayed above:

[Draft resister in response to question about his parents' disciplinary practices]: They would yell at me in one instance and slap me in another. . . .

And I lighted the cherry bomb and I tossed it out onto the street. The problem was that when I tossed it out of the window it exploded in the air right next to the guy painting on the ladder. Fortunately he was a young cat, you know, and he went like he fell off the ladder but he didn't hurt himself. You know, my mother comes in and blah-blah, and she just knew I did it. She just figured it out. And my mother had a hang-up about lying. She couldn't stand lies. And she said, "You used the money that you were supposed to put in the church collection," and I said, "no," you know, but she was really furious. She was really furious. She really thought that I was lying to her and had taken that money and had said that I was giving it to that church thing, you know. And that I had just, you know, turned around and had gone and spent it. And on firecrackers no less! [slight laugh]. And she really—she started to hit me, you know, and I had to put my hands up. She was—she was—I was amazed, she was really furious. She gave me a black eye [slight laugh]. Yeah. And of course afterwards, you know, I was still really pissed at her because she found out afterwards, you know, my father came home and like I didn't want to just blow it and say that my father gave me the money. He came home and, you know, "What happened? The kid's mad. You can tell that something is wrong." My mother must have explained it to him and he said, "Aw, I gave him an extra quarter. What did you do? I gave him the money, you know." And then my mother apologized, but then I was really pissed. Like I was mad because she didn't really give me any chance, you know. And she really flew off the handle.[36]

Note that in this war resister's family, physical violence per se is not prohibited. But it occurs within a context in which the child also has rights. Even though he had admittedly exploded the cherry bomb, which caused the painter to fall off the ladder, the boy felt himself wronged by his mother for not stopping to learn his side of the story. When the father came home, he was aware that his son was "mad" about something and inquired about the problem, indicating a concern for the boy's subjective feelings. In the end, the mother recognized that she was wrong and apologized—an occurrence apparently unthinkable in the Green Beret families, where the parents were always right. The war resister in this account, by contrast, expected to have his point of view taken into account and his rights as a subject respected. The body of Mantell's evidence indicates that this respect for their children also existed in the other war resister families.

We might conclude two things from the contrast between these two kinds of families. First, if a society wished to educate its children for war, it should follow the example of the parents of the Green Berets, who made excellent soldiers. It should ask parents to arbitrarily assign themselves the role of only subjects, their children (with varying degrees of physical violence to emphasize the point) the roles of degraded objects. These parents should never inquire about their children's internal subjective states, but should instead beat (literally or figuratively) them into subjection. They should ask for unswerving loyalty and obedience, but give only whimsical dictates in return. They would thus be likely to produce the kinds of men described by Mantell to Colonel X, a Special Forces officer, in the following exchange:

> [Interviewer, in answer to a question about his overall impression of the Green Beret interviewees]: The Special Forces soldier had been accustomed since early childhood to very hard, severe, and arbitrary discipline . . . in the form of whippings, intimidation, beatings. . . . There was little or no warmth in their families. . . . Punishments took violent forms. . . . There were weapons in the homes. . . . They've been accustomed to the use of weapons since early childhood. . . . They hunted and used the weapons to kill. . . . They did not have strong ties to anything beyond the rest of the family. . . . The families were isolated units. . . . There were no positive expressive emotional ties within the family. . . . They began their sexual experience at a remarkably early age. . . . Average age for first intercourse would be about fifteen and a half. . . . Although they had intercourse frequently throughout adolescence they did not have emotional ties to these girls. . . . They don't report having had deep friendships with anyone. . . . They enjoy the service. . . . They have respect for law enforcement agencies and clearly know what can happen to them if they do something criminal. . . . They've killed many people, men, women and children in Vietnam and have no guilt feelings or nightmares.

> [Colonel X]: You know, you have described Americanism at its best. But somehow you have twisted it around to almost make it sound derogatory. We're so proud of having that kind of individual in Special Forces, it's unbelievable.[37]

Just so, for such individuals are extremely useful in fighting wars.

If, on the other hand, a society wished to educate its children for peace, it would not need to ask that its parents be perfectly loving and gentle at all times, but merely that they exhibit a basic respect for their children as subjects. It should ask that they listen to their children, take their viewpoints into account, and be willing to apologize when they themselves were wrong. The children of such parents would develop a capacity for positive reciprocity, taking into account the point of view of each as the same as self, as a prelude to understanding others on the world scene. So long as one's initial experiences of the Other do not require one to defend oneself against being made a degraded object by distancing and reifying the Other, then such positive reciprocity will, I believe, naturally develop.

Mantell contrasts the war resisters with Green Berets and draftees in their responses to tests designed to measure psychological needs:

> The relatively strongest need among the war resisters was to help others (Nurturance). This need occupies the tenth position in the draftees' hierarchy and the next to last position in that of the volunteers [Green Berets]. The need for many close friendships (Affiliation) occupies positions 4, 11, and 12 respectively in each group. The need to be free in thought and action (Autonomy) occupies positions 2, 5, and 7 respectively in each group. The resisters had their strongest needs in these areas, whereas for the draftees they occupy middle and for the Green Berets low positions. The draftees' and volunteers' relatively strongest need was for heterosexual contact whereas this need was of secondary strength for the war resisters. Finally, the need to complete a task (Endurance) was among the volunteers' strongest, the draftees' second, and the resisters' weakest needs.[38]

Interestingly, as Mantell notes, the need for heterosexual contact demonstrated by the Green Berets and draftees in these test results was not based on deprivation, for most draftees and volunteers were living with wives or girl friends. Nor could this need among the Green Berets be correlated with a desire for intimacy. Indeed one is struck by the Green Berets' lack of feeling for women, American women as well as Vietnamese women, as demonstrated by their answers to interview questions.

Their answers provide a striking contrast to the war resisters' answers, thereby suggesting that strong intimacy-needs positively correlate with a childhood in which one's parents respect one as a subject. Obviously, also, persons whose greatest needs are for nurturing others, forming friendships, and acting independently, as indicated by the war resisters' test results, are not likely to be attracted by hierarchical military discipline or by war. Providing our children with the kind of respectful childhood enjoyed by the war resisters might therefore be a way of educating them for peace.

IMPLICATIONS FOR PEACE EDUCATION

This discussion so far gives cause for both optimism and pessimism with respect to the prospects for creating a peaceful world. On the optimistic side, the possibility that aggression is not an innate drive but a response to being with other persons, that it is an ontological possibility rather than a biological necessity, leads me to hope that the problem of international aggression can be solved through peace education.

On the pessimistic side, leaving aside the enormous difficulties of solving the problems of oppression based on scarcity, which Sartre mentions in the initial quote concerning the Demonic Double, there is also the fact that many persons in the contemporary world have from earliest childhood been educated for war rather than for peace. They have therefore come to need the aggressive reification of others as Demonic Doubles as a way of staving off the recognition that they themselves can be hurt and humiliated. They are also more likely than others to continue this tradition with their own children. The question, I suppose, is whether the necessary changes in childrearing practices and early childhood education for peace can take place in time.

Oddly enough, it seems that the peril of possible annihilation may force some changes in the brutal practices of war and the thinking that leads to war. It is becoming clear to many who do not otherwise agree on politics that nuclear war is a real and totally devastating possibility. The Green Party in Germany, for example, consists of a coalition of persons from the political left, right, and center who have an overriding interest in saving the environment from nuclear and other forms of devastation.

Perhaps there is some cause for hope, even, in the ironic christening of a former movie star president's defense plan with the name of a science fiction movie. "Star Wars" suggest both the impracticality of the plan and disbelief that a defense plan of this magnitude is not secretly an invitation to war. That this same president could refer to the Soviet Union as the "Evil Empire," after the science fiction villains in this same movie, only doubles the irony.

Possibly the U.S. public is beginning to see the fallacy in Demonic-Double thinking as it concerns the Soviet Union. Various "sister city" and other projects for getting to know and find an affinity with Soviet citizens provide a positive counterforce. And the November 1985 summit meeting between the U.S. and Soviet heads of state also provides some glimmerings of hope that the two superpowers can transcend their mutual antagonisms in favor of a project of preventing mutual annihilation.

On the other hand, the problems inherent in both U.S. and Soviet relationships with underdeveloped countries (the "have-nots"), together with the problems among those countries and between their various political factions, are real and provide genuine obstructions to world peace.

The present essay does not pretend to offer political or economic solutions to these problems. Instead it suggests a direction that peace education must take vis-à-vis children if it is to produce world leaders and citizens who are less inclined toward war and more inclined toward peace. I have pointed out that individuals who enjoy war tend to be those with a great need to reify others. Their difficulties are existential, not instinctual. If we could change the childrearing practices that tend to produce such individuals (perhaps recent public concern about child abuse, physical and psychological, is a step in the right direction) and institute corrective measures designed to challenge basic levels of defensiveness and fear in dealing with others, then perhaps the aggressive life stance that inclines individuals and nations toward war would diminish. Educational exercises, for instance, that would lead to experiencing and being experienced by others as a subject should prove corrective.

We should also remember that not all aggression is inappropriate, as psychologist Eric Fromm has pointed out.[39] As a mode of clearing away obstacles for creative activity, aggression can also be helpful. As a therapist, I am frequently amazed at the fact that getting in touch with rage does not destroy a patient's relationships, so long as he or she maintains touch with the subjectivity of the persons involved. In fact, anger in an interpersonal situation, where the aim is to share oneself or to change intolerable conditions rather than to hurt or humiliate the other person, can open positive lines of communication. Of course, the equation of anger (feeling) with aggression (action) is a false equation in the first place: each can exist without the other, although they often exist together. My point is that only negatively aggressive acts, those informed by a negative reciprocity, which refuses to regard the Other as a subject like oneself, is unequivocally destructive in human relationships—individual or group. To learn to see the Other, even in the most provoking of circumstances, as an other self rather than as an antihuman Other is therefore the sine qua non of educating for peace. We must dispose of the Demonic Double if we are to survive.

Obviously the basic principles of existentialist peace education, which involve learning positive reciprocity and unlearning damaging reification, must be put into practice if they are to yield positive results. The preceding discussion might suggest the following ideas for parents and teachers interested in educating for peace. They are for the most part necessarily general, although I think readers should have no difficulty devising their own plans for applying them to specific situations:

1. Treat children as individuals, listening to and regarding their thoughts and feelings, rather than giving commands or otherwise acting as if they were objects rather than subjects. Avoid authoritarianism. Respect children as persons.

2. Encourage children to face the anguish of their freedom by making choices and accepting responsibility for those choices. (Responsibility is not punishment, but natural consequences.)

3. Educate children to identify less with their social roles than with their tasks as complete human beings. Point out, for instance, that one creates one's own unique way of living a particular profession or family role—that one can never be a doctor or a parent as a table is a table, that every marriage and every family are what the individuals involved make of it, and so on. (Such education would diminish the need for the Demonic Double as a reinforcement to a life lived as an escape from freedom—that is, in "bad faith.")

4. Provide an educational milieu that values and encourages the talents of *all* children.

5. Provide games and educational materials that encourage the development of cooperation as well as competition.

6. Develop educational materials that encourage children to see into the minds of persons very different from themselves.

7. Encourage and teach children to carry on genuine dialogue among themselves and with adults, especially with persons of different cultural, racial, or other backgrounds.

8. Allow older children, both boys and girls, to share in caring for and teaching younger children; also allow children to have and care for animals.

9. Teach children to deal with conflict and anger in a direct, nonreifying manner.

10. Encourage children to face and evaluate their own cultural biases in learning about other cultures and other nations. Use educational materials (stories, role-playing, games) that allow children to identify with a wide variety of persons from different cultures, stations in life, races, gender roles, and so on. (Educational games involving setting aside one's own culture or identifying with a person from a different culture might be one possibility for doing this. Creative anthropological studies might be another. Still another might be to encourage children to participate in friendship city projects or to have pen pals in other nations or cultures, especially those that seem to be "enemies." A fourth might involve planned supervised travel that includes cross-cultural dialogue.)

I do not mention direct education about war and peace, although it might certainly be included, because I believe the more subtle human teachings are more significant in encouraging a prediliction toward peace. Obviously, the first of the suggestions listed above is the most important in the light of the ideas discussed in this essay. If one respects children as persons, then it should follow that they will have less of a tendency to reify others. In place of the Demonic Double, our children might then develop an inclination toward positive reciprocity, which precludes seeing others as aliens to oneself, at the same time that it encourages respect for legitimate differences. Such education might even make possible a cooperative solution to the problems of scarcity and oppression, which could make war obsolete. At least we owe it to ourselves as a species to try to find some such solution, considering what appear to be its dire alternatives.

NOTES

1. Jean-Paul Sartre, *Critique of Dialectical Reason* (London, Verso/NLB, 1982), pp. 131–32.

2. Ibid., p. 132.

3. Richard J. Barnet, in *The Giants: Russia and America* (New York, Simon and Schuster, 1977), has given a chilling account of how the United States and the Soviet Union have mirrored each other, acting each as the other's Demonic Double, for sixty years. His conclusion gives one pause for thought, considering the gravity of the issues: "The cold war is a history of mutually reinforcing misconceptions" (p. 94). Similarly, Jerome Frank, M.D., in "Psychological Aspects of International Violence" (in Jan Fawcett, M.D., ed., *Dynamics of Violence,* [Chicago, American Medical Association, 1972]), catalogues the way in which American public opinion has added to this categorization of various other nations as Demonic Doubles, with greater and lesser justification in fact. He points out that in 1942, Americans picked adjectives like "warlike," "treacherous," and "cruel" to describe the Germans and the Japanese. In 1966,

however, all three of these adjectives had disappeared from descriptions of Germans and Japanese (now allies), but Russians were conceived to be "warlike and treacherous" and the mainland Chinese to be "warlike, treacherous and sly" (pp. 34–35).

4. "Existential psychoanalysis" is Sartre's term for his own non-Freudian approach to an individual's history and behavior. Sartre accepts Freud's idea that an individual's "project" (complex, in Freudian terms) is a whole and that the original choice (determination, in Freudian terms) of a way of being in the world derives from childhood, but denies Freudian determinism, together with the existence of the unconscious and universal symbols. Originally published separately in English, "Existential Psychoanalysis" is described specifically on pages 557–74 of *Being and Nothingness* (New York, Philosophical Library, 1956). The whole of *Being and Nothingness* is much concerned with matters of individual psychology, whereas *Critique of Dialectical Reason* attends more to the sociology, psychology, and history of groups and to social science theory in general. *Saint Genet: Actor and Martyr* (New York, George Braziller, 1963) is an application of the principles of existential psychoanalysis to the life of Jean Genet. The volumes of the Flaubert biography (vol. 1, *The Family Idiot*, University of Chicago Press, 1980) combine Marxism with existential psychoanalysis to a greater extent than the earlier biography of Genet. In this respect, the Flaubert biography is the culmination of Sartre's work, for it combines the themes and methodology of existential psychoanalysis from *Being and Nothingness* with the social responsibility that is a persistent theme in *Critique*. The present essay follows this tradition in attempting a psycho-social analysis of the psychology of aggression as this leads to a propensity toward war.

5. Innate aggressionism is a favorite explanation of war from Sigmund Freud to Desmond Morris. Freud, in *Civilization and its Discontents* (New York and London, Norton, 1961), presents a theory of aggression in which all human aggression is the result of a death instinct or primary masochism. According to Freud, the two great principles of Eros (life, sexuality in the broad sense) and Thanatos (the death instinct) are warring together for possession of the future of humankind. Thanatos is responsible for war and could lead to the annihilation of the race. Writers like Konrad Lorenz (*On Aggression*, New York, Harcourt Brace and World, 1966) and Desmond Morris (*The Naked Ape*, New York, McGraw-Hill 1967) say much the same thing in less cosmic terms. According to Lorenz and Morris, human nature has an inborn tendency toward aggression inherited from the lower animals. Ashley Montagu, in *The Nature of Human Aggression* (New York, Oxford University Press, 1976), has attempted to discredit the evidence of the innate aggressionists bit by bit in favor of a more humanly responsible theory of aggression.

6. B.F. Skinner, in *Beyond Freedom and Dignity* (New York, Vintage Books, 1972), argues that aggression is not a matter of instinct but of conditioning. War and other evils, he believes, could be prevented by an adequate technology of behavior that has no use for concepts like "freedom" and "dignity." Indeed Skinner believes these get in the way of a "scientific" approach to problems. In my opinion, it is just such a propensity toward reification as that displayed by behaviorism in its more extreme forms that leads to war in the first place.

7. *Saint Genet*, p. 29.

8. "Bad faith," which is an ontological category in Sartre (see *Being and Nothingness*, pp. 47–70), is defined as the tendency to deny reality in one of two ways: (1) by overemphasizing facticity at the expense of freedom, as when a person identifies with a role (doctor, lawyer, parent, etc.) or his or her own past, or (2) by overemphasizing freedom at the expense of facticity, as when a person denies all responsibility for his or

her past. Later in this essay, we shall see how the first form of bad faith applies to the persons described here.

9. David Mark Mantell, *True Americanism: Green Berets and War Resisters* (New York and London, Teachers College Press, 1974).

10. See John A. Sanford, *Evil: The Shadow Side of Reality* (New York, Crossroad, 1981), p. 25.

11. Ibid., p. 30.

12. See C.G. Jung, "A Psychological Approach to the Trinity," in *Psychology and Religion*, Collected Works, vol. 11; *Psychology and Alchemy*, vol. 12; and *Mysterium Coniunctionis*, vol. 14 (Princeton University Press). Jung also proposed "archetypes" of evil, including an archetype of pure evil, which was purely destructive. It was thus that he explained really disastrous events, such as the rise of Hitler. But it was only if one failed to individuate, ignoring the shadow and failing to bring its messages into conscious awareness, that such phenomena could occur. The *coincidentia oppositorum* thus became highly significant for Jung's own theory of individuation.

13. Mircea Eliade, *The Two and the One* (London, Harvill Press, 1965), pp. 82–88.

14. *Critique*, p. 133.

15. *Being and Nothingness*, pp. 361–430.

16. Jean-Paul Sartre, *Anti-Semite and Jew* (New York, Shocken Books, 1970), p. 13.

17. Ibid., p. 40.

18. Yale University Press, 1943.

19. *Saint Genet*, p. 31.

20. Ibid., p. 34.

21. Ibid., p. 29.

22. Ibid., p. 44.

23. Ibid., pp. 598–99.

24. Ibid., p. 30.

25. Sartre, like Freud, would trace certain life stances back to childhood. Indeed, while he insists on a combination of existential psychoanalysis and Marxism for any valid view of individual/historical processes, he believes that the trouble with contemporary Marxists is that "they have forgotten their own childhoods" (*Search for a Method*, New York, Vintage Books, 1968, p. 62): "It is childhood which sets up unsurpassable prejudices, it is childhood which, in the violence of training and the frenzy of the tamed beast, makes us experience the fact of our belonging to our environment *as a unique event.* . . . [Hence] psychoanalysis alone allows us to discover the whole man in the adult; that is, not only his present determination but the weight of his history" (ibid., p. 60). It is therefore by using the method of existential psychoanalysis that we can discover the early childhood precedents for the propensity toward war and aggression.

26. Mantell speculates on the amazing frequency with which Green Berets had witnessed violent death during childhood and adolescence, suggesting that perhaps not all their exposures were accidental. "I think it more logical," he says, "to assume that the Green Berets felt drawn to this kind of violence and that death held a fascination for them" (p. 97). This would accord with my experience as a therapist, which suggests that persons manage to subtly involve themselves in all kinds of improbable life events that seem exactly tailored to their issues.

27. I am aware, of course, that opposition to the policies of one's own government can on occasion be a sign of psychological illness rather than health. Dogmatic leftism is as suspicious as neo-Nazism. Robert Lindner, for example, reports a case involving

therapy with a communist party member who used the party to give vent to his hatred and aggression (*The Fifty Minute Hour*, New York, Bantam Books, 1955), and Richard D. Chessick reports on the "Psychotherapy of a Terrified Communist" who made the Chinese communists the good guys and the American government the Demonic Double (in Fawcett, *Dynamics* [n. 3, above], pp. 123–27).

28. Mantell, *True Americanism*, p. 39.

29. *Being and Nothingness*, pp. 252–302.

30. Ibid., pp. 405–6.

31. *True Americanism*, p. 24.

32. Ibid., pp. 29–30.

33. Ibid., p. 48.

34. Ibid., p. 62.

35. Anna Freud added this defense to her father's list in *The Ego and the Mechanisms of Defense*, revised edition (New York, International Universities Press, 1966).

36. Mantell, *True Americanism*, p. 68.

37. Ibid., pp. 177–78.

38. Ibid., pp. 308–9.

39. Eric Fromm, *The Anatomy of Human Destructiveness* (New York, Holt, Rinehart and Winston, 1973). See esp. chap. 9, "Benign Aggression."

14

Antony Flew

Peace, "Peace Movements," and "Peace Studies": A Dissenting Voice

FOUR FUNDAMENTALS AND TWO FURTHER POINTS

My concern is with peace as opposed to war, rather than with peace of mind. In this sense certainly peace, like liberty and perhaps health also, is something essentially negative; albeit a necessary precondition for all manner of other more positive goods.[1] Yet in all three cases there are those, uneasy with the idea that anything they rightly recognize as an important good should be negative, who insist on intruding their own positive values into these concepts. Immanuel Kant, for instance, objected to his own first and provisional account of freedom of will: "The preceding definition of freedom is *negative* and therefore unfruitful for the discovery of its essence; but it leads to a *positive* conception which is so much the more full and fruitful."[2] Again, the World Health Organization stated in its original constitution: "Health is a state of complete physical, mental, and social well-being, and not merely the absence of disease or infirmity."[3]

Peace therefore, in my understanding, is, quite simply and very straightforwardly, the absence of war. Whereas peace of mind, or the lack of it, characterizes individuals, wars are started, waged, and stopped by collectives. This point too, like that of the essential negativity of peace, is both in a sense philosophical and, once made, undeniably obvious. Nevertheless, like so many similarly obvious and philosphical points, it does carry practical implications.

Most relevantly it suggests that the study of individual psychology is not going to be able to throw much light upon the causes of wars—something to remember if and when all the established academic interest groups start to demand a slice of the peace studies pie!

A third similarly obvious yet fundamental point is that—with some short-lived exceptions and others of no contemporary interest—wars are waged by and between states. In their turn, states—again with certain exceptions that may for present purposes be ignored—are under the control of governments; and it is their governments that decide whether wars are to start, continue, or stop. The short-lived and contemporary exceptions are civil wars, in which the party opposing what remains of the previous central government and state machinery makes haste to establish its own alternatives—as was the case, for instance, in the Spanish civil war of 1936-39.

Different governments make their different decisions in different ways, and under various constraints. A precious few—a tiny minority of the nearly two hundred represented in the United Nations—are ultimately accountable to a mass electorate. This kind of accountability constitutes a most powerful constraint, making it almost impossible for such a government to start or to conduct a war that is not perceived as wholly defensive. And it makes it very difficult to maintain a military establishment adequate to deter the hostile advances of powers the governments of which are not so constrained. We have here considerations that would, surely, be central to the long-term thinking of any peace campaign, which—unlike, for instance, the World Peace Council—was not in effect and even in intention an instrument of Soviet foreign policy.

The other present relevance of our third glimpse of the too often neglected obvious is to remind enthusiasts for new programs of peace studies that an enormous amount of work bearing upon the stated aims of those programs has been and is being done by persons employed as historians or as political scientists.[4] That reminder given, it becomes incumbent upon those enthusiasts to provide generous hospitality both for that work and for the disciplines required to do it. They also need to think much harder than has been done in Britain of what substantially different and equally or more relevant sort of work it would be appropriate to do as peace studies research.

In fact here neither of these obligations is being met. Where, for instance, in any of the proliferating syllabi can we discover recommendations of works by mainstream historians; works such as *Studies in War and Peace* or *The Causes of Wars* by Michael Howard, sometime Chichele Professor of the History of War and now Regius Professor of Modern History, at Oxford University?[5] And what do we find when we look down the list of current postgraduate research programs published by the School of Peace Studies at the University of Bradford? They range from "British Civil Defense Programs" through "Women in the Peace Movement" and "Asian Education in Bradford" to "Water Resources on the Palestinian Left Bank." Then in the list of dissertations submitted in 1983 we have such remote and esoteric gems as "The Failed

Life and Achieved Poetry of Sylvia Plath" and "The Informal Education of the Postschool Adolescent."[6]

Nowhere, it seems, at any level are the students of the School of Peace Studies directed to attend to the history and hegemonic expansion of the U.S.S.R., or to the proclaimed objectives of its rulers, or to its governmental decision-making processes.[7] These are objectives and processes that are, surely, most relevantly different from those of or in the most important states standing in the way of Soviet power—states therefore by it standardly described and denounced as "imperialist." Instead it appears that the main interests of this Bradford school at graduate and faculty level are either peace studies themselves or what they choose to identify as peace movements.

Continuing to review conceptual truths and factual truisms, the fourth such proposition to take on board is that it has been many years since any government, much less any people, has been even inclined to rate war any kind of good in itself. None now, surely, would contemplate war save insofar as the perceived alternatives were by them regarded as even more intolerable. To say this, of course, is to say, not that there is everywhere an overwhelming reluctance to wage war, but that all governments would, if possible, prefer to achieve their objectives by other means.

It is important to underline this fourth truth. For it is implicitly denied by those who accuse political opponents of war mongering. It is here wryly significant, and significant in many ways, that this charge has been and is loudly and widely urged against President Reagan, who is subject to every democratic constraint, and by persons who never think to bring the same accusation against the government of the U.S.S.R., which is currently conducting a quite extraordinarily savage colonial war in and against Afghanistan. But even that imperial government presumably regards the waging of war as very much the lesser evil as compared with (to them) the intolerability of Afghan independence.

Those who implicitly or explicitly deny this fourth truth often support their denial with an unsound argument, urging that it is governments that launch and maintain wars, whereas peoples are always antiwar. But the first of these two claims is true only in an interpretation that makes it effectively tautological, and the second is false unless it is construed as meaning only that peoples do not regard war as a good in itself. (Certainly in the summer of 1940 the British people was at least as resolved as the British government not to surrender; nor, after Pearl Harbor, were there many voices heard in the U.S.A. urging the president to arrange terms of capitulation!)

This fourth fundamental thus duly grasped, we are ready to appreciate two further points, at least one of which might be seen as a corollary. The first and more consequential is that, until and unless you have assessed the possible alternatives, it is silly to conclude that the initiation or continuation of war is the worst of all possible courses of action. This is again a point that, once made, might seem too obvious to be worth putting. It is, nevertheless, commonly and, in some circles, universally overlooked. Where, for instance, is the film or television critic who has not said of every latest realistic war movie that it demonstrates the futility of war? Yet how could the typical treatment, confined to the actual waging of a war, and without attending to the later consequences of that war, even begin to demonstrate anything of the sort? This piece of conventional foolishness provides an ever welcome occasion to quote the poet-scholar A. E. Housman's blistering rebuke: "Three minutes thought would suffice to find this out; but thought is irksome, and three minutes is a long time."[8]

In the 1930s the conclusion that wars are always futile was standardly supported by a bold generalization, itself usually sustained by no historical knowledge at all: "No war ever settles anything."[9] Because World War I had been billed as the war to end all wars, some of these drastic generalizers perhaps were recklessly confounding two vastly different propositions: "no war ever settles anything"; and "no war settles everything."

There is another equally worthless argument, employed only since World War II, and then only with reference to nuclear weapons. It consists in urging that it is crazy for the superpowers to add or to update their arsenals of these armaments, for both sides already have enough to kill all their enemies several times over. Such superpower moves may or may not be in some ways infatuated. But certainly, and by itself, the argument does nothing to prove that they are.

In this case the begrudged moments of preliminary thought should have been about what it is now conventional to call conventional weapons: ordinary shells and bullets or, for that matter, arrows and spears. Powers going to war have almost always had enough of these to kill all their enemies several times over—if only those enemies were willing to position themselves suicidally, making no efforts either to resist or to reciprocate!

The second and less consequential further point is that it is sometimes downright false, and almost always very misleading, to describe all military budgets as providing for expenditure on defense. This particular kind of confusion, along with many others, can be seen at perhaps its most confounded in the Report of the Brandt Commission. In a characteristically uncritical aphorism the commission contends: "More arms do not make mankind safer, only poorer."

Suppose that the UN, perhaps inspired by a speech from the first prime minister of independent Grenada, had, against that prophet's predicted invasion of UFOs from outer space, launched a fabulous and fabulously expensive program for the defense of planet earth. Then the commission's aphorism would have been apt.

As a contribution to thought about problems of the real world, which is what the whole Brandt Report pretends to be, it is not. For the various separate military budgets thus fallaciously summed to yield a total expenditure on the defense of "humankind" are, of course, all budgets spent by more or less sovereign, separate governments on behalf not of humankind but of their own states.[10] It now becomes obvious that at least some states have been and are made much safer by their military expenditure. Suppose that the state of Israel, for instance, had followed the Brandt Commission in eschewing all military spending as unacceptably impoverishing. Then, certainly, the state of Israel would have ceased to exist long since; and, probably, much of its population would have survived, if at all, only in a condition substantially more wretched than anything suffered in consequence of its enormously burdensome actual defense spending.

When in this way we descend from fictitious global collectivities to concrete and individual fact, it also becomes clear that it is not correct to describe all military expenditure as defense expenditure. If it really were, then how could there be actual or possible threats for all the defense provision to be defensive against? But, of course, it is not. There are actual threats, and real possibilities of future threats. To cite only two of the least disputable and Third World cases, both Colonel Qaddafi, ever since seizing power, and the presidents of Egypt, after the six-day and before the Yom Kippur wars, spent hugely. But no one seriously pretends either that Egypt's expenditure was for any purpose other than to make possible the offensive with which President Sadat opened that later war, or that any of Libya's neighbors have been or are more threatening than threatened.

The way in which talk about defense can be misleading, as opposed to being false, is by suggesting that the main object of the exercise must be to fight and to win any defensive war in which the state to be defended might find itself engaged. This does not have to be and, it seems, increasingly is not so. For the main objective, even the sole objective, may be to deter possible attackers, and thus to prevent rather than to win wars. It is entirely consistent with the pursuit of this objective to hold that the outbreak of the war that you are laboring to prevent would be an unmitigated catastrophe, or that it would not be in any real sense winnable by either party. Indeed the more firmly you hold to these opinions, the stronger your reasons for seeking and maintaining some effective deterrent.

Therefore, however emotionally effective, it is rationally absurd to present the unspeakably appalling consequences of bombardment by a salvo of multi-megaton nuclear missiles—as members of what call themselves "antinuclear campaigns" or "peace movements" so regularly do present them—as knock-down, decisive reasons for abandoning your own deterrents, and leaving such ultimate weapons in hands potentially or actually hostile. It cannot be too often reiterated that both Hiroshima and Nagasaki were de facto "nuclear-free zones."[11] Though paradoxical there was a deal of truth in the old Roman maxim, *si vis pacem para bellum,*[12] a maxim later adapted and adopted for a motto by the aircrew of the USAAF Strategic Air Command: "peace is our profession."

Here the important and crucial distinction is between, on the one hand, actually waging a defensive war, and, on the other hand, deterring an actual or potential enemy from either attacking or securing compliance by threatening to do so. Once this distinction is grasped—as it seems that by the more militant peaceniks it rarely if ever is—then it ceases to be any longer possible honestly to misrepresent the position of all those opposed to unilateral (and always non-Soviet) nuclear disarmament as epitomized in the nutshell slogan, "better dead than red." It would be more, although not perfectly, correct to sum it up as "better some chance, and that not necessarily a very big chance, of being dead, rather than the near certainty of being red." (In any case those of us who are active friends of freedom and enemies of socialism must expect under a Marxist-Leninist regime to be consigned to the slow death of the Gulag. So why should it be thought that we see the situation in the way that these "peace movements" say that we see it?)

DISARMAMENT PROPOSALS

Confronted by the many and various groups customarily calling themselves part of the peace movement, and usually accepted by the media at this their own valuation, some outsiders, but too few, have resented the implicit suggestion that a sincere concern for the maintenance of peace is narrowly proprietary and confined to the militants of this movement.

In the perspectives opened above, I should also perceive it as strange, in countries that have in fact been at peace for many years and in which no one is advocating war, that nevertheless there are nowadays often strong and vociferous movements so describing themselves. In a free society, although only to the extent that it is indeed such, you might expect to find peace movements on two conditions: if a war was already in progress, or if a proposal to start one was being seriously and actively debated. But why now, and why in several countries of western Europe (although not equally in all)?

1. Part of the answer must lie in failures to appreciate points made in the first section above, points that, though elementary and, once made, obvious, just as obviously do escape many persons not otherwise egregiously obtuse. But the clue to another part of the answer is a corollary of one of these same truisms. For wherever it is the case that no government holds war to be somehow good in itself, there one could presumably hope to find an absolute guarantee of permanent peace in ensuring that all demands made under threat of military force shall be accepted immediately.

This is indeed the openly proclaimed policy of the Antitax Party in Denmark, which proposes the installation of a hotline with its prerecorded answer to any ultimatum: "We surrender." It is, surely, significant that everyone identifies one and only one considerable source of ultimata to Denmark! Certainly it does simplify matters if we can ignore both the theoretical possibilities of incompatible ultimata, and the more practical possibility that surrender would leave the captive nation still liable to be involved in the wars of its captors.

2. It appears, furthermore, to be characteristic of all these self-styled peace movements, not only in western Europe but also—curiously and notably—in the socialist block, to demand the one-sided nuclear disarmament of western Europe, and to denounce alleged American or allied (but very rarely if not

quite never Soviet) imperialists, revanchists, and warmongers. This demand may be made for various and widely different reasons, differences that anyone genuinely embarking on study of the issues needs to take account of.

Quakers and other pacifist supporters, for example, regardless of whatever beliefs they may hold about the consequences of alternative courses, reject all employment of military force, whether nuclear or not, as absolutely and indefensibly wrong. Others, though not committed to this total rejection, are convinced that war, or at any rate nuclear war, is the worst of all possible evils. They recognize that it necessarily takes two sides to wage a war, that there is no chance whatsoever of unilateral disarmament by the U.S.S.R., and little chance of its agreement to any really substantial progress toward verifiable multilateral disarmament. So, in hopes of removing all danger of the occurrence of so catastrophic a conflict, they call for the immediate one-sided disarmament of the side that just might be persuaded so to disarm. Whatever their other merits and demerits, both of these are well thought-out positions deserving of some respect. But the great mass of members and supporters appear to belong to one or other of two further groups, whom opponents may agree to nickname the ninnies and the nasties.

The first of these two labels can be applied not unfairly to all who, not wishing to be troubled by hard facts or harder argument, respond to seeing *The Day After* or its like with a knee-jerk reaction: Ban the Bomb! By this intellectual abdication they make themselves available for exploitation by anything calling itself an antinuclear or peace movement.

The second and much less friendly label applies to all those who are consciously and deliberately working for that further and decisive shift in balance of power that must result from further successes for the policies of these movements. (I say "further successes" because, for instance, they have already succeeded in delaying or preventing the development and deployment of the neutron bombs that could, without totally devastating a given district, by simply killing their crews, render the massively superior tank armies of the Warsaw Pact impotent.)

At one time this second group would have consisted almost entirely of members or fellow travelers of communist parties presently in full communion with Moscow. Thanks to the growth of many, if not quite fifty-seven, other varieties of Marxist-Leninists, some of whom profess to disown what they indefinitely describe as Stalinism, that is no longer true. Unsurprisingly, members of this group, who appear to exercise a disproportionate organizational influence, are not all willing to admit aiming to produce a decisive shift in the balance of power.[13] Yet, with straight faces, they can scarcely deny that such must be—"objectively"—the consequence of the implementation of their policies, whatever—"subjectively"—the professed intents of individuals. Those boldly claiming the Trotskyite name, of course, actually boast that, in all external conflicts, they still stand "unconditionally" at the side of the U.S.S.R., characterized, a little oddly, as a "workers' state."[14]

Extreme socialists of all stripes are usually predominant, if not always correspondingly prominent, in the leadership and control of these self-styled antinuclear and peace movements. They also play a similarly disproportionate part in the business of inducing labor unions and other organizations to commit themselves to support their political campaigns. Indeed, whereas it would be utterly wrong to assert that all their members and supporters have been and are either Marxist-Leninists or any other kind of ultrasocialist, it would by contrast be very nearly the exact truth to say that all socialist ultras do support the unilateral dismantling of all (non-Soviet) nuclear weapons.[15] So much so that strength of support for this policy has become one chief criterion for the application of the expression "very left-wing."

3. The very left-wing persons who now control both the national conferences and (what North Americans might think of as) the district or riding locals of the British Labour Party have captured it for the unilateral renunciation of the British nuclear deterrent, the expulsion of all U.S. nuclear forces, and for (what it is trying to sell as) "a nonnuclear defense policy."

This political phenomenon is, surely, intelligible only to those willing to open their eyes to the fact that these very left-wing persons do positively desire that decisive shift in the balance of power. For it must be impossibly difficult for persons apprised of the enormous destructive potential of nuclear weapons to persuade themselves that, in a conflict in which one side enjoyed a monopoly of such weapons and was not somehow effectively constrained from using them, the other side could be anything but totally at the mercy of those nuclear monopolists. How many hours was it, after those first two demonstrations at Hiroshima and Nagasaki, before Japan surrendered unconditionally?

That these persons are not in fact themselves persuaded of this foolishness can be brought out by resolving another puzzle. The writers of op ed columns in the British press all expressed astonishment when Mr. Anthony Wedgewood-Benn and other able but very left-wing members of the National Executive Committee of the Labour Party proclaimed that no threat is either coming or likely to come from the U.S.S.R. How, these editorializers asked, could otherwise intelligent and well-informed politicians be so complacent and so blind?

Theirs was a perplexity that takes only a small tincture of philosophy to ease. It is a matter of the logic of threats and promises. Which of your foretellings of your future behavior toward me shall I perceive as threats and which as promises? My answer is determined in large part by what I myself happen to relish or disrelish. Nor, reviewing the whole continuing record of the Soviet regime from Georgia in 1920 to Afghanistan today, is it possible to deny that the rulers of the U.S.S.R. have been and remain resolved to impose their social system wherever they are able to extend their power. And precisely, or at any rate roughly, that same system of total and therefore totalitarian socialism is that to which such very left-wing persons are by their cloth themselves dedicated. Why should they, therefore, perceive unbalanced Soviet power as a threat? In truth, they do not.

SYLLABI FOR PEACE STUDIES PROGRAMS

1. Suppose we are concerned to construct a program of peace studies. Suppose too that the object is, as it certainly ought to be, to help students to think better and more fruitfully about the great issues of war and peace. Then one thing that we shall certainly want to include is some basic training in the sort of analytical work exemplified in the first two sections of this paper. In the waspish words of one of the greatest of intellectual coaches, J. L. Austin:

> There is nothing so plain boring as the constant repetition of assertions that are not true, and sometimes not even faintly sensible; if we can reduce this a bit, it will be all to the good.[16]

But those syllabi that I and my friends have so far been able to inspect allow no room for any such conceptual training. On the contrary, those who construct and teach these courses seem to be themselves clients, if not to say aggressive promoters, of most of the most popular of these misconceptions and mistakes, falsehoods and fallacies.

For this, and many much more compelling reasons, it becomes hard to avoid the conclusion that to these persons the name of the game is not education but indoctrination.[17] Insofar as that truly is the case, they will not want their students either to learn relevant facts or to acquire critical capacities; not, that is, if those acquisitions are likely to undermine convictions recommended by the indoctrinators. Nor is the indoctrination restricted to the beliefs and attitudes of propaganda for defenselessness. In the first section of this paper I noted how the adoption of a perversely positive redefinition of "peace" licenses the subsumption of all manner of other perceived goods under that term. It is also usual to redefine "violence" in a way similarly perverse, distorting, and enormously overextended.

In the traditional sense, the sense in which violence has acquired and deserves its traditional ill repute, doing violence is the essentially intentional infliction of grievous bodily or sometimes other harm. In the new sense of "violence," occasionally qualified as structural or institutional, although the suggestion of sinister intent is retained, almost anything of which the speaker disapproves (however caused) can be rated (an effect of) violence.

As Stephanie Duzcek observes, "the extended definition of 'violence' . . . enables an extended definition of 'peace.' "[18] It does indeed. For, as she also remarks, "this could include bad housing, poor educational and medical provision, systems of apartheid and discrimination, high unemployment, and poverty. At the international level one could name systems of imperialism, the arms race, or even the international monetary system."[19] The expression "structural violence," like the expression "institutionalized racism," can be a formula for finding violence, like racism, everywhere; including, perhaps especially, places where, in the ordinary and ordinarily obnoxious understandings of these words, there is in truth neither violence nor racism to be found.

2. So far I have settled on one element that, to be genuinely educational, any program of peace studies ought to contain. However, those who have fully grasped the point that the concept of peace is essentially negative can scarcely fail to notice that this means that the innumerable situations to which it can correctly be applied may have little or nothing positively in common. In fact, of course, they do not. But then, that being so, how can we be sure that there is a possible, practically important, intellectual discipline that this nominal expression can conveniently be recruited to designate?

It is a question that may profitably be generalized to embrace also women's studies and black studies.[20] There is no doubt but that peace and women and blacks are all very important. Nor is there any doubt but that there are similarly important questions to be asked and answered about each and all of them. But none of this is by any means sufficient to warrant the desired conclusion. It is not, that is to say, sufficient to show that all the questions thus picked out should be investigated together in the same context. For neither a particular gender nor a particular pigmentation nor the absence of war constitutes an adequate uniting bond. Indeed those who would deny this in the first two cases expose themselves to charges of, respectively, sexism and racism.

Again, even if it be allowed that we do have in peace studies the makings of an integrated and viable academic discipline, to allow this is very different from allowing that it is one that can properly and profitably be pursued at every level—from primary to graduate school. It is, no doubt, always rash to assert that there is anything that no one would be prepared to maintain. Yet, surely, there cannot be many who would want to maintain that sex education should have a place in the curriculum at every level from primary to graduate school. So, once it is admitted that not every subject that has a place at some level has a place at every level, those who want peace studies to be pursued from top to bottom of the educational system will have this further claim to validate.

3. I return now to the question of what, always supposing that we have to have programs of peace studies, these programs ought to contain. Here I have three further suggestions, in addition to a course in *Straight and Crooked Thinking,* with particular reference to questions of war and peace.[21] First, we should need a course in moral philosophy, with particular reference to the medieval doctrine of the just war and contemporary criticism thereof. Yet it would be a maimed and aborted course in either ethics or moral philosophy that confined itself to issues of war and peace. Nor has anyone any business silently to ignore Aristotle's warnings against attempts to teach material of this kind to the immature:

Again, each person judges correctly those matters with which he is acquainted . . . . Hence the young are not fit to be students of Public Affairs. For they have no experience of life and conduct, and it is these that supply the premises and subject matter of this discipline. They are, moreover, followers of their feelings and will, therefore, get no profit from the study—since its end is not knowledge but practice.[22]

Secondly, there is the very practical theoretical study both of strategy in conflict and of conflict-resolution through bargaining. Those wishing to conciliate the Third World First lobby could do this, with absolutely no sacrifice of intellectual quality, by stipulating as required reading for the former not only Clausewitz's *On War* but also Sun Tzu's *The Art of War*. For the latter I can think of no better required reading than Thomas Schelling's *The Strategy of Conflict*.[23]

Thirdly, the indispensable background can be provided only by history and, in particular the history of modern Europe and of North America, of World War II, and of the U.S.S.R. and its expansion. To be fully and effectively relevant this study would have to attend especially to the differences between governmental decision-making and the constraints upon it in NATO and in the Warsaw Pact; to the global objectives of the ruling elite in the U.S.S.R;[24] to the opinions about armament and disarmament of dissidents who have themselves suffered under the absolute and irremovable power of such elites;[25] and to the experiences of those who have lived through *The Day After* a Soviet military occupation.[26]

4. Inasmuch as the four essentials listed in subsections 1 and 3, just above, add up to a lot, it becomes doubly desirable to list a few things that British courses in peace studies insist upon including but could with advantage omit. Take, for a start, the list of lecure topics for the taught, as opposed to thesis, master's degree at the University of Bradford. It is provided by an official brochure, *The School of Peace Studies*. This list includes "Critical Sociology and the Idea of a Just Society," and "Problems of Third World Development," but no reference to the structure and aims of the U.S.S.R. and other states of the socialist bloc.[27] Both are no doubt important topics. But what, other than the adoption of a factitious positive concept of peace, gives them a place in a program of peace studies?

Descending to the second and third years of the undergraduate course we find a list including "Social Alternatives," "Race Relations," "Politics of Developing Areas," and "Social Psychology of Industrialism and Militarism."[28] Once again there seems to be no direct treatment of any of the four matters that I have put forward as essential. Nor is it easy to discern why the first three of the four topics quoted from the Bradford list are thought to be essential to an undergraduate study of peace; nor why industrialism is thought to be significantly related to militarism; nor yet why, if it is, we are still supposed to welcome industrial development.

At the school level again almost anything can be fitted in. Or, rather, almost anything can be fitted in except what might possibly lead pupils to question crucial elements in the standard package of contemporary left-wing convictions and commitments. Document after document claims that peace educa-

tion includes everything from teaching children courtesy and good manners to
"equal opportunities" (always confused with equal outcomes), "human rights,
justice, underdevelopment, ecology, militarism, arms spending, North/South,
United Nations, cooperation"; even "a different history," together with the
study of "conflict between nations" and of the "threat of mass destruction
from nuclear weapons, etc., and choices for action."[29]

In fact the materials are often selected carefully, and then always or almost
always with specific indoctrinative objectives. The same examples, for instance, occur again and again—Northern Ireland, Central and South America,
South Africa, and the Middle East. Yet we never find so much as a passing
mention of Afghanistan, Poland, Cambodia, or the Sino-Soviet conflict. And
even in the Middle East it is always a matter of Israel and its Arab neighbors
and enemies, never the Iran-Iraq war; which is, interestingly, an exclusively
Third World affair, having nothing to do with either superpower confrontation
or class or economics. Sadly, it appears that no one in this professedly educational movement has, or wants to encourage, the curiosity to ask why Indian
nationalists were so quick, and Irish are so interminably reluctant, to accept the
fact of partition. Why is there no Indian Republican Army engaged in a
terrorist war designed to bring the entire subcontinent under a single (and, of
course, Marxist-Leninist) government?

It is deeply significant of the true aims and nature of the entire peace studies
movement in Britain that by far the largest of the labor unions in what would
like to be rated as the profession of schoolteaching, the National Union of
Teachers, at its 1982 conference rejected a motion to affiliate with the unilateralist Campaign for Nuclear Disarmament by the very modest card vote majority of 114,000 to 108,000. This formal affiliation was opposed by the union
president on the revealing grounds that "teachers are not supposed to indoctri-
nate children and we shall demonstrate our bias if we pass this."[30] It is not,
apparently, disputed that indoctrination is being done. But it must not, or not
too obviously, be seen to be done.

NOTES

1. "For above all it will not do to assume that the 'positive' word must be around to
wear the trousers; commonly enough the 'negative' (looking) word that makes the
(positive) abnormality, while the 'positive' word, if it exists, merely serves to rule out the
suggestion of that abnormality"(J. L. Austin, in *Philosophical Papers* [Oxford, Clarendon, 1961], p. 140).

2. This is the first sentence of the second paragraph of the third section of Kant's
Foundations of the Metaphysic of Morals. The demand for a positive conception of
political freedom leads inevitably to one that is in truth the negation of that great
negative good. For a critique of one such illiberal exercise, see 'Freedom is Slavery': a
Slogan for Our New Philosopher Kings," in A. P. Griffiths, ed., *Of Liberty* (Cambridge
University Press, 1983).

3. For an examination of the logical and practical consequences of a definition so excessively comprehensive and positive, see, for instance, my *Crime or Disease?* (London, Macmillan, 1973).

4. See, for instance, *Peace Studies: A Critical Survey,* by Caroline Cox and Roger Scruton (London, Institute for European Defence and Strategic Studies, 1984).

5. London, Temple Smith, 1970 and 1983.

6. Cox and Scruton, *Peace Studies,* pp. 12ff.

7. Consider, as one sobering example, this statement by Admiral Gorshkov, Commander in Chief of the Soviet Fleet: "Soviet sea power, merely a minor defensive arm in 1953, has become the optimum means by which to defeat the imperialist enemy and the most important element in the Soviet arsenal to prepare the way for a communist world." For much more of the similar, see *They Mean What They Say,* edited by Ian Greig (London, Foreign Affairs Research Institute, 1981). This "compilation of Soviet statements on ideology, foreign policy, and the use of military force" ought to be on every peace studies or peace movement reading list. I have yet to find either it or any tolerable substitute on even one.

8. *Juvenalis Saturae* (Cambridge University Press, rev. ed., 1931), p. xi.

9. Those who have visited the Lincoln Memorial in Washington, D.C., should need no further reminder that the American Civil War did achieve, albeit at most grievous cost, its originally stated aim—to preseve the union. Emancipation was a very far from negligible bonus.

10. Critical readers of J. S. Mill's *Utilitarianism* will be reminded of the way in which the psychological hedonists' insistence that everyone individually pursue their own greatest happiness leaves no one available for the collective pursuit of the greatest happiness of the greatest number.

11. Before U. S. readers begin to indulge in orgies of national self-abuse, let it be said by a friendly foreigner: first, that the casualties on these two single bomb raids were rather lower than in some other attacks on Japanese cities; and, secondly and more to the point, that dropping the atomic bombs saved the heavier casualties, both Japanese and American, expected in contested landings on the main islands.

12. "If you want peace, prepare for war."

13. See, for instance, Alun Chalfont, "The Great Unilateralist Illusion," *Encounter* (April 1983); and compare Eric and Rael Jean Isaac, "The Counterfeit Peacemakers: Atomic Freeze," *The American Spectator* (June 1982). Both articles have also been separately reprinted as pamphlets in London, England, and Bloomington, Indiana.

14. See, for instance, Blake Baker, *The Far Left* (London, Weidenfeld and Nicolson, 1981), passim.

15. Not quite, however; because those for whom Peking (Beijing) rather than Moscow is the Third Rome are sometimes eager to maintain resistance against the imperialism of "the new czars."

16. J. L. Austin, *Sense and Sensibilia* (Oxford, Clarendon, 1962), p. 5.

17. See, for instance, John Marks, *"Peace Studies" in our Schools: Propaganda for Defencelessness* (London, Women and Families for Defence, 1984); and Cox and Scruton, *Peace Studies.* As far as what has been going on in Britain is concerned, these two publications are together entirely decisive.

18. "Peace Education," in John Thacker, ed., *Perspectives. No. 11* (University of Exeter, School of Education, 1983).

19. Stephanie Duzcek, "A Practitioner's Perspective," a speech to a National Council of Women conference, "Peace Education in Schools" (March 3, 1984).

20. See Cox and Scruton, *Peace Studies,* pp. 9–10.

21. I mention, honoris causa, R. H. Thouless, *Straight and Crooked Thinking* (London, Hodder and Stoughton, 1930). But what was in its day a minor masterpiece is by now badly outdated. So instead compare, perhaps, my own, *Thinking Straight* (Buffalo: Prometheus Books, 1977).

22. *Nicomachean Ethics,* 1094B28–1095A7.

23. Harvard University Press, 1963.

24. See, for instance, *They Mean What They Say,* mentioned in n. 7, above.

25. See, for instance, Vladimir Bukovsky, *The Peace Movement and the Soviet Union* (London, Coalition for Peace through Security, 1982). For examinations of the twists and evasions of the chief guru of that movement in Britain, see Scott McConnell, "The 'Neutralism' of E. P. Thompson," *Commentary* (April 1983) and Gerald Frost, "Portrait of a Peace-Fighter," *Encounter* (May 1984).

26. From an overwhelmingly abundant and correspondingly frightful literature take, for instance *The Captive Mind* by the Nobel Prize-winning Polish poet Czesla Milosz (New York, Vintage Books, 1981). Published first in 1951 it contains material not only on the occupation of Poland but also on the occupation and incorporation into the U.S.S.R. of the three Baltic republics. Compare too, as always, Alexander Solzenitsyn, *The Gulag Archipelago* (London, Collins Fontana, 1976–78).

27. P. 2. It must be noted both that "critical sociology" is a code expression for a kind of Marxist sociology, and that Bradford's study of Third World development shows no sign of attending either to Peter Bauer's criticism of "development economics" and government-to-government economic aid, or to the success stories of those previously poor countries that have heeded the advice of Adam Smith rather than that of J. K. Galbraith.

28. Ibid., p. 7.

29. All these quotations come from what the Campaign for Nuclear Disarmament teachers' affiliate, Teachers for Peace, offers as a definition of "peace education." But they could be paralleled in many other documents issued, often by Local Education Authorities, for the misguidance of teachers. See Marks, *"Peace Studies,"* passim.

30. *The Times* (London), April 14, 1982. Of the six national officers elected at the 1984 CND conference, all were socialist activists of some stripe. Of the twenty new council members, sixteen were socialist activists, two of them members of the Communist Party (Muscovite). The two conference organizers were also recent members. Of the remaining six new council members, one professed to be a Liberal, another an Ecologist, and a third a Christian but a contributor to the Communist Party daily paper *Morning Star.* It is, therefore, not surprising that, whereas the CND June 1984 turnout against President Reagan numbered 50,000, the movement mustered only 300 when on December 8, 1985, it was shamed into a token demonstration against Soviet missiles. It can never be repeated too often that these Soviet SS20s are the ones targeted on us; or that the sole purpose of installing the Cruise and Pershing IIs, which give such offense to the Soviet government and to its backers in the NATO countries, is to neutralize this threat.

15

Haim Gordon

Peacemaking in Action

Recently I received a chain letter that originated in Hiroshima and Nagasaki; it appealed to scholars around the world to call for complete prohibition and elimination of nuclear weapons. Shortly after receiving the letter I duly wrote ten letters to colleagues in Israel and other countries encouraging them to continue the chain. But while going through the motions of sending these letters, I had a vague feeling of futility. The letter might arouse the awareness of some of my colleagues, yet this, in itself, was not peacemaking in action. Something essential was missing. I can best describe this essential lack by words such as "spiritual depth" or "direction," or "philosophy and vision of peace." But for these words to attain meaning in the context of peacemaking, one must indicate how they can be translated into daily acts, into educational and political acts.

One recognizes the need of peacemaking when one realizes that every war or revolt, every buildup of nuclear arsenals, in any country in the world, has global implications. Shootings and bombings in Nicaragua, Iran, Iraq, Lebanon, Afghanistan, or South Africa affect us all. Nuclear buildups anywhere threaten all human existence. This situation may be disheartening, but it also indicates that every person in the world can contribute to peacemaking. One can begin to work for peace in one's immediate milieu by addressing the causes and justifications given for war: hatred, exploitation, bigotry. One can and should also address the justifications given for the devastating nuclear buildup. In such work the peacemaker must address specific issues, and must address them with a depth of understanding, with a direction for development in mind, and with a philosophy and vision of peace nurtured by the spiritual traditions treated in this book.

Put differently, many persons who have been active in the peace movement, or who have attempted to educate for peace have mainly reacted to political or social developments. Only a few have sought to initiate new approaches that address the basic problems underlying our living on the brink of war. As reactors, peacemakers are essentially in a weak position: they are *not* calling the moves; they are merely reacting to the acts of others. And when one merely reacts to events, one is usually not affecting the essential social and political structures that led to, say, the terrifying nuclear arsenals that the superpowers wield. For instance, even if the peace movement in Western Europe had recently succeeded in convincing the governments involved not to station Pershing missiles in Europe, one wonders if anything essential would have changed in the balancing game of nuclear brinkmanship that currently characterizes East-West relations. Antony Flew makes an important point when he holds that given the totalitarian tendencies of the Soviet Union, given its history of a blatant quest for domination and of oppression of human rights, given the political cynicism that has characterized many of the decisions of the leaders of the Soviet Union in the past half century, conceding to the demands of the Soviet Union may often lead the West closer to war than to peace. All this is not to suggest that the peoples of Western Europe should agree to the stationing of Pershing missiles near their homes. Rather my point is that, if they wish to be peacemakers, they must address the problem of peace on a level that allows them to take initiatives. This can be done only when one lives peacemaking not only as a reaction to developments, but also as a way of life.

One of the few areas where a person can initiate is education. At all levels, education can be an oasis of humane interaction in the desert of ruthlessness that encompasses human existence. The structure of, what Sartre calls, the social and political ensembles in which humankind finds itself, often leaves a person impotent in the face of social, economic, or political developments. In his life Sartre did not accept this impotence; he struggled against it, while struggling for justice. But he often equated struggling and initiating change with bloodletting, with war and rebellion, with violence. He overlooked the fact that educating for peace can also be a way of struggling, of initiating change.

Educating for peace without relating to injustice and to evil is not only an attempt to evade one of the major issues that leads to war, it is also a watering down of the entire venture of education for peace. In the twentieth century, after Hitler and Stalin, few persons will need convincing that evil exists, and that certain regimes, in certain countries, at certain times, are bastions of evil. Without going into details it is safe to say that any regime whose manifestations are described by words such as "totalitarian," "fanatic," "genocide," "concentration camps," "torture of prisoners," is governed by persons who themselves are evil and who are propagating evil. Educating for peace loses its significance and its ultimate meaning if it does not teach persons to condemn, to struggle against, and—if need be—to combat such manifestations of injustice and evil.

Now, if one is not careful, everything can become sticky. If combating evil is also education for peace, where are the limits? Cannot Ayatollah Khomeini hold that by sending young Iranian teenagers to clear Iraqi minefields with their bodies so that regular troops can cross mine-infested areas safely, he is combating evil and educating for peace? Of course Khomeini can hold such views, but if he does he is wrong for two basic reasons. In educating for peace one not only assumes responsibility for world history, but also for every individual life. Such is the attitude one must assume in combating evil. Furthermore, one cannot educate for peace if one accepts the oppressing of freedom which is central to Khomeini's regime. In short, a person, like Khomeini, who squanders human life and oppresses human freedom is propagating evil and not combating it.

Contrary to Khomeini, the major religions teach that peacemaking can be blended with a struggle against evil and an initiating of just and meaningful ways of life, when it is motivated by a celebration of human life and of personal freedom. Such a celebration, which demands courage, is rare in the world of alienation and oppression that encompasses us, hence its power of attraction. Love is such a celebrating.

Peacemaking can attain depth, direction, and vision when it is an expression of joy in life, when it is motivated by a passionate love for earthly existence. Fear of war or of other persons is not a source of personal strength from which the peacemaker can draw the power to act. Anyone from a Western democracy who has traveled to countries subject to totalitarian regimes or to ruthless dictators will immediately sense the lack of joy in life among the inhabitants (of course, not on the tourist track). They may be polite and attentive; but they will never let go and be happy-go-lucky. Hannah Arendt has shown how the totalitarian regime breaks down all meaningful interaction between persons until a Kafkaesque chiaroscuro of insipid human relations prevails. No expressions of joy in life or of a passionate love for this earthly existence can emerge in such a regime; because joy in life is a manner of sharing oneself with others, and a passionate love for this earthly existence can be expressed only through giving oneself to nature, to other persons, or to a life of spirit. In short, totalitarian regimes are a wasteland of human communion, joy, and love. In such desolateness no peacemaker can thrive. Think of the failure of Andrei Sakharov's call for peace to arouse even a faint echo among his fellow citizens of the Soviet Union.

Yet how do peacemakers' joy in life and passionate love for this earthly existence help them attain depth, direction, and vision? In her essay above, Betty Cannon shows how a lack of joy and love characterizes the Green Berets, who feel comfortable waging war and are indifferent to killing and inflicting suffering. Following Cannon's insight one perceives that when a person lives joyfully and lovingly, the Demonic Double will find it difficult to attain a dominant role in one's consciousness. This finding supports my tenet, but it still does not answer the question posed.

Peacemakers can attain depth, direction, and vision in their endeavors when they act as whole beings. Even before discussing this point, one can now understand why my continuing the chain of letters that originated in Hiroshima and Nagasaki was not very meaningful to me. It was not an act of my whole being, because I was merely a number in a series. It was not my personality, my joy in life, or my love for this earthly existence that I was expressing; rather, I was using myself as an object to transmit my fear of nuclear annihilation to my colleagues.

I have purposely stressed joy and love because these are experiences in which a person's entire being is united—there is no division in one's soul or between one's body and one's soul. Persons who act with their entire being are pursuing a specific direction; their act emerges from the depths of their being and allows them to penetrate deeply into the matter at hand. I shall give examples of such peacemaking shortly, but first it is important to indicate that relating with one's entire being is at the core of the religious experience. Religions have often buried this core experience under centuries of dogmatic sediment, but as shown in part 2 of this book, it need not remain buried.

Peacemakers are thus faced with a two-step challenge. They must first learn to unite their entire being; then they must learn to direct themselves, as a united being, to action within the political realm, and to education. But one should point out immediately that the realm of politics is usually not amenable to such a way of life. The vast majority of politicians are concerned with developing strategies that will allow them to remain in power, and to enlarge their power. Peacemakers are not out to seek power, or to find ways of benefiting their supporters; they are not speaking the language of most politicians, they are not playing that game. Hence, peacemakers can thrive only on the border area of mainstream politics. That is their strength, but also their weakness.

In the realm of education peacemakers who unite their being can be powerful and influential. The educational sayings on peace spoken by the Hebrew prophets, Jesus, Buddha, Gandhi, and Muhammad, who spoke as whole beings, can be as inspirational today as when they were first spoken. Something of such inspiration emanates from educators who act from their entire being. Before progressing with the general theme of my argument, let me give a concrete example that will present much of what I have said up to this point in a more earthly perspective.

A CONCRETE EXAMPLE

In 1979 I began to work on establishing relationships of dialogue between Jews and Arabs living in Israel. I soon perceived that the relationships between many Jews and Arabs were characterized by existential mistrust, which may be defined as a relationship arising between two persons or groups when one of them believes that the other denies it the right to exist and to realize its potentials in that part of the world where they both live. The relationship is expressed by the attitude: if I intend to continue living here, I cannot trust you. This mistrust hinders attempts to establish sincere relationships between Jews and Arabs, and often distorts the mistrusting person's way of life. I soon learned that very little had been done to diminish this mistrust.

I have described my attempts to initiate Buberian dialogue between Jewish and Arab adults, so as to diminish the existential mistrust between them, in my book *Dance, Dialogue, and Despair: Existentialist Philosophy and Education for Peace in Israel* (University of Alabama Press, 1986). Here I shall briefly review my attempts to transfer the knowledge I attained in working with adults to pupils in Jewish and Arab secondary schools in Israel. My initial idea was to develop a curriculum for dialogue between Jewish and Arab secondary school students, to be adopted as a course of studies for all Israeli secondary schools by the Ministry of Education. I succeeded in developing the curriculum; an experimental program, which tested the curriculum, diminished mistrust between many of the three hundred Jewish and Arab pupils who participated, in addition to teaching them about their prejudices concerning the other group. But I totally failed in my attempts to attain a hearing where I could describe these successses to the Ministry of Education. The successes reemphasize the points made in my book that Buberian dialogue can significantly diminish existential mistrust. Yet I believe that peacemakers have much more to learn from my failures.

Yes, my failures are instructive, because as a person who was working for peace I refused to accept that once peacemakers begin to succeed they will find themselves locked in a power struggle—a struggle against devious bureaucrats and dishonest politicians, bigots and liars who will do everything in their power to isolate them and minimize their influence. I could have learned this simple truth from history: Gandhi, Martin Luther King, Jr., and Sakharov found themselves locked in such a power struggle despite their wish to live and work solely as peacemakers. But in my myopia I refused to believe that it could happen in Israel. I was wrong, dead wrong. But in order to learn from this failure, and from the successes, I must briefly review the curriculum developed for peacemaking in Israeli secondary schools.

The curriculum was centered around the philosophy of Martin Buber, which holds that in dialogical encounter a person learns to relate to one's own otherness and to the otherness of one's partners. A dialogical encounter does not occur when a person merely learns some facts about the other person or persons, or, in contrast, identifies fully with the other person, such as occurs in empathy. What is more, neither the learning of facts about another person nor identification with that person can lead to the diminishing of mistrust. Trust, according to Buber, emerges when a person learns to accept other persons in their otherness.

Creating opportunities for a dialogical encounter between Jewish and Arab eleventh graders was logistically problematic. In Israel Jewish education is in Hebrew, Arab education in Arabic. The schools of each community are separate. Arab pupils learn Hebrew from an early age, few Jewish pupils learn Arabic. Although they might meet in the street, on the beach, at a movie, or in the market, Jewish and Arab teenagers usually evade any personal exchange. They warily watch each other, viewing each other as potential enemies. Hence, the curriculum had to not only teach Jewish and Arab teenagers the signifi-cance of Buberian dialogue for their own life, but also to create circumstances in which Jews and Arabs could meet and attempt to relate to each other dialogically.

Buber's philosophy influenced the three focal areas of the curriculum: learning, meeting, and assuming responsibility for relating dialogically outside class. The pupils learned *about* dialogical encounter and its significance for each person's life through the reading of essays by Buber, and works by novelists who describe such encounters. In exercises in class, they were given the opportunity to relate dialogically to each other. In other words, after learning *about* dialogue, Jewish pupils first attempted to relate dialogically to fellow Jews, and Arabs to fellow Arabs.

Another area of learning was about the other group. Some history and literature of the other group was read and discussed in class, but the main learning came about through the regular meetings of Jewish and Arab teenag-ers. Arab and Jewish classes were paired, and their pupils met every six weeks for, at least, a three-hour workshop. During these meetings the concepts that Buber developed on dialogical relationships became vivid, for the otherness of the other immediately struck one's eye. Later in the school year these meetings were extended to include an overnight stay at the house (or tent) of a member of the other group, a one-day trip together to the holy places of each religion, and a week-long trip together to Egypt. During these trips quartets made up of Jewish and Arab teenagers were assigned learning exercises to perform in the streets of Jerusalem, Cairo, and Alexandria. In addition to their intellectual challenge, these exercises also taught the pupils how to act responsibly and dialogically outside class.

I was not surprised at the positive results of this intense educational program, especially because I had succeeded in establishing Buberian dia-logue between Jewish and Arab adults in a similar program. I was somewhat surprised at how rapidly mistrust vanished in those teenagers who were willing to give themselves to the educational process. The ontological results of these findings are clear: there are ways of diminishing existential mistrust between Jewish and Arab teenagers, and bringing them to relate to each other dialogically and trustfully. The pivot of a dimishing of mistrust cannot be intellectual learning; it must be live encounters in which Jewish and Arab teenagers confront each other while confronting the difficult questions of their mutual existence in an area where Jewish-Arab strife is a common occurrence. At the first meeting between Jews and Arabs, six weeks into the school year, the pupils were divided into quartets of two Jews and two Arabs, and were asked to discuss in the quartet why they mistrusted members of the other group. Soon they were trustfully discussing the problems of their mutual mistrust.

No. The positive results did not surprise me. Dialogue, as Buber had shown and as I had proven in similar undertakings, is a powerful force. It can break down barriers of mistrust. What did surprise me was what one might call—to borrow an image from Bertolt Brecht—the "Galileo telescope" effect. Let me explain.

In his play *Galileo,* Brecht reenacts the official response to the announcement by Galileo, who had focused his telescope on Jupiter, that he had discovered moons circling that planet. These moons were not mentioned in Aristotle's work or in the Scholastic studies based on Aristotle. Hence members of the religious and political establishment denied Galileo's findings. When he asked them to look through the telescope and report what their eyes saw, they refused. He set up a telescope, focused on Jupiter, in court, but the religious and political leaders passed by it without daring to look through it.

The problem that many peacemakers face has nothing to do with their arguments or their findings or their convictions or their presentation of the truth. The problem they face is that members of the political and religious establishment will pass by their "Galileo telescope" and refuse to look through it. This happened with my curriculum for Jewish-Arab dialogue in Israeli secondary schools. The general manager of the Israeli Ministry of Education, Mr. Shmueli, met with me willingly as long as the curriculum was in its development stage, as long as my research was in progress. But once the data and conclusions were in—once there was need for him and his staff to look through the telescope and see the moons circling Jupiter—I became persona non grata. The fact that one could teach Jewish and Arab teenagers to reach mutual trust was a truth too difficult for their myopic minds to ingest. Hence Mr. Shmueli refused to read my findings, refused to grant me a meeting, and did everything in his power to erase my research from the horizon of the Ministry of Education.

One may, of course, argue that my experience is limited. It is. But again and again one encounters the "Galileo telescope" effect. Consider the televised discussion that followed the ABC presentation of the film *The Day After,* which portrayed a partial nuclear holocaust and the ensuing mass deaths from radiation, the destruction of an entire social and economic structure, and the return to barbarism. The attitudes that emerged in the discussion of the film were in many respects as depressing as viewing an actual nuclear holocaust. The discussants were six or seven middle-aged white men, dressed in elegant suits, who had attained some prominence in politics, or science, or the arts. No blacks, women, hispanics, teenagers, or young persons were invited to respond to the filming of a partial destruction of the planet. And these well-dressed men bypassed the horror, the barbarism, and the devastation depicted in the film, just as the elite of Florence bypassed Galileo's telescope. Except perhaps for the scientist, all of them presented to their hundred million viewers platitudes that allowed them to evade confronting the issue of nuclear annihilation.

The above example supports a major conclusion: peacemaking must begin at the grassroots level, because that level is its power base. The quest for depth, direction, and vision may succeed, as all religious leaders have advocated, when it is linked to the day-to-day life of the persons involved. Furthermore, when such a quest stems from the way of life of the peacemaker, it will possibly encourage others to undertake peacemaking. Thus, there is no essence of peacemaking—there is only a series of daily acts. Peacemaking acquires depth when persons address issues that engage them at the deepest possible level; it acquires direction through those daily deeds by which persons struggle to extract themselves from the quagmire of hatred and war in which all persons on this globe find themselves. And such daily acts, with other persons, can occur only at the level where persons meet each other as persons, not as functions.

I am not arguing that continuing a chain of letters against nuclear weapons, or writing to one's representative about arms control, is not, at times, helpful. Rather, I maintain that these actions are secondary or tertiary. They attain some significance when they are supported by a struggle at the grassroots level—such as attempts to educate persons not to relate to others as Demonic Doubles. Recall once again the failure of Sakharov's call for peace to arouse any response in the Soviet Union. One reason for this failure is that the Communist Party and the Soviet regime, through organized terror, have done their utmost to totally destroy the grassroots level of interaction and political involvement in the Soviet Union. I suspect that what particularly enraged the Soviet regime about Lech Walesa's Solidarity Movement in Poland is that it emerged as a grassroots movement and succeeded in that capacity. In the process of doing everything in their power to annihilate the possibility of any grassroots involvement and interaction, totalitarian regimes are also sterilizing the ground upon which peacemaking can flourish.

The inevitable objection that immediately arises is: if one begins peacemaking at the grassroots level, one may perhaps never influence the political establishment that is leading the world to the brink of a nuclear disaster. And the inevitable answer to this objection is: if work at the grassroots level were no threat to a political establishment, totalitarian regimes would not expend such energies to hem in this area of human interaction. The founders of the world religions recognized the powers that may emerge at the grassroots level; hence their message appealed to persons at that level. What is more, they emerged as challengers of the political establishment; in the monotheistic religions Moses challenged the pharoah, Jesus the Pharisees and the Romans, Muhammad the pagan leaders of the Arab peninsula. They knew that the spirit of a religion reveals itself at the grassroots level; they knew the political establishment often interferes with such revelation—Buddha left his kingdom to seek enlightenment—and that this spiritual power, which religious leaders have revealed and which emerges among the people, can threaten a political establishment and, at times, even conquer it. Think of the role of "people power" in the overthrow of Ferdinand Marcos in the Philippines.

Peacemaking at the grassroots level is a spiritual undertaking. It requires that a person relate as a whole being, express one's joy in life and one's love of this earthly existence in the concrete day-to-day reality that one encounters. Peacemakers will succeed only when they can partially change that daily reality, so that space be made for relationships that allow the spirit to emerge.

Once such relationships arise, they have a life of their own; they can influence persons and processes profoundly; they can bring about changes years later. But there are no two ways about it. Without space being made for persons to relate as whole beings, peacemaking is merely an intellectual exercise. To clarify what I mean by "the emerging of spirit," let me return to my experience of developing a curriculum for dialogue between Jewish and Arab teenagers.

BANALITY AND EVIL

As a peacemaker, I realized that the racist, the fanatic, and the cynic are enemies of dialogue and peace. Hence I tried to evade working with such Jews and Arabs. But I did not grasp that many of these enemies of peace donned liberal robes and mingled with liberals in order to acquire an aura of legitimacy. I saw a situation and what needed to be done, but I did not perceive the broad prevalence of two points that Hannah Arendt repeatedly stressed: (1) in the twentieth century we are often confronted with the banality of evil; (2) the promoters of this evil frequently attain legitimacy among intellectuals and liberals through linguistic manipulations by which they attempt to conceal both their banality and their evil. But in order to concretely describe what I mean, and to show how all this is connected to the emergence of spirit in my work, I must give some background information concerning Jewish-Arab relations in Israel and the Middle East.

Around three million one hundred thousand Jews and six hundred fifty thousand Arabs are citizens of Israel. On the West Bank and in the Gaza Strip live a million and a quarter Palestinian Arabs, some of whom are citizens of Jordan. Israel is a parliamentary democracy, but the West Bank and the Gaza Strip are under Israeli military rule. The bureaucratic administration that deals with Jews and Arabs is, for the most part, in Jewish hands. It was with this large, well-entrenched bureaucracy (which is in close communication with the Israeli Secret Service) that I was confronted with the banality of evil.

What does Hannah Arendt mean by the banality of evil? She means that Mephistopheles, as the clever seducer of a person to freely choose evil, has all but disappeared. Instead, many of the persons who participate in doing evil do it as if it were a normal daily chore—hence they have no pangs of conscience. Like the Green Berets whom Betty Cannon describes, as long as somebody with authority gives them the order to do something, they will perform without considering whether the deed is just or not. Hannah Arendt showed that this lack of conscience is linked to an unwillingness or an inability to think. Thinking, she argued, ontologically counters the banality of evil. Here is where the bureaucrat comes in. To be a perfect bureaucrat one must learn to *not* think, but to administer; to *not* make decisions of conscience, but to make decisions of prudence; to not worry about being moral, but to be effective.

Because they refuse to think, or to consider the morality of a decision, perfect bureaucrats will never speak straightforwardly. They develop a language and a system of signs, clichés, and cues that hint at their intentions, but do not explicitly say what they mean. Such a language, such a constant emphasis on prudence, such an unwillingness to think, allow bureaucrats to do evil, seemingly without its ever coming to their attention. Instead of seeing what actually happens and responding to it, bureaucrats plunge into administrative tasks, conceal the outcome and meaning of their deeds with administrative language, and answer with clichés all questions concerning the morality of their doings. In short, by selling their freedom to the regime, and by refusing to think, these promoters and perpetuators of evil become puppets of the establishment.

I need not go on. We have all met these bureaucrats; they surround us and like leeches suck the blood of our freedom. In totalitarian regimes these puppets become the backbone of the power structure—hence all ethical considerations disappear. Such leeches, both Jewish and Arab, did their best to hinder my attempts to educate for peace and dialogue. But they often fail, because in a democratic society banal perpetuators of evil often—by arousing the scorn of free persons—encourage a rebellion that allows the spirit of peace and dialogue to emerge.

One Bedouin school at which I worked was a group of concrete-slab buildings atop a hill in the middle of a dusty desert. No paved roads, electric or telephone wires connected the school to the rest of the world, although there was a bus stop on the road that passed half a kilometer from the school. There were no buildings in the neighborhood, neither were there Bedouin tents. The pupils and some of the teachers resided in tents scattered about in an area of seventy square kilometers. To reach school, the pupils had to get to a main road, at times four kilometers from their family tent, and catch the school bus. And yet, a few of these pupils had a much deeper openness to the need of Jewish-Arab dialogue than adults such as the principal of the school, many of their teachers, and the bureaucrats at the Ministry of Education.

After two years the education for peace curriculum was terminated in this school—because it succeeded. The principal of the school, a perfect bureaucrat, was afraid of any innovative program that threatened to bring about change. He had no inkling as to how one copes with personal development. What particularly threatened him was that the Arab pupils, through their experience of dialogue, were learning to live and to think as free human beings. Yes, the perfect bureaucrat will be happy with a program for peace if it fails to appeal to pupils as free persons. Thus, many of the peace programs taught at universities and secondary schools are superficial. They must be superficial in order to please the bureaucrats in charge—and I suspect that many teachers comply with this bureaucratic approach in their classroom work. For a program to be successful, it must be profound—it must appeal to the deeper levels of a person's being, which include freedom and the ability to think, to evaluate, to decide.

Bureaucrats and superficial teachers also fear an innovative program because it will demand of them personal change and the attempt to bring about change in their immediate milieu. They dread this new responsibility, this need to act courageously. But only when one acts and speaks courageously will the possibility for an emergence of the spirit arise. The quicksand of mendacity and cowardice that these contemporary Pharisees entice others to is a continual attempt to bring down all believers in spirit. —Enough. Analyzing these enemies of justice and peace will not indicate how the spirit may emerge in the work and life of the peacemaker. Here is where a new problem arises. As long as one is discussing the enemies of peacemaking, one can analyze. But to describe the emergence of the spirit, one must tell a story.

TWO WAYS OF LEARNING

In the next chapter in this book, "Fun, Fantasy, and Failure in Educating for Peace," I tell the story of Diana Dolev's work as a peacemaker. Here I will add to that story, albeit briefly. Yet why is it that one can convey the spirit of peacemaking in a story and not in an essay? And how is a story linked to interaction at the grassroots level?

In order to describe *who* a specific person is as a whole being, one must tell a story. Otherwise one is merely describing *what* he or she is. He is a businessman, a carpenter, a drug addict; she is a banker, a cab driver, a lesbian—these appellations merely describe *what* a person is. They describe the person as a finished product that one can label, in short, as an object. But consider: "It happened, late one afternoon, when David arose from his couch and was walking upon the roof of the king's house, that he saw from the roof a woman bathing; and the woman was very beautiful" (2 Sam. 11:2). This sentence is the beginning of a story. It describes two persons, David and Bathsheba, who are developing, making decisions, changing—in short, who actively live their freedom, hence can express themselves as spiritual beings.

Peacemaking in action is *actively* living one's freedom. The emphasis is on *actively;* because if persons do not act and speak for peace, if they do not continually initiate and create, they are sympathizers, not actors. There are no stories to tell about sympathizers. Only persons who act have stories to tell, only they may taste glory or bite the dust. In education the distinction is significant. Often pupils believe or feel that by acquiring knowledge they are already altering the situation at hand. But they are not. Acquiring knowledge may alter a situation only if this knowledge guides one's actions and words while interacting with other persons.

In Israel there are a few educational programs that teach Jews and Arabs *about* each other, describing the different cultural and religious heritages. But all these programs—because they educate sympathizers and ignore the importance of meeting and acting, because they relate to Jews and Arabs as objects and not as persons who have a specific story to tell—all these programs are merely a form of intellectual masturbation.

Consider the following story: Joseph (fictitious name), a pupil in Diana Dolev's class, told his fellow pupils at the beginning of the year that he believed that all Arabs should either be forced to emigrate from Israel or be killed—

"There is no need for them here in Israel, and I want them to disappear from my life." When asked why he chose to participate in the education for peace program, he answered that the class fitted perfectly into his daily schedule. Despite this attitude, he participated actively in what was being taught. He was late to the first Jewish-Arab meeting in the Arab school and had to reach the desert school, described above, on his own. Only after he arrived did he realize that "three months ago I would have been scared to come to an Arab school alone and would never have agreed to meet with those Arabs." Some of his fellow pupils, who had adorned themselves with liberal feathers from the beginning of the program, responded: "How did it come into your mind to be afraid of Arabs?" They ignored his authentic response and the story of his personal development. Nor did they acknowledge that the program had created the space and the opportunity for the emergence of new relationships between Joseph and Arabs.

The spirit of peacemaking emerges when persons recognize their own difficulties in relating to other persons as partners in this world, with whom they must share their existence. It emerges when one acknowledges the significance of every human life as contributing to the manifoldness of the human world. But acknowledging and recognizing are acts of peacemaking only when one's passion is involved; if one strives merely for intellectual acknowledgment or recognition, nothing of the spirit will emerge. Yet how does one act and strive for peace in one's everyday reality? How does one educate for peace while living one's everyday life? Few, after all, can initiate educational programs, or be crusaders for peace. To answer this question, let us briefly recall Brecht's story of Galileo's telescope.

Was stupidity the reason why the religious and political leaders refused to look through Galileo's telescope? They knew very well that they would see Jupiter's moons through the telescope. They refused to look through it because they sensed that by this act of looking they might initiate a dialectical development that would change their entire conception of the place of humankind in the universe. The role of peacemakers, in their immediate milieu, is to initiate a somewhat similar dialectical development. They must change the conception of the human being as a warmaker and of war as the inevitable way of solving power struggles—and they must change this conception while rejecting injustice and battling evil. Their means and strengths in initiating such processes may seem flimsy and vulnerable when compared with the ingrained prejudices they are rejecting and with the powers they are battling. And often they are. Peacemakers must be aware that the vulnerability of their power does not always diminish its ability to initiate new developments.

The power of peacemakers is dialectical. By showing new directions, which may stem from the core of one's religion, they can threaten accepted assumptions. This showing of new directions has great influence when it is an expression of the way of life of the peacemaker. Hence, peacemaking is both a struggle to develop oneself so that one can relate wholly, express joy in life and one's passionate love for this earthly existence, and a response to the developments that one encounters in a manner that will encourage others to live together in justice, freedom, and peace. Peacemakers' self-education and acting should be coupled with an urging and teaching of other persons to undertake a similar way of life.

In such acting many tensions are involved: political, personal, social, religious. But the honest seeking of a way to bring justice in peaceful ways must face these tensions squarely and unremittingly. Consider briefly two recent Nobel Peace Prize laureates and the tensions they face: Lech Walesa and Bishop Desmond Tutu.

Both Desmond Tutu and Lech Walesa know that they are living under a grossly unjust regime, in apartheid South Africa or communist Poland. But they also know that violent manners of opposing the regime may lead to more oppression, destruction, and bloodshed; hence their emphasis on peaceful methods of opposition. All this seems simple to us, overlooking the rage a Tutu or Walesa must feel when he is constantly oppressed by a group of banal evil leaders who have no other goal but holding on to their power by whatever unjust means. Without the passion that sustains this rage, neither Walesa nor Tutu could work for peace, or appeal to others to follow their lead. They must allow their rage to appear, yet direct it to a constructive working for change—even while openly opposing the propagators of violence and destruction among their enemies and supporters. If peacemaking were not a way of life for these two persons, one doubts that they could continually walk the tightrope between the oppressive evil that they reject, and the wish to violently wreak havoc on the manifestations and the props of that evil, which they need to suppress.

EDUCATING PEACEMAKERS

How does one *begin* to educate a peacemaker? Betty Cannon's essay provides some worthy suggestions. Antony Flew is right that much of what passes for peace education is probably indoctrination, because it is devoid of critical analysis. But his essay is also instructive in that one cannot divorce peace education from the political, historical, and social context in which one exists. Betty Cannon is right that the Demonic Double is central to one's ontological relationships to other persons, and that when such an attitude dominates a person's being, the result may lead to enjoying all the brutal manifestations of war, which include killing, rape, inflicting pain, destroying. But her essay also indicates that the peacemaker and peace educator must relate to ontology, and to the manner of being-in-the-world of the persons with whom they are interacting. In short, these essays will allow me to give some suggestions as to how to begin to educate a peacemaker.

Following Antony Flew I would hold that "peace studies," as they are currently pursued in many educational institutions, will not educate peacemakers. Such studies are deficient inasmuch as they do not educate persons to think clearly and critically, and do not encourage them to develop historical awareness, understanding, or knowledge. Historical awareness and knowledge will not allow the peacemaker to ignore the cynicism and expansionist motives that led to the Soviet invasion and domination of Afghanistan, or the evil manifested in Pol Pot's massacre of two million Cambodians, or the fact that the atomic bomb was used against the Japanese, who were Hitler's partners and themselves conducted a war accompanied by enslavement and torture and murder of innocent persons. Thus, although passion is central to the action of the peacemaker, it must be tempered and guided by the type of critical thinking and self-immersion in history that Flew suggests—even if one may not agree with all his explicit and implicit views.

Distorted and impure passions live congenially with uncritical and banal thinking; it is no wonder that fanaticism is a bedfellow of erroneous thought. Thinking clearly often demands courage; the results of such thinking are not always what one wishes them to be. Such courage can lead to new acts of courage. Educating for human integrity, which must be one of the major goals of the peacemaker, cannot be done by embracing the superficial approaches offered by some peace studies programs. As Socrates indicated, clear thinking, and especially clear thinking that leads to action, is crucial to a person's striving to live honestly and with integrity.

Such clear thinking and historical awareness and knowledge will also help a person distinguish between a Demonic Double, with which Betty Cannon deals, and a true enemy of peace. The enemy of the peacemaker embraces a clearly defined attitude, which refuses to acknowledge the freedom of each person, and each person's right to pursue and express one's freedom. The rulers and propagators of totalitarian and dictatorial regimes in the world today are enemies of the peacemaker. In contrast, the Demonic Double is the projection onto others of one's inability to cope with evil, of one's distorted relationships to oneself. Thus religious fanatics are enemies of the peacemaker, even if they are members of one's own community of faith or one's own nation. The fanatic is not the Demonic Double of the peacemaker; the approach of peacemakers, both to their religious heritage and to other persons, is in clear contradiction to the approach of the fanatic. Still, Cannon reminds us that persons have a tendency to grasp and to treat the Other as an object, as an embodiment of Satan, as a Demonic Double. Hence the danger of the Demonic Double in the life and work of the peacemaker is that almost without one's sensing it, such an attitude can creep into one's ontology.

As Cannon shows, such an ontology is often rooted in childhood experiences and in a superficial grasping of the authentic religious message of one's faith. A childhood in which the child's subjectivity is continually reified, in which one's value as a person and a subject is continually trampled upon, in which there is no love at all—such a childhood is an apt breeding ground for the inclination to see war as a way of life. When, in addition, faith is not grasped as the complement of human love, as its blood brother or sister, but rather as a manner of eradicating human freedom and human worth, so as to make the person part of a mass of believers, then the warmaker and warmonger will epitomize this distorted "faith."

Educating peacemakers means, therefore, teaching them that they may have enemies—and if one struggles and works for peace one probably will have enemies—but one should strive not to relate to other persons as Demonic Doubles. Ayatolla Khomeini is an enemy of the peacemaker. But to brand all the Iranians who are fighting for his cause as warmongers is to resort to the Demonic Double. A few of these fighters may be warmongers, some may be afraid to act otherwise in a totalitarian regime, others may be victims of indoctrination, and still others may be perpetuators of the banality of evil. Few are an embodiment of Satan.

But remember! One can begin to educate a person to be a peacemaker if one follows the suggestions of Flew and Cannon. Yet, to fulfill the task of peace education one must surpass these suggestions and strive to embody—and to educate one's pupils to embody in their everyday actions—the peacemaking core of one's religious heritage. I have already noted that this striving needs to be nourished by living dialogue, by relating wholly as a person, by passionately expressing one's joy in life and love for other persons and for worldly existence. Such a way of life emerging, as shown in this book, from the immortal truths of one's heritage can lead one to engage in authentic education for peace. Of course, many pitfalls await such a peacemaker—I have pointed out some of them. But accepting the challenge of living such a life is a blessing for all involved.

Verse 11 of Psalm 29 is usually translated: "The Lord will give strength to his people; the Lord will bless his people with peace." But the translation is gravely lacking in relation to one unique word in Hebrew. The Hebrew word, *oz,* which is here translated "strength," means much more. *Oz* is both a daring spiritual strength and a joyful fortitude. Thus the psalmist indicated that only if persons could realize in their life a joyful fortitude coupled with daring spiritual strength would the people be blessed with peace. No writer since has expressed peacemaking in action more succinctly.

16

Diana Dolev and Haim Gordon

Fun, Fantasy, and Failure
in Educating for Peace

What follows is a series of letters written by Diana Dolev to Haim Gordon, drawing out some of the fun, fantasy, and failures one is bound to encounter when educating for peace. The letters describe the developments during the second year of Project Shalom, which was initiated by the two authors under the academic leadership of Haim Gordon, in order to examine the possibility of developing a secondary school curriculum that would educate Jewish and Arab teenagers to relate dialogically, trustfully, and peacefully toward each other. In many respects Project Shalom was an offshoot of a previous project entitled "Education for Peace on the Basis of Martin Buber's Philosophy," which taught adult Jews and Arabs to relate dialogically to each other in the sprit of Martin Buber's philosophy of dialogue.[1] The letters were written during the period when Haim Gordon was on sabbatical leave. We have inserted background information between and in the letters only where we feel it is essential for clarification.

In Israel Jewish education is in Hebrew, Arab education in Arabic. The schools of each community are separate. Arab pupils learn Hebrew from an early age, few Jewish pupils learn Arabic. There are very few opportunities for Jewish and Arab high school pupils to meet each other; there are even fewer opportunities for them to engage in meaningful dialogue. Project Shalom was the first attempt, in Israel's short, difficult history, to teach Jewish and Arab teenagers the significance of Buberian dialogue for their own life and to create circumstances in which they could meet and attempt to relate to each other dialogically. It should be remembered that genuine dialogue, as Buber envi-

*sioned it, occurs when no participant in the encounter tries to manipulate the
conversation, or another participant, while conversing.*

*In the classroom pupils were taught how to realize many of Buber's thoughts
using methods Haim Gordon had developed in his work with adults. Every
four to six weeks each Jewish class met with its Arab twin class for a joint
educational encounter. The "twin classes" were taught by the same teacher:
Diana taught a Jewish class in Arad and an Arab class in Kseifa; Ilana Freifel
taught a Jewish class in Beer Sheva and an Arab class in Rahat. The four
participating schools were in the south of Israel, the Negev, in or near Beer
Sheva. Most of the Jewish teenagers came from a middle-class background; the
Arabs were all Bedouins. We also attempted to set up a similar program in
central areas of Israel, where Arab towndwellers reside. But we failed.*

September 1983

Dear Haim,

When you ascended the steps to the departure gates at Ben Gurion Airport
and turned to wave goodbye for a year and a half, I must admit that I was
elated. At last, I was fully in charge of Project Shalom, which I believed could
make an impact on what is going on here between Jews and Arabs, could
diminish mistrust and some of the hatred. I was elated, but also a bit fright-
ened. No; I was scared to death. As I drove home from the airport, I once again
felt how turned off I am with what we denoted as conventional encounters,
where Jews and Arabs merely played with meeting each other; I firmly reas-
serted my belief in the significance of dialogue and of a Buberian encounter
between Jewish and Arab teenagers. Don't worry; it's not that I like that you
are out of the picture; it is just that I like the new power to try to do good with
which I have been endowed. But let me stop talking about my feelings and tell
you what has been happening.

I want to write about the things that haven't been going well, because the
things that are going well are not news. But let me mention that in the Negev
Ilana and I are doing well with the four classes in the Beer Sheva area. They are
undergoing the educational process that we developed in accordance with
Buber's philosophy and seem quite interested. They also want to meet members
of their twin class. Again, I was surprised how little Jews and Arabs of this age
meet each other. In my Jewish class only two Jews had ever talked as friends
with an Arab, and they admitted that the conversation was superficial. In my
Arab class no one had ever spoken as a friend to Jews. I was shocked, even
though I knew about it from last year. Repeatedly I had to remind myself that
these Jews and Arabs go to schools that are a mere twenty-minute bus ride
from each other.

In the classes that we wanted to set up in the center of Israel, in the Wadi Ara
area, nothing seems to be happening. At the Jewish school there are teachers
who are willing to undertake teaching our program. But in the Arab schools it
seems that N. has not the power to cope with the bureaucratic subtleties that the

Arab principals pile in his way. Even though he knows our program well, he is a
new teacher in that system and area and does not yet have tenure. Whatever the
reasons, nothing is occurring there. I am mad at N. because I waited for him for
an hour in a filthy café in the central bus station in Tel Aviv and he didn't show
up. Later, I learned that in one of his classes the vice principal described the
project as learning about the Israeli-Egyptian peace treaty and subsequent
peace; N. got so angry that he decided to give up. You know that many of the
pupils believe that the Palestinian cause—and they call themselves
Palestinians—demands that they reject the peace treaty with Egypt. So N.
gave up and I don't know what to do; I'll have to look into it when I get back
from the trip to Egypt with a group from last year's participants in Project
Shalom. . . .

October 1983

Dear Haim,

Going to Egypt with a group of pupils was great, and we did it without you—
two Israeli women in charge, and a third woman as a helper in that male
chauvinistic Egyptian society. I'm sick of the lusty glances of those Egyptian
males, which sort of rape you as you pass by them. And their damnable habit
of trying to touch you and pinch you is obnoxious. But let me get back to the
story of our trip to Egypt with fifteen Jewish and Arab pupils, in order to test
them as dialogical persons.

As you know, we went to Egypt with some of last year's pupils in Project
Shalom. We wanted to check the strength of the dialogical encounters in Israel
in an entirely new milieu—an Arab milieu, where Arabs and Arabic dominate
the entire scene. We also wanted to check what they had internalized from
Buber's philosophy on relating to the other as a person, even in adverse
conditions.

Well, it was an overwhelming success. Jewish and Arab teenagers, who a
year ago had never spoken with members of the other community—these Jews
and Arabs, who had only undergone a two-hour course weekly for a year in
education for peace—functioned together beautifully in Egypt. In accordance
with the methods that you developed for adults, we divided the fifteen teenagers into three groups of five, with Jews and Arabs in each group. An adult
accompanied each group, but she was there more for the record. The decisions
were made by the teenagers without her interference. Each group had to learn
about an aspect of Egyptian life each day, in accordance with exercises we had
prepared; these stipulated that the participants visit certain parts of the city or
certain cultural areas and write a report on what they had learned.

I was wrong in saying that they "functioned" together—they lived together
as friends, as partners, as future Israeli citizens, as future neighbors in the
Middle East. I know that there is not much new in what we did, but for us, for
whom Israeli-Arab mistrust and hatred has become a fact of life, seeing that
trusting each other is a real possibility enhances our faith in our capability of

living together, as human beings. I'm perhaps overenthused, but who cares?

By the way, on the way back from Egypt the teenagers felt as if they were returning from a good dream together to a harsh reality. They didn't want to wake up to the exigencies of Israeli society, of Jewish-Arab mistrust. When they reached Tel Aviv, they refused to go home before sitting together one last time for an hour in a café and talking quietly. . . .

Buber's philosophy, which is central to the educational approach developed in Project Shalom, holds that genuine dialogue is a commitment, an accepting of responsibility for one's partner in dialogue. Such responsibility emerged on the joint trips to Egypt, against the background of Egyptian society, which is male-dominated, chauvinistic, and hardly congenial to dialogue.[2]

November 1983

Dear Haim,

At times I just want to go back to teaching the history of art and forget about Arabs and Jews. I've been teaching for twelve years and this is the first time pupils threw stones at me—and for what?—because I want to educate for Jewish-Arab dialogue. They gathered pebbles during the break, and whenever I turned my back to write something on the blackboard, I'd be hit by a few pebbles. I'm talking about this year's class of Arab pupils in Kseifa. The reason they are so aggressive is that they are against education for peace, some of them for ideological reasons, and others because it is an added burden in their curriculum. One of them, T., went to the supervisor to complain.

We thought we were succeeding when this year a class opened in Kseifa. You remember that last year they refused to teach the subject because we suggested a Druze teacher and there is a blood feud between Bedouins of the tribe around Kseifa and Druze Arabs. But our success is no victory; it is stupid and often hard work, which, at times, I hate. It isn't only the uncomfortable feeling I get as a Jewish woman teaching a class of forty Bedouins, most of them teenage boys, with all the problems of that age, in a rundown shack way out there in the desert. It isn't only the fact that they don't understand what the hell I want from them, and why do they have to sit an additional two hours to hear me and to read some Buber, which they don't understand. It's the whole futility of the undertaking: What can I change, what can we change, when the government and the rightist movements in Israel are breeding hatred as badly as the terrorist movements in the Arab world?

But I won't give up, dammit, it isn't my style. Let me tell you what is happening. I made a mistake this year at the first meeting in which Jewish and Arab pupils from my two schools got together. Instead of asking them to discuss the nitty-gritty—hated, mistrust, etc.—as we did in our Buberian learning groups for adults, I asked the pupils to just talk about neutral subjects with each other. Don't get angry—I learned from all of this. Anyhow it was a failure, except for one of the small groups into which we divided the pupils. In that group of five Jews and Arabs, one Jewish girl started talking about her fear of Arabs. When she learned that the Arabs sitting there also feared Jews, suddenly the entire gestalt of her perceptions was transformed—she suddenly grasped herself not only as being scared, but also as threatening—because she is a Jew. I know that this is just a beginning and has nothing yet to do with dialogue as Buber described it, but I was thankful for even that shift, when everything else was so stale.

Ilana tried to organize a similar meeting, but the Arab pupils didn't show up. When she went to school the next day, she learned that the principal had canceled the meeting without notifying her, or the Jewish pupils from their twin school. Ilana got so angry that she started crying and screaming at the principal in the middle of the teacher's room. As an Arab male, that is probably the first time a woman dared scream at him in front of a group of men. He was beside himself and didn't know how to respond. But suddenly, true to Buber, he responded by letting go of himself and screaming back. It was like two hawkers in the marketplace. Then Ilana quit; and then he tried to pacify her. To make a long story short she is now treated with velvet gloves at school and he apologized for canceling her class; he probably learned a lesson of aggressive feminism in the bargain. And many of the class, who learned of Ilana's courage, now appreciate her, and are interested in what she has to say. . . .

December 1983

Dear Haim,

It was good I spoke to you on the phone, but now I want to make things clear for the record. As I told you, I was called to a meeting with two of your colleagues, among them the director of the Humphrey Center (which is administratively in charge of Project Shalom). At the meeting the director played around with me, saying that I had not given him enough information on what was going on. Then he suddenly started arguing that he cannot administer the project in its current format, with you abroad. The primary reason is that, since you demanded an inquiry into the mess at the university budget department, everyone in that department hates you and they are giving trouble to any research connected with your doings. I believe that they are especially angry at the fact that the Israeli press found out, as a result of your complaint, how incompetent the university administration is, and they also broke the story on corruption in the budget department. Anyway, the director of the Humphrey Center wanted to change the name of our project and by such camouflage to get the budget department to do their work. What a coward!

I rejected his proposal, but then I learned that what he really wants is to find someone to take over the project instead of you, or find a way for using our money for another research topic. In short, what he really wants is to either close down the project or to kick you out of it. I suspect that if our project did not have to do with Jewish-Arab dialogue, the response would have been different. . . .

Unfortunately, many of the fears and anxieties expressed in the above letter proved all too true. After some international calls, and threats that legal proceedings would be commenced if any change was made in the initial contract, Project Shalom continued as planned.

February 1984

Dear Haim,

You probably remember how difficult it is to get Jewish pupils to be overnight guests of a Bedouin family. The greatest resistance comes from the parents. As the date for this activity drew near, and as we discussed it in class, I started receiving letters from parents in which they notified me that they will not permit their teenage child to spend a night in a Bedouin home. They wrote clearly: "We don't trust these Arabs with our children." Last year I organized a meeting with the parents; but they only came in order to express their vague fears—fears which I could not pin down in order to refute. This fear is their justification; and when I explain that such a vague fear cannot be a justification if there are no facts to support it—they simply don't listen.

Like last year, I was once again determined not to give up. So last Friday afternoon, in cloudy weather, I drove to Kseifa with four pupils, two boys and two girls, and with my nine-year-old daughter. To my surprise, only five pupils from Kseifa came to invite us to their homes. Since one Jewish teenage girl wanted to visit together with her boyfriend, we went to four homes. With my daughter, I visited W.'s home; she is one of my best pupils.

W. lives in a tin shack in the middle of the desert. You can see the lights of Beer Sheva from her home. She has ten brothers and sisters, most of them younger than she. They all sleep in one room. The only other room in the shack has three walls and that is where they do the cooking and eat. The Bedouin day is divided into hours during which they work or attend to their chores, and hours during which they sit around the fire and eat or talk. At times they watch TV, which gets its power from a car battery. They have their own private water tank, on wheels, which they fill by attaching it to their truck and driving to the nearest watering place.

We arrived at around 5:00 in the afternoon. They were very happy, since this was the first time that a Jewish woman and her daughter had come to spend the night with them. The younger children were a bit shy. Serving as hosts for a Jewish woman was something new and out of the ordinary for them. Guests in Bedouin society are always men; and then the men sit around the fire and converse while the women sit in the sleeping room. With me they had a problem. They solved it by formally anouncing that I was a member of the family, and then I could sit with the entire family. I enjoyed our conversations, even though some of the discussions had to be translated. W.'s nine-year-old brother decided to teach me the correct intonations in Arabic, and whenever I uttered a name he corrected me, demanding that I get it right. We had fun together.

At night we all slept in the sleeping room, except the father and two older brothers who slept beside the fire in the other room. My daughter, who slept beside me, whispered to me before she fell asleep that she hoped we wouldn't be murdered during the night. Around midnight it started to rain. The raindrops hit the tin roof like bullets and woke us up. The rain continued for some hours. In the morning everything was muddy, and we could hardly walk. I couldn't drive to see the other pupils. Fortunately, the sun came out strong, and around noon I could get my car to move without skidding too much on the dirt roads. I decided to try to visit the other pupils but gave up when my exhaust pipe hit a rock during a skid. In the afternoon we started driving home. When I had to drive through the flowing wadi my knees shook—but somehow we got across. When I got to Arad my mud-covered car attracted attention—but I was happy. So were the Jewish pupils. One told me: "On that weekend I discovered a new world."

April 1984

Dear Haim,

Since you were with us in Egypt, flying seventeen hours from southern Alabama, I don't want to report on what you saw. I believe, though, that we can best summarize the success of taking twenty-seven Jewish and Arab pupils to Egypt by comparing the bus ride to Egypt with the bus ride back.

Going to Egypt Arabs and Jews did not sit together. One reason might have been that all the Arab teenagers were boys and all the Jewish teenagers were girls. I seemed to sense that for the Arab youths, the tension on the bus also had to do with their not knowing how to interact with Jewish girls. Some probably wondered if this interaction might lead to sexual adventure.

In Egypt the learning experience dominated everybody's interest; it demanded personal involvement, thinking and discussing together—the entire fantasy of sex evaporated, as you saw simple dialogue prevail.

On the way back Jews and Arabs sat together, chatted, told jokes, teased each other, quarreled as teenagers quarrel, and taught each other songs. It is a long twelve-hour bus ride.

When we reached the Israeli border, reality hit us in the face like a policeman's fist. The Israeli customs officials divided the Jews and Arabs in our group. They led the Arabs into another room. We Jews thought that the reason for the division was that the Arabs had bought many goods in Egypt and they might have to pay customs. But it turned out that no one looked at how much they had bought; the real reason for the division was to instill some fear into them. In that room they sat for an hour, then were told to strip to their tights, and in such a situation underwent a sadistic interrogation—questions like: What did you do in Egypt? You better tell us the truth, since we already know about your doings! Why did you go to Egypt? Did any terrorist approach you? If he would have approached you, would you help him? Who exactly did you meet in Egypt? In short, the secret service officials at the terminal tried to instill terror in their hearts for two hours.

It was such a terrible ending to such a good trip. It was such a horrible thing to do that shame and anger overwhelmed me. Fortunately, the Arabs did not take out all of their frustrations on members of the group, but shared some of their pain with us. . . .

After the incident on the Israeli border, Diana tried to get the Arabs who had been interrogated to lodge an official complaint. They refused. One reason is that many Arabs do not yet know their basic rights in a democratic society— they let the bureaucrats rule them. Furthermore, they hesitate to engage in a conflict over a minor issue, or inconvenience, or shame, or frustration—even if it has been purposely inflicted upon them—because they sense that they do not know the rules of the game of democracy and they fear greater frustrations will result from their conflict. Diana did write to some members of the Israeli Knesset (parliament), but there was no response.

June 1984

Dear Haim,

It is difficult to summarize what I learned during such an eventful year in educating for peace. I do want to mention three points. First of all, doing is much more difficult and satisfying than talking about the need for peace. By going through all the shit that I went through this year, I learned that I have the power to do, to make changes in persons' lives, changes for the better. Such an approach was and still is in sharp contrast to what transpires in many places in Israel that bear the banner of peace and talk about Jewish-Arab understanding. For instance, the International Center for Peace in the Mideast in Tel Aviv is a cave of impotent talkers about peace. Doing something to change persons is beyond their horizon. They sit in their plush offices and discuss. I'm thankful my work had nothing of such an approach to it.

I also learned how enhancing the building of dialogical relations with other persons can be, despite the political differences that exist. I had learned this much earlier, but here I was the initiator of many such relations and I found myself growing while assuming such a responsibility. Where this growth will lead I do not know. You would probably say that it doesn't matter.

But perhaps the most important thing that I learned is to trust myself when I am doing good. You remember the pupil T. who went to the superintendent at the beginning of the year and complained about the course in education for peace. In Egypt he told me that he learned through this course not to hate Jews. I wanted to hug him, but I held back. In the final paper in class he wrote that he really thanks me for the course and he wishes that all Jews and Arabs could learn to educate for peace. He has learned to use his courage in order to do good.

No, I didn't learn much, but yet maybe I did. The last point seems to me most significant. I now believe that most persons don't trust themselves to do good in a difficult situation. They are afraid that their fantasy of the good will evaporate, or that they will be confronted with failure. They don't imagine that if they learn to trust themselves to do good, much fun may also come their way. Yes, doing good can be fun, and I'm thankful for having had the opportunity to learn this.

NOTES

1. For more information, see Haim Gordon, *Dance, Dialogue and Despair: Existentialist Philosophy and Education for Peace In Israel* (University of Alabama Press, 1986).

2. Ibid.; the chapter on Mahfouz explains much more about Egypt.

Contributors

INGO BALDERMANN is professor of theology at the Universität-Gesamthochschule, Siegen, West Germany. He is the author of numerous works on the Bible and Protestant theology including *Die Bibel—Buch des Lernens* (1982) and *Der Gott des Friedens und die Götter der Macht* (1983).

BETTY CANNON is assistant professor of humanities and social services at the Colorado School of Mines and a practicing psychotherapist. She has written on the relationship of the philosophy of Jean-Paul Sartre to psychotherapy and has recently co-edited a volume entitled *Gandhi in the Postmodern Age: Issues in War and Peace* (1984).

MAYA CHADDA is associate professor in the department of political science at William Patterson College, Wayne, New Jersey. Born in Gandhi's ashram in India, she completed her early education in India. Dr. Chadda is a scholar who has published widely in the areas of foreign policy, Third World development, and the thought of Gandhi.

DIANA DOLEV is a graduate student at the University of Tel Aviv in Israel. She assisted in the Education for Peace Project in Accordance with Martin Buber's Philosophy and served as director of its second phase as a pilot program for Arab and Jewish secondary students in Israel.

EUGENE FISHER is executive secretary of the Secretariat for Catholic-Jewish Relations, National Conference of Catholic Bishops (U.S.A.). He is the author and editor of several books, including *Faith Without Prejudice* (1977), *Liturgical Foundations of Social Policy in the Catholic and Jewish Traditions* (1983), and *Seminary Education and Christian-Jewish Relations* (1983). He is a consultor to the Holy See's Commission for Religious Relations with the Jewish People.

ANTONY FLEW is professor emeritus of philosophy, University of Reading, England, and Distinguished Research Fellow at the Social Philosophy and Policy Center, Bowling Green State University, Ohio. He is the author of numerous books including *Thinking Straight* (1975), *A Rational Animal* (1978), *The Politics of Procrustes* (1981), *Darwinian Evolution* (1984), and *Thinking about Social Thinking* (1985).

TIMOTHY GEORGE is associate professor of church history and historical theology at the Southern Baptist Theological Seminary, Louisville, Kentucky. He is the author of four books and numerous articles on religious themes. He serves as coordinating editor of *Baptist Peacemaker,* a quarterly journal with an ecumenical readership of around 30,000.

LEAH GOLDBERG (1911–1970) was a leading Hebrew author, poet, and translator. Born in Lithuania, Dr. Goldberg came to Palestine in 1935 and later became head of the department of comparative literature at the Hebrew University. Many of Dr. Goldberg's poems are considered classics of the modern period of Hebrew literature.

HAIM GORDON is senior lecturer in the department of education at Ben Gurion University of the Negev, Beer Sheva, Israel. He is the author of numerous works on existential philosophy and, in particular, on the philosophy of Martin Buber. He is co-editor of *The Martin Buber Centenary Volume* (1984) and for several years directed a peace education project with Arab and Jewish Israelis, which provides the basis for his most recent book, *Dance, Dialogue, and Despair* (1986).

LEONARD GROB is associate professor of philosophy at Fairleigh Dickinson University, Rutherford, New Jersey. He has written in the areas of leadership studies, the philosophy of Martin Buber, and peace studies. In 1986 he led a "dialogue group" consisting of black and Jewish city personnel at Newark, New Jersey.

RIFFAT HASSAN is associate professor of religion at the University of Louisville and (1986–87) visiting lecturer and research associate at the Harvard Divinity School. She is the author of numerous articles and two books on the Muslim thinker Allama Muhammad Iqbāl and, for the past dozen years, a scholar of feminist theology in Islam. She is currently completing a book *Equal Before Allah?,* a study of issues relating to woman-man equality discussed in light of the Qur'ān and the Judeo-Christian-Islamic traditions.

NAGUIB MAHFOUZ is the most celebrated writer in the Arab world. His numerous novels and short stories depict aspects of life in contemporary Egyptian society. He has also written on Israeli-Arab relations in the Egyptian newspaper *Al Ahram,* and was the first writer in Egypt to advocate publicly the adoption of peace initiatives toward Israel.

MANJUVAJRA was born in England in 1947. He received degrees from Imperial College (physics) and University College, London (transportation studies). In 1974 he was ordained into the Western Buddhist Order by the Venerable Maha Sthavira Sangharakshita. Until 1977 he ran a Buddhist center in Cornwall, England, and then worked at the London Buddhist Centre. In 1981 he cofounded the Boston Buddhist Center. He now lives and works at Aryaloka, a seminary in Newmarket, New Hampshire.

ICHIRO MORITAKI is professor emeritus of ethics at Hiroshima University. A survivor of the atomic blast in which he lost one eye, he has been an active member of the peace movement in Japan, chairing both the Hiroshima Anti-Nuclear Movement and the Society of Atom Bomb Survivors. He is the author of *My Thirty Years Struggle against Nuclear Weapons* (1976).

RAMAKRISHNA PULIGANDLA is professor of philosophy at the University of Toledo, Ohio. Born in India and educated in his native land and in the U.S.A., Dr. Puligandla has published sixty papers and seven books in the areas of logic and philosophy of science, as well as in comparative philosophy and religion, with special reference to the Indian tradition.

MYRA SHAPIRO is a poet. In 1983 she was a recipient of a MacDowell fellow-ship. She was also the winner of the Dylan Thomas Poetry Award from the New School in 1981.

Index

Abraham, Rabbi, 40
Advaita Vedanta, 155
Afghanistan, 12, 197, 202, 206, 222
Africa, 23, 156
Ahemedabad, 152
Ahimsa, 218
Ahmad, 126
Al Ahram, 109
Al Azhar, 111, 112
Alexandri, Rabbi, 38
Alexandria, 214
Aloni, Shulamit, 54
America. *See* United States
Anabaptists, 69-71
Anglican religion, 13
Anti-Semite, 178, 179
Applefeld, A., 53
Aquinas, T., *Summa,* 69
Arendt, Hanna, 211, 217
Argentina, 157
Aristotle, 204, 215
Armenians, 11
Asia, 14
Asoka (emperor), 142
Aswan, 109
Atman, 141, 142, 145, 146, 148
Augustine, St., 15, 68, 175
Aurobino, S., 143
Austin, J. L., 203
Azad, Abu'l Kalam, 100
Babylon, 114
Babylonians, 175
Bacon, F., 129
Baez, J., 23
Bahais, 14
Baharain, 109
Baptists, 72
Baptist tradition, 65
Barth, K., 63
Beer Sheva, 90, 225, 229
Begin, M., 11
Bellow, S., 54
Ben Gurion University of the Negev, 90

Ben Levi, Joshua, 36
Benn, A. W., 202
Ben Zakkai, Yochanan, Rabbi, 37
Bernard of Clairvaux, 69
Bible, 9, 17, 18, 19, 37, 51, 55, 56, 79-85.
  See New Testament; Old Testament
Bihar, 152
Bondurant, J., 150, 154
Bradford, University of, 169, 197, 205
Brahma, 123, 141, 142, 145, 146, 148, 176
Brandt Commission, 199
Brandt Report, 198
Brecht, B., 215, 220; *Galileo,* 215
Brethren, the, 63
Britain, 196
Bruyn, de, G., 79
Buber, M., 6, 8, 20, 23, 40-43, 54, 58, 213,
  214, 224-228
Buberian dialogue, 213, 214, 224
Buddha, 115, 116, 120, 121, 126, 129-134,
  216
Buddhagaya, 130
Bunam, Rabbi, 40
Cahane, M., 57
Cairo, 46, 109-111, 214
Cambodia, 206, 222
Campaign for Nuclear Disarmament, 206
Camp David accords, 11
Canaan, 31, 39
Canada, 182
Carter, J., 11, 50
Casablanca, 109
Cathari, 69
Celsus, 67, 68
Central America, 160, 161, 206
Champaran, 152
China, 12, 15, 16, 93, 143, 157
Chinese boycotts, 16
Christ, 66-72, 81, 85, 86, 129. *See also*
  Jesus
Clausewitz, Karl von, *On War,* 205
Clement of Alexandria, 67
Coleridge, W., 173

236